# HOLT SCIENCE & TECHNOLOGY

# Forces, Motion, and Energy

**HOLT, RINEHART AND WINSTON**

A Harcourt Classroom Education Company

Austin · New York · Orlando · Atlanta · San Francisco · Boston · Dallas · Toronto · London

# Acknowledgments

## Chapter Writers

**Christie Borgford, Ph.D.**
*Professor of Chemistry*
University of Alabama
Birmingham, Alabama

**Andrew Champagne**
*Former Physics Teacher*
Ashland High School
Ashland, Massachusetts

**Mapi Cuevas, Ph.D.**
*Professor of Chemistry*
Santa Fe Community College
Gainesville, Florida

**Leila Dumas**
*Former Physics Teacher*
LBJ Science Academy
Austin, Texas

**William G. Lamb, Ph.D.**
*Science Teacher and Dept. Chair*
Oregon Episcopal School
Portland, Oregon

**Sally Ann Vonderbrink, Ph.D.**
*Chemistry Teacher*
St. Xavier High School
Cincinnati, Ohio

## Lab Writers

**Phillip G. Bunce**
*Former Physics Teacher*
Bowie High School
Austin, Texas

**Kenneth E. Creese**
*Science Teacher*
White Mountain Junior High School
Rock Springs, Wyoming

**William G. Lamb, Ph.D.**
*Science Teacher and Dept. Chair*
Oregon Episcopal School
Portland, Oregon

**Alyson Mike**
*Science Teacher*
East Valley Middle School
East Helena, Montana

**Joseph W. Price**
*Science Teacher and Dept. Chair*
H. M. Browne Junior High School
Washington, D.C.

**Denice Lee Sandefur**
*Science Teacher and Dept. Chair*
Nucla High School
Nucla, Colorado

**John Spadafino**
*Mathematics and Physics Teacher*
Hackensack High School
Hackensack, New Jersey

**Walter Woolbaugh**
*Science Teacher*
Manhattan Junior High School
Manhattan, Montana

## Academic Reviewers

**Paul R. Berman, Ph.D.**
*Professor of Physics*
University of Michigan
Ann Arbor, Michigan

**Russell M. Brengelman, Ph.D.**
*Professor of Physics*
Morehead State University
Morehead, Kentucky

**John A. Brockhaus, Ph.D.**
*Director, Mapping, Charting and Geodesy Program*
Department of Geography and Environmental Engineering
United States Military Academy
West Point, New York

**Walter Bron, Ph.D.**
*Professor of Physics*
University of California
Irvine, California

**Andrew J. Davis, Ph.D.**
*Manager, ACE Science Center*
Department of Physics
California Institute of Technology
Pasadena, California

**Peter E. Demmin, Ed.D.**
*Former Science Teacher and Department Chair*
Amherst Central High School
Amherst, New York

**Roger Falcone, Ph.D.**
*Professor of Physics and Department Chair*
University of California
Berkeley, California

**Cassandra A. Fraser, Ph.D.**
*Assistant Professor of Chemistry*
University of Virginia
Charlottesville, Virginia

**L. John Gagliardi, Ph.D.**
*Associate Professor of Physics and Department Chair*
Rutgers University
Camden, New Jersey

**Gabriele F. Giuliani, Ph.D.**
*Professor of Physics*
Purdue University
West Lafayette, Indiana

**Roy W. Hann, Jr., Ph.D.**
*Professor of Civil Engineering*
Texas A&M University
College Station, Texas

**John L. Hubisz, Ph.D.**
*Professor of Physics*
North Carolina State University
Raleigh, North Carolina

**Samuel P. Kounaves, Ph.D.**
*Professor of Chemistry*
Tufts University
Medford, Massachusetts

**Karol Lang, Ph.D.**
*Associate Professor of Physics*
The University of Texas
Austin, Texas

**Gloria Langer, Ph.D.**
*Professor of Physics*
University of Colorado
Boulder, Colorado

**Phillip LaRoe**
*Professor*
Helena College of Technology
Helena, Montana

**Joseph A. McClure, Ph.D.**
*Associate Professor of Physics*
Georgetown University
Washington, D.C.

**LaMoine L. Motz, Ph.D.**
*Coordinator of Science Education*
Department of Learning Services
Oakland County Schools
Waterford, Michigan

**R. Thomas Myers, Ph.D.**
*Professor of Chemistry, Emeritus*
Kent State University
Kent, Ohio

**Hillary Clement Olson, Ph.D.**
*Research Associate*
Institute for Geophysics
The University of Texas
Austin, Texas

**David P. Richardson, Ph.D.**
*Professor of Chemistry*
Thompson Chemical Laboratory
Williams College
Williamstown, Massachusetts

**John Rigden, Ph.D.**
*Director of Special Projects*
American Institute of Physics
Colchester, Vermont

# Acknowledgments (cont.)

**Peter Sheridan, Ph.D.**
*Professor of Chemistry*
Colgate University
Hamilton, New York

**Vederaman Sriraman, Ph.D.**
*Associate Professor of Technology*
Southwest Texas State University
San Marcos, Texas

**Jack B. Swift, Ph.D.**
*Professor of Physics*
The University of Texas
Austin, Texas

**Atiq Syed, Ph.D.**
*Master Instructor of Mathematics and Science*
Texas State Technical College
Harlingen, Texas

**Leonard Taylor, Ph.D.**
*Professor Emeritus*
Department of Electrical Engineering
University of Maryland
College Park, Maryland

**Virginia L. Trimble, Ph.D.**
*Professor of Physics and Astronomy*
University of California
Irvine, California

**Martin VanDyke, Ph.D.**
*Professor of Chemistry, Emeritus*
Front Range Community College
Westminster, Colorado

**Gabriela Waschewsky, Ph.D.**
*Science and Math Teacher*
Emery High School
Emeryville, California

## Safety Reviewer

**Jack A. Gerlovich, Ph.D.**
*Associate Professor*
School of Education
Drake University
Des Moines, Iowa

## Teacher Reviewers

**Barry L. Bishop**
*Science Teacher and Dept. Chair*
San Rafael Junior High School
Ferron, Utah

**Paul Boyle**
*Science Teacher*
Perry Heights Middle School
Evansville, Indiana

**Kenneth Creese**
*Science Teacher*
White Mountain Junior High School
Rock Springs, Wyoming

**Vicky Farland**
*Science Teacher and Dept. Chair*
Centennial Middle School
Yuma, Arizona

**Rebecca Ferguson**
*Science Teacher*
North Ridge Middle School
North Richland Hills, Texas

**Laura Fleet**
*Science Teacher*
Alice B. Landrum Middle School
Ponte Vedra Beach, Florida

**Jennifer Ford**
*Science Teacher and Dept. Chair*
North Ridge Middle School
North Richland Hills, Texas

**Susan Gorman**
*Science Teacher*
North Ridge Middle School
North Richland Hills, Texas

**C. John Graves**
*Science Teacher*
Monforton Middle School
Bozeman, Montana

**Dennis Hanson**
*Science Teacher and Dept. Chair*
Big Bear Middle School
Big Bear Lake, California

**David A. Harris**
*Science Teacher and Dept. Chair*
The Thacher School
Ojai, California

**Norman E. Holcomb**
*Science Teacher*
Marion Local Schools
Maria Stein, Ohio

**Kenneth J. Horn**
*Science Teacher and Dept. Chair*
Fallston Middle School
Fallston, Maryland

**Tracy Jahn**
*Science Teacher*
Berkshire Junior-Senior High School
Canaan, New York

**Kerry A. Johnson**
*Science Teacher*
Isbell Middle School
Santa Paula, California

**Drew E. Kirian**
*Science Teacher*
Solon Middle School
Solon, Ohio

**Harriet Knops**
*Science Teacher and Dept. Chair*
Rolling Hills Middle School
El Dorado, California

**Scott Mandel, Ph.D.**
*Director and Educational Consultant*
Teachers Helping Teachers
Los Angeles, California

**Thomas Manerchia**
*Former Science Teacher*
Archmere Academy
Claymont, Delaware

**Edith McAlanis**
*Science Teacher and Dept. Chair*
Socorro Middle School
El Paso, Texas

**Kevin McCurdy, Ph.D.**
*Science Teacher*
Elmwood Junior High School
Rogers, Arkansas

**Alyson Mike**
*Science Teacher*
East Valley Middle School
East Helena, Montana

**Donna Norwood**
*Science Teacher and Dept. Chair*
Monroe Middle School
Charlotte, North Carolina

**Joseph W. Price**
*Science Teacher and Dept. Chair*
H. M. Browne Junior High School
Washington, D.C.

**Terry J. Rakes**
*Science Teacher*
Elmwood Junior High School
Rogers, Arkansas

**Beth Richards**
*Science Teacher*
North Middle School
Crystal Lake, Illinois

**Elizabeth J. Rustad**
*Science Teacher*
Crane Middle School
Yuma, Arizona

**Rodney A. Sandefur**
*Science Teacher*
Naturita Middle School
Naturita, Colorado

**Helen Schiller**
*Science Teacher*
Northwood Middle School
Taylors, South Carolina

**Bert J. Sherwood**
*Science Teacher*
Socorro Middle School
El Paso, Texas

**Patricia McFarlane Soto**
*Science Teacher and Dept. Chair*
G. W. Carver Middle School
Miami, Florida

**David M. Sparks**
*Science Teacher*
Redwater Junior High School
Redwater, Texas

**Larry Tackett**
*Science Teacher and Dept. Chair*
Andrew Jackson Middle School
Cross Lanes, West Virginia

**Elsie N. Waynes**
*Science Teacher and Dept. Chair*
R. H. Terrell Junior High School
Washington, D.C.

**Sharon L. Woolf**
*Science Teacher*
Langston Hughes Middle School
Reston, Virginia

**Alexis S. Wright**
*Middle School Science Coordinator*
Rye Country Day School
Rye, New York

**Lee Yassinski**
*Science Teacher*
Sun Valley Middle School
Sun Valley, California

**John Zambo**
*Science Teacher*
Elizabeth Ustach Middle School
Modesto, California

# M Forces, Motion, and Energy

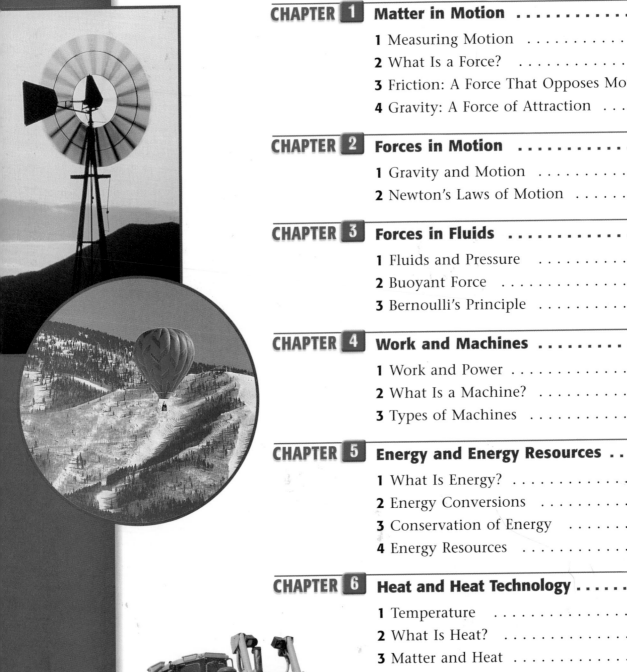

# Skills Development

## Process Skills

### QuickLabs

### Chapter Labs

# Skills Development *(continued)*

## Research and Critical Thinking Skills

### Apply

### Feature Articles

**Science, Technology, and Society**

**Across the Sciences**

**Eureka!**

**Careers**

**Science Fiction**

## Connections

## Mathematics

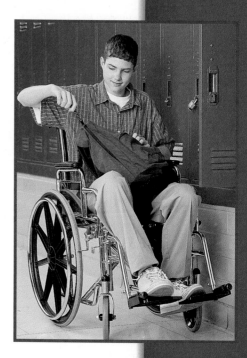

# To the Student

**This book was created to make your science experience interesting, exciting, and fun!**

## Go for It!

Science is a process of discovery, a trek into the unknown. The skills you develop using *Holt Science & Technology*—such as observing, experimenting, and explaining observations and ideas—are the skills you will need for the future. There is a universe of exploration and discovery awaiting those who accept the challenges of science.

## Science & Technology

You see the interaction between science and technology every day. Science makes technology possible. On the other hand, some of the products of technology, such as computers, are used to make further scientific discoveries. In fact, much of the scientific work that is done today has become so technically complicated and expensive that no one person can do it entirely alone. But make no mistake, the creative ideas for even the most highly technical and expensive scientific work still come from individuals.

## Activities and Labs

The activities and labs in this book will allow you to make some basic but important scientific discoveries on your own. You can even do some exploring on your own at home! Here's your chance to use your imagination and curiosity as you investigate your world.

## Keep a ScienceLog

In this book, you will be asked to keep a type of journal called a ScienceLog to record your thoughts, observations, experiments, and conclusions. As you develop your ScienceLog, you will see your own ideas taking shape over time. You'll have a written record of how your ideas have changed as you learn about and explore interesting topics in science.

## Know "What You'll Do"

The "What You'll Do" list at the beginning of each section is your built-in guide to what you need to learn in each chapter. When you can answer the questions in the Section Review and Chapter Review, you know you are ready for a test.

## Check Out the Internet

You will see this ![sciLINKS logo] logo throughout the book. You'll be using *sci*LINKS as your gateway to the Internet. Once you log on to *sci*LINKS using your computer's Internet link, type in the *sci*LINKS address. When asked for the keyword code, type in the keyword for that topic. A wealth of resources is now at your disposal to help you learn more about that topic.

In addition to *sci*LINKS you can log on to some other great resources to go with your text. The addresses shown below will take you to the home page of each site.

---

### internet**connect**

**This textbook contains the following on-line resources to help you make the most of your science experience.**

 **go. hrw .com**

Visit **go.hrw.com** for extra help and study aids matched to your textbook. Just type in the keyword HST HOME.

 **SC*i*LINKS. NSTA**

Visit **www.scilinks.org** to find resources specific to topics in your textbook. Keywords appear throughout your book to take you further.

 Smithsonian Institution® **Internet Connections**

Visit **www.si.edu/hrw** for specifically chosen on-line materials from one of our nation's premier science museums.

 **CNN fyi.com**

Visit **www.cnnfyi.com** for late-breaking news and current events stories selected just for you.

# Matter in Motion

Pre-Reading
Questions

1. How is motion measured?
2. What is a force?
3. How does friction affect motion?
4. How does gravity affect objects?

## SWOOSH!!

Have you ever watched a speed skating race during the Winter Olympics? Speed skaters are extremely fast. In fact, some speed skaters have been known to skate at a rate of 12 meters per second! Speed skaters, like the one you see in this photograph, must have a great deal of athletic skill and ability. First of all, they have to be very strong in order to exert the force needed to move so fast. Secondly, speed skaters skate on ice, which is very slippery. These athletes must be able to overcome the lack of friction between their skates and the ice—so they won't fall during the race! In this chapter, you will learn more about motion, including speed and acceleration, and the forces that affect motion, such as friction and gravity.

## Activity

## THE DOMINO DERBY

Speed is the rate at which an object moves. In this activity, you will determine the factors that affect the speed of falling dominoes.

### Procedure

1. Set up **25 dominoes** in a straight line. Try to keep equal spacing between the dominoes.

2. Using a **meterstick,** measure the total length of your row of dominoes, and write it down.

3. Using a **stopwatch,** time how long it takes for the entire row of dominoes to fall. Record this measurement.

4. Repeat steps 2 and 3 several times, using distances between the dominoes that are smaller and larger than the distance used in your first setup.

### Analysis

5. Calculate the average speed for each trial by dividing the total distance (the length of the domino row) by the time taken to fall.

6. How did the spacing between dominoes affect the average speed? Is this result what you expected? If not, explain.

*What You'll Do*

◆ Identify the relationship between motion and a reference point.
◆ Identify the two factors that speed depends on.
◆ Determine the difference between speed and velocity.
◆ Analyze the relationship of velocity to acceleration.
◆ Interpret a graph showing acceleration.

# Measuring Motion

Look around you—you're likely to see something in motion. Your teacher may be walking across the room, or perhaps a bird is flying outside a window. Even if you don't see anything moving, motion is still occurring all around you. Tiny air particles are whizzing around, the moon is circling the Earth, and blood is traveling through your veins and arteries!

## Observing Motion

You might think that the motion of an object is easy to detect—you just observe the object. But you actually must observe the object in relation to another object that appears to stay in place. The object that appears to stay in place is a *reference point*. When an object changes position over time when compared with a reference point, the object is in **motion.** When an object is in motion, you can describe the direction of its motion with a reference direction, such as north, south, east, west, or up and down.

**Common Reference Points**  The Earth's surface is a common reference point for determining position and motion. Nonmoving objects on Earth's surface, such as buildings, trees, and mountains, are also useful reference points, as shown in **Figure 1.**

A moving object can also be used as a reference point. For example, if you were on the hot-air balloon shown below, you could watch a bird fly by and see that it was changing position in relation to your moving balloon. Furthermore, Earth itself is a moving reference point—it is moving around the sun.

**Figure 1** *During the time it took for these pictures to be taken, the hot-air balloon changed position compared with a reference point–the mountain.*

## Speed Depends on Distance and Time

The rate at which an object moves is its **speed.** Speed depends on the distance traveled and the time taken to travel that distance. Look back at Figure 1. Suppose the time interval between the pictures was 10 seconds and the balloon traveled 50 m in that time. The speed (distance divided by time) of the balloon is 50 m/10 s, or 5 m/s.

The SI unit for speed is meters per second (m/s). Kilometers per hour, feet per second, and miles per hour are other units commonly used to express speed.

**Determining Average Speed** Most of the time, objects do not travel at a constant speed. For example, you probably do not walk at a constant speed from one class to the next. Therefore, it is very useful to calculate *average speed* using the following equation:

$$\text{Average speed} = \frac{\text{total distance}}{\text{total time}}$$

**Recognizing Speed on a Graph** Suppose a person drives from one city to another. The blue line in the graph below shows the distance traveled every hour. Notice that the distance traveled every hour is different. This is because the speed (distance/time) is not constant—the driver changes speed often because of weather, traffic, or varying speed limits. The average speed can be calculated by adding up the total distance and dividing it by the total time:

$$\text{Average speed} = \frac{360 \text{ km}}{4 \text{ h}} = 90 \text{ km/h}$$

The red line shows the average distance traveled each hour. The slope of this line is the average speed.

**MATH BREAK**

**Calculating Average Speed**

Practice calculating average speed in the problems listed below:

1. If you walk for 1.5 hours and travel 7.5 km, what is your average speed?

2. A bird flies at a speed of 15 m/s for 10 s, 20 m/s for 10 s, and 25 m/s for 5 s. What is the bird's average speed?

### A Graph Showing Speed

Actual ━━  Average ━━

Distance (km): 400, 300, 200, 100, 0

Time (h): 1, 2, 3, 4

# Velocity: Direction Matters

*Here's a riddle for you: Two birds leave the same tree at the same time. They both fly at 10 km/h for 1 hour, 15 km/h for 30 minutes, and 5 km/h for 1 hour. Why don't they end up at the same destination?*

Have you figured it out? The birds traveled at the same speeds for the same amounts of time, but they did not end up at the same place because they went in different directions. In other words, they had different velocities. The speed of an object in a particular direction is the object's **velocity** (vuh LAHS uh tee).

Be careful not to confuse the terms *speed* and *velocity;* they do not mean the same thing. Because velocity must include direction, it would not be correct to say that an airplane's velocity is 600 km/h. However, you could say the plane's velocity is 600 km/h south. Velocity always includes a reference direction. **Figure 2** further illustrates the difference between speed and velocity.

**Figure 2** *The speeds of these cars may be similar, but their velocities are different because they are going in different directions.*

**Velocity Changes as Speed or Direction Changes** You can think of velocity as the rate of change of an object's position. An object's velocity is constant only if its speed and direction don't change. Therefore, constant velocity is always along a straight line. An object's velocity will change if either its speed or direction changes. For example, if a bus traveling at 15 m/s south speeds up to 20 m/s, a change in velocity has occurred. But a change in velocity also occurs if the bus continues to travel at the same speed but changes direction to travel east.

## ✔ Self-Check

Which of the following are examples of velocity?

1. 25 m/s forward
2. 1,500 km/h
3. 55 m/h south
4. all of the above

*(See page 232 to check your answer.)*

**Combining Velocities** If you're riding in a bus traveling east at 15 m/s, you and all the other passengers are also traveling at a velocity of 15 m/s east. But suppose you stand up and walk down the bus's aisle while it is moving. Are you still moving at the same velocity as the bus? No! **Figure 3** shows how you can combine velocities to determine the *resultant velocity.*

**Figure 3 Determining Resultant Velocity**

**15 m/s east**

1 m/s east

When you combine two velocities that are **in the same direction**, add them together to find the resultant velocity.

**Person's resultant velocity**

15 m/s east + 1 m/s east = 16 m/s east

1 m/s west

**15 m/s east**

When you combine two velocities that are **in opposite directions**, subtract the smaller velocity from the larger velocity to find the resultant velocity. The resultant velocity is in the direction of the larger velocity.

**Person's resultant velocity**

15 m/s east − 1 m/s west = 14 m/s east

## SECTION REVIEW

1. What is a reference point?

2. What two things must you know to determine speed?

3. What is the difference between speed and velocity?

4. **Applying Concepts** Explain why it is important to know a tornado's velocity and not just its speed.

**BRAIN FOOD**

The space shuttle is always launched in the same direction that the Earth rotates, thus taking advantage of the Earth's rotational velocity (over 1,500 km/h east). This allows the shuttle to use less fuel to reach space than if it had to achieve such a great velocity on its own.

# Acceleration: The Rate at Which Velocity Changes

Imagine that you are in-line skating and you see a large rock in your path. You slow down and swerve to avoid the rock. A neighbor sees you and exclaims, "That was great acceleration! I'm amazed that you could slow down and turn so quickly!" You're puzzled. Doesn't *accelerate* mean to speed up? But you didn't speed up—you slowed down and turned. So how could you have accelerated?

**Defining Acceleration** Although the word *accelerate* is commonly used to mean "speed up," there's more to its meaning scientifically. **Acceleration** (ak SEL uhr AY shuhn) is the rate at which velocity changes. To *accelerate* means to change velocity. You just learned that velocity changes if speed changes, direction changes, or both. So your neighbor was right! Your speed and direction changed, so you accelerated.

Keep in mind that acceleration is not just how much velocity changes. It is also *how fast* velocity changes. The faster velocity changes, the greater the acceleration is.

**Calculating Acceleration** You can calculate acceleration by using the following equation:

$$\text{Acceleration} = \frac{\text{final velocity} - \text{starting velocity}}{\text{time it takes to change velocity}}$$

Velocity is expressed in meters per second (m/s), and time is expressed in seconds (s). Therefore, acceleration is expressed in meters per second per second (m/s/s).

Suppose you get on your bicycle and accelerate southward at a rate of 1 m/s/s. (Like velocity, acceleration has size and direction.) This means that every second, your southward velocity increases by 1 m/s, as shown in **Figure 4** on the next page.

**Figure 4** **Acceleration at 1 m/s/s South**

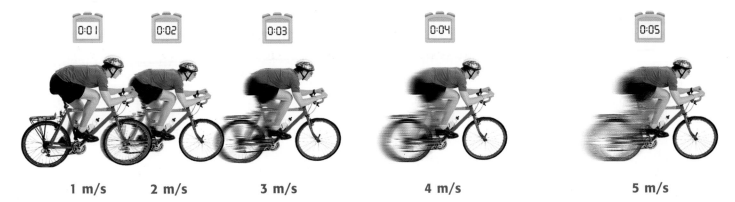

1 m/s      2 m/s      3 m/s      4 m/s      5 m/s

After 1 second, you have a velocity of 1 m/s south, as shown in Figure 4. After 2 seconds, you have a velocity of 2 m/s south. After 3 seconds, you have a velocity of 3 m/s south, and so on. If your final velocity after 5 seconds is 5 m/s south, your acceleration can be calculated as follows:

$$\text{Acceleration} = \frac{5 \text{ m/s} - 0 \text{ m/s}}{5 \text{ s}} = 1 \text{ m/s/s south}$$

You can practice calculating acceleration by doing the MathBreak shown here.

**Examples of Acceleration**  In the example above, your velocity was originally zero and then it increased. Because your velocity changed, you accelerated. Acceleration in which velocity increases is sometimes called *positive acceleration*.

Acceleration also occurs when velocity decreases. In the skating example, you accelerated because you slowed down. Acceleration in which velocity decreases is sometimes called *negative acceleration* or *deceleration*.

Remember that velocity has direction, so velocity will change if your direction changes. Therefore, a change in direction is acceleration, even if there is no change in speed. Some more examples of acceleration are shown in the chart below.

**MATH BREAK**

**Calculating Acceleration**

Use the equation shown on the previous page to do the following problems. Be sure to express your answers in m/s/s and include direction.

1. A plane passes over Point A with a velocity of 8,000 m/s north. Forty seconds later it passes over Point B at a velocity of 10,000 m/s north. What is the plane's acceleration from A to B?

2. A coconut falls from the top of a tree and reaches a velocity of 19.6 m/s when it hits the ground. It takes 2 seconds to reach the ground. What is the coconut's acceleration?

| Example of Acceleration | How Velocity Changes |
| --- | --- |
| A plane taking off | Increase in speed |
| A car stopping at a stop sign | Decrease in speed |
| Jogging on a winding trail | Change in direction |
| Driving around a corner | Change in direction |
| Standing at Earth's equator | Change in direction |

Figure 5 *The blades of this windmill are constantly changing direction as they travel in a circle. Thus, centripetal acceleration is occurring.*

**Circular Motion: Continuous Acceleration**   Does it surprise you to find out that standing at Earth's equator is an example of acceleration? After all, you're not changing speed, and you're not changing direction . . . or are you? In fact, you are traveling in a circle as the Earth rotates. An object traveling in a circular motion is always changing its direction. Therefore, its velocity is always changing, so acceleration is occurring. The acceleration that occurs in circular motion is known as *centripetal* (sen TRIP uht uhl) *acceleration.* Another example of centripetal acceleration is shown in **Figure 5.**

**Recognizing Acceleration on a Graph**   Suppose that you have just gotten on a roller coaster. The roller coaster moves slowly up the first hill until it stops at the top. Then you're off, racing down the hill! The graph below shows your acceleration for the 10 seconds coming down the hill. You can tell from this graph that your acceleration is positive because your velocity increases as time passes. Because the graph is not a straight line, you can also tell that your acceleration is not constant for each second.

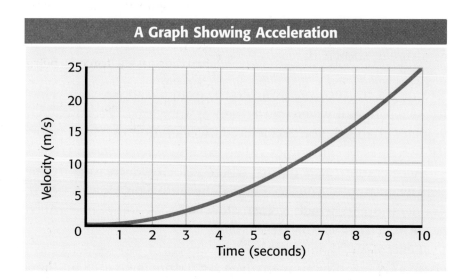

**A Graph Showing Acceleration**

**internet connect**

**SC*i*LINKS.**
**NSTA**

**TOPIC:** Measuring Motion
**GO TO:** www.scilinks.org
***sci*LINKS NUMBER:** HSTP105

## SECTION REVIEW

1. What is acceleration?

2. Does a change in direction affect acceleration? Explain your answer.

3. **Interpreting Graphics**  How do you think a graph of deceleration would differ from the graph shown above? Explain your reasoning.

## Terms to Learn

force                    net force
newton

## What You'll Do

- Give examples of different kinds of forces.
- Determine the net force on an object.
- Compare balanced and unbalanced forces.

# What Is a Force?

You often hear the word *force* in everyday conversation:

"That storm had a lot of force!"
"Our basketball team is a force to be reckoned with."
"A flat tire forced me to stop riding my bicycle."
"The inning ended with a force-out at second base."

But what exactly is a force? In science, a **force** is simply a push or a pull. All forces have both size and direction.

Forces are everywhere. In fact, any time you see something moving, you can be sure that its motion was created by a force. Scientists express force using a unit called the **newton (N).** The more newtons, the greater the force.

## Forces Act on Objects

All forces are exerted by one object on another object. For any push to occur, something has to receive the push. You can't push nothing! The same is true for any pull. When doing schoolwork, you use your fingers to pull open books or to push the buttons on a computer keyboard. In these examples, your fingers are exerting forces on the books and the keys. However, just because a force is being exerted by one object on another doesn't mean that motion will occur. For example, you are probably sitting on a chair as you read this. But the force you are exerting on the chair does not cause the chair to move. That's because the Earth is also exerting a force on the chair. In most cases, it is easy to determine where the push or pull is coming from, as shown in **Figure 6.**

**Figure 6** *It is obvious that the bulldozer is exerting a force on the pile of soil. But did you know that the pile of soil also exerts a force, even when it is just sitting on the ground?*

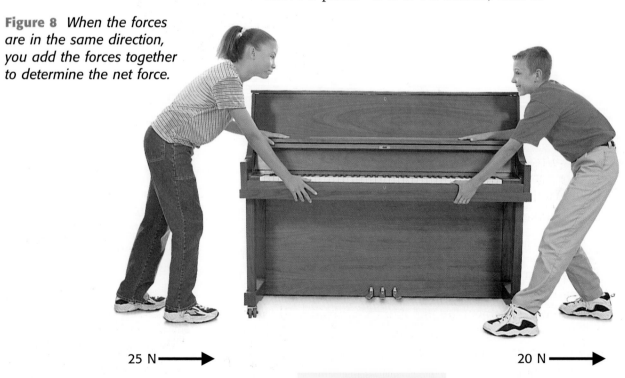

**Figure 7**
*Something unseen exerts a force that makes your socks cling together when they come out of the dryer. You have to exert a force to separate the socks.*

It is not always so easy to tell what is exerting a force or what is receiving a force, as shown in **Figure 7.** You cannot see what exerts the force that pulls magnets to refrigerators, and the air you breathe is an unseen receiver of a force called *gravity.* You will learn more about gravity later in this chapter.

## Forces in Combination

Often more than one force is exerted on an object at the same time. The **net force** is the force that results from combining all the forces exerted on an object. So how do you determine the net force? The examples below can help you answer this question.

**Forces in the Same Direction**  Suppose you and a friend are asked to move a piano for the music teacher. To do this, you pull on one end of the piano, and your friend pushes on the other end. Together, your forces add up to enough force to move the piano. This is because your forces are in the same direction. **Figure 8** shows this situation. Because the forces are in the same direction, they can be added together to determine the net force. In this case, the net force is 45 N, which is plenty to move a piano—if it is on wheels, that is!

**Figure 8** *When the forces are in the same direction, you add the forces together to determine the net force.*

25 N ➤

20 N ➤

**Net force**
25 N + 20 N = 45 N
to the right

**Forces in Different Directions** Consider two dogs playing tug of war with a short piece of rope. Each is exerting a force, but in opposite directions. **Figure 9** shows this scene. Notice that the dog on the left is pulling with a force of 10 N and the dog on the right is pulling with a force of 12 N. Which dog do you think will win the tug of war?

Because the forces are in opposite directions, the net force is determined by subtracting the smaller force from the larger one. In this case, the net force is 2 N in the direction of the dog on the right. Give that dog a dog biscuit!

## Science

## C O N N E C T I O N

Every moment, forces in several directions are exerted on the Golden Gate Bridge. For example, Earth exerts a powerful downward force on the bridge while elastic forces pull and push portions of the bridge up and down. To learn how the bridge stands up to these forces, turn to page 33.

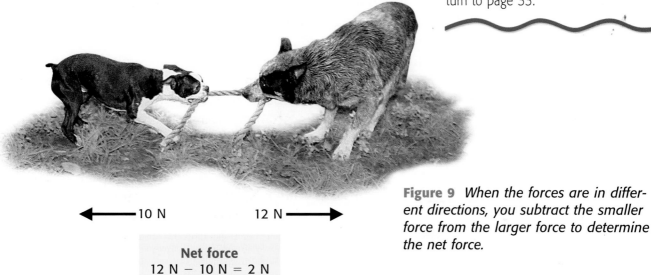

**Net force**
12 N − 10 N = 2 N
to the right

**Figure 9** *When the forces are in different directions, you subtract the smaller force from the larger force to determine the net force.*

## Unbalanced and Balanced Forces

If you know the net force on an object, you can determine the effect the force will have on the object's motion. Why? The net force tells you whether the forces on the object are balanced or unbalanced.

**Unbalanced Forces Produce a Change in Motion** In the examples shown in Figures 8 and 9, the net force on the object is greater than zero. When the net force on an object is not zero, the forces on the object are *unbalanced*. Unbalanced forces produce a change in motion (acceleration). In the two previous examples, the receivers of the forces—the piano and the rope—move. Unbalanced forces are necessary to cause a non-moving object to start moving.

## Self-Check

What is the net force when you combine a force of 7 N north with a force of 5 N south? *(See page 232 to check your answer.)*

Unbalanced forces are also necessary to change the motion of moving objects. For example, consider a soccer game. The soccer ball is already moving when it is passed from one player to another. When the ball reaches the second player, the player exerts an unbalanced force—a kick—on the ball. After the kick, the ball moves in a new direction and with a new speed.

Keep in mind that an object can continue to move even when the unbalanced forces are removed. A soccer ball, for example, receives an unbalanced force when it is kicked. However, the ball continues to roll along the ground long after the force of the kick has ended.

**Balanced Forces Produce No Change in Motion** When the forces applied to an object produce a net force of zero, the forces are *balanced*. Balanced forces do not cause a nonmoving object to start moving. Furthermore, balanced forces will not cause a change in the motion of a moving object.

Many objects around you have only balanced forces acting on them. For example, a light hanging from the ceiling does not move because the force of gravity pulling down on the light is balanced by an elastic force due to tension that pulls the light up. A bird's nest in a tree and a hat resting on your head are also examples of objects with only balanced forces acting on them. **Figure 10** shows another case where the forces on an object are balanced. Because all the forces are balanced, the house of cards does not move.

**Figure 10** *The forces on this house of cards are balanced. An unbalanced force on one of the cards would cause motion—and probably a mess!*

## SECTION REVIEW

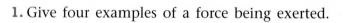

1. Give four examples of a force being exerted.

2. Explain the difference between balanced and unbalanced forces and how each affects the motion of an object.

3. **Interpreting Graphics** In the picture at left, two bighorn sheep push on each other's horns. The arrow shows the direction the two sheep are moving. Describe the forces the sheep are exerting and how the forces combine to produce the sheep's motion.

**Terms to Learn**

friction

**What You'll Do**

◆ Explain why friction occurs.
◆ List the types of friction, and give examples of each.
◆ Explain how friction can be both harmful and helpful.

# Friction: A Force That Opposes Motion

Picture a warm summer day. You are enjoying the day by wearing shorts and tossing a ball with your friends. By accident, one of your friends tosses the ball just out of your reach. You have to make a split-second decision to dive for it or not. You look down and notice that if you dove for it, you would most likely slide across pavement rather than the surrounding grass. What would you decide?

Unless you enjoy scraped knees, you probably would not want to slide on the pavement. The painful difference between sliding on grass and sliding on pavement has to do with friction. **Friction** is a force that opposes motion between two surfaces that are touching.

## The Source of Friction

Friction occurs because the surface of any object is rough. Even surfaces that look or feel very smooth are actually covered with microscopic hills and valleys. When two surfaces are in contact, the hills and valleys of one surface stick to the hills and valleys of the other surface, as shown in **Figure 11.** This contact causes friction even when the surfaces appear smooth.

The amount of friction between two surfaces depends on many factors, including the roughness of the surfaces and the force pushing the surfaces together.

**Figure 11** *When the hills and valleys of one surface stick to the hills and valleys of another surface, friction is created.*

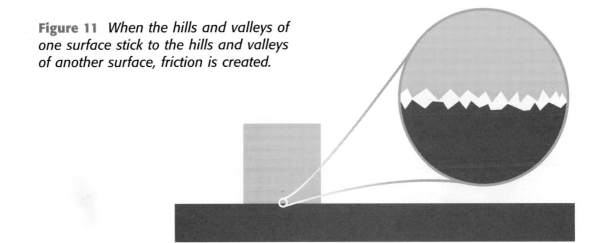

**Rougher Surfaces Create More Friction**  Rougher surfaces have more microscopic hills and valleys. Thus, the rougher the surface, the greater the friction. Think back to the example on the previous page. Pavement is much rougher than grass. Therefore, more friction is produced when you slide on the pavement than when you slide on grass. This increased friction is more effective at stopping your sliding, but it is also more painful! On the other hand, if the surfaces are smooth, there is less friction. If you were to slide on ice instead of on grass, your landing would be even more comfortable—but also much colder!

**Greater Force Creates More Friction**  The amount of friction also depends on the force pushing the surfaces together. If this force is increased, the hills and valleys of the surfaces can come into closer contact. This causes the friction between the surfaces to increase. Less massive objects exert less force on surfaces than more massive objects do, as illustrated in **Figure 12**. However, changing the amounts of the surfaces that touch does not change the amount of friction.

**Figure 12  Force and Friction**

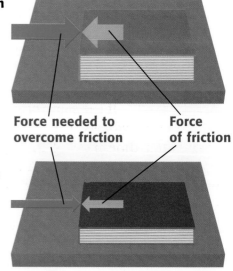

**a**  There is more friction between the more massive book and the table than there is between the less massive book and the table. A harder push is needed to overcome friction to move the more massive book.

Force needed to overcome friction

Force of friction

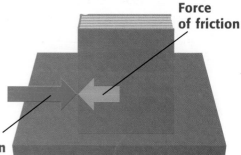

**b**  Turning the more massive book on its edge does not change the amount of friction between the table and the book.

Force of friction

Force needed to overcome friction

# Types of Friction

The friction you observe when sliding books across a tabletop is called sliding friction. Other types of friction include rolling friction, fluid friction, and static friction. As you will learn, the name of each type of friction is a big clue as to the conditions where it can be found.

**Sliding Friction** If you push an eraser across your desk, the eraser will move for a short distance and then stop. This is an example of *sliding friction*. Sliding friction is very effective at opposing the movement of objects and is the force that causes the eraser to stop moving. You can feel the effect of sliding friction when you try to move a heavy dresser by pushing it along the floor. You must exert a lot of force to overcome the sliding friction, as shown in **Figure 13.**

You use sliding friction when you go sledding, when you apply the brakes on a bicycle or a car, or when you write with a piece of chalk.

**Rolling Friction** If the same heavy dresser were on wheels, you would have an easier time moving it. The friction between the wheels and the floor is an example of *rolling friction*. The force of rolling friction is usually less than the force of sliding friction. Therefore, it is generally easier to move objects on wheels than it is to slide them along the floor, as shown at right.

Rolling friction is an important part of almost all means of transportation. Anything with wheels—bicycles, in-line skates, cars, trains, and planes—uses rolling friction between the wheels and the ground to move forward.

**Figure 13  Comparing Sliding Friction and Rolling Friction**

Moving a heavy piece of furniture in your room can be hard work because **the force of sliding friction is large.**

It is easier to move a heavy piece of furniture if you put it on wheels. **The force of rolling friction is smaller** and easier to overcome.

Figure 14 *Swimming provides a good workout because you must exert force to overcome fluid friction.*

**Fluid Friction** Why is it harder to walk on a freshly mopped floor than on a dry floor? The reason is that on the wet floor the sliding friction between your feet and the floor is replaced by *fluid friction* between your feet and the water. In this case, fluid friction is less than sliding friction, so the floor is slippery. The term *fluid* includes liquids, such as water and milk, and gases, such as air and helium.

Fluid friction opposes the motion of objects traveling through a fluid, as illustrated in **Figure 14.** For example, fluid friction between air and a fast moving car is the largest force opposing the motion of the car. You can observe this friction by holding your hand out the window of a moving car.

**Static Friction** When a force is applied to an object but does not cause the object to move, *static friction* occurs. The object does not move because the force of static friction balances the force applied. Static friction disappears as soon as an object starts moving, and then another type of friction immediately occurs. Look at **Figure 15** to understand when static friction affects an object.

**Figure 15** **Static Friction**

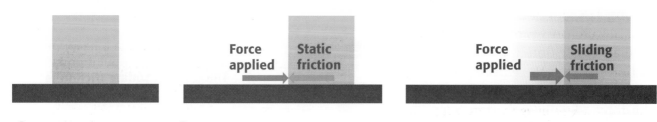

**a** There is no friction between the block and the table when no force is applied to the block to move it.

**b** If a small force—shown in blue—is exerted on the block, the block does not move. The force of static friction—shown in orange—exactly balances the force applied.

**c** When the force exerted on the block is greater than the force of static friction, the block starts moving. Once the block starts moving, all static friction is gone, and the force applied opposes sliding friction—shown in green.

## Self-Check

What type of friction was involved in the imaginary situation at the beginning of this section? *(See page 232 to check your answer.)*

# Friction Can Be Harmful or Helpful

Think about how friction affects a car. Without friction, the tires could not push against the ground to move the car forward and the brakes could not stop the car. Without friction, a car is useless. However, friction can cause problems in a car too. Friction between moving engine parts increases their temperature and causes the parts to wear down. A liquid coolant is added to the engine to keep it from overheating, and engine parts need to be changed as they wear out.

Friction is both harmful and helpful to you and the world around you. Friction can cause holes in your socks and in the knees of your jeans. Friction by wind and water can cause erosion of the topsoil that nourishes plants. On the other hand, friction between your pencil and your paper is necessary for the pencil to leave a mark. Without friction, you would just slip and fall when you tried to walk. Because friction can be both harmful and helpful, it is sometimes necessary to reduce or increase friction.

**Some Ways to Reduce Friction**   One way to reduce friction is to use lubricants. *Lubricants* (LOO bri kuhnts) are substances that are applied to surfaces to reduce the friction between them. Some examples of common lubricants are motor oil, wax, and grease. **Figure 16** shows why lubricants are important to maintaining car parts.

Friction can also be reduced by switching from sliding friction to rolling friction. Ball bearings are placed between the wheels and axles of in-line skates and bicycles to make it easier for the wheels to turn by reducing friction.

**Figure 16** *Motor oil is used as a lubricant in car engines. Without oil, engine parts would wear down quickly, as the connecting rod on the bottom has.*

**Figure 17** *No one enjoys cleaning pans with baked-on food! To make this chore pass quickly, press down with the scrubber to increase friction.*

Another way to reduce friction is to make surfaces that rub against each other smoother. For example, rough wood on a park bench is painful to slide across because there is a large amount of friction between your leg and the bench. Rubbing the bench with sandpaper makes it smoother and more comfortable to sit on because the friction between your leg and the bench is reduced.

**Some Ways to Increase Friction** One way to increase friction is to make surfaces rougher. For example, sand scattered on icy roads keeps cars from skidding. Baseball players sometimes wear textured batting gloves to increase the friction between their hands and the bat so that the bat does not fly out of their hands.

Another way to increase friction is to increase the force pushing the surfaces together. For example, you can ensure that your magazine will not blow away at the park by putting a heavy rock on it. The added mass of the rock increases the friction between the magazine and the ground. Or if you are sanding a piece of wood, you can sand the wood faster by pressing harder on the sandpaper. **Figure 17** shows another situation where friction is increased by pushing on an object.

## APPLY

### Friction and Tires

The tire shown here was used for more than 80,000 km. What effect did friction have on the rubber? What kind of friction is mainly responsible for the tire's appearance? Why are car owners warned to change their car tires after using them for several thousand kilometers?

**internetconnect**

SCi**LINKS**
NSTA

**TOPIC:** Force and Friction
**GO TO:** www.scilinks.org
*sci***LINKS NUMBER:** HSTP110

## SECTION REVIEW

1. Explain why friction occurs.

2. Name two ways in which friction can be increased.

3. Give an example of each of the following types of friction: sliding, rolling, and fluid.

4. **Applying Concepts** Name two ways that friction is harmful and two ways that friction is helpful to you when riding a bicycle.

*What You'll Do*

◆ Define gravity.
◆ State the law of universal gravitation.
◆ Describe the difference between mass and weight.

# Gravity: A Force of Attraction

If you watch videotape of astronauts on the moon, you will notice that when the astronauts tried to walk on the lunar surface, they bounced around like beach balls instead.

Why did the astronauts—who were wearing heavy spacesuits—bounce so easily on the moon (as shown in **Figure 18**), while you must exert effort to jump a few centimeters off Earth's surface? The answer has to do with gravity. **Gravity** is a force of attraction between objects that is due to their masses. In this section, you will learn about gravity and the effects it has on objects.

**Figure 18** *Because gravity is less on the moon than on Earth, walking on the moon's surface was a very bouncy experience for the Apollo astronauts.*

**Biology**

**C O N N E C T I O N**

Scientists think seeds can "sense" gravity. The ability to sense gravity is what causes seeds to always send roots down and the green shoot up. But scientists do not understand just *how* seeds do this. Astronauts have grown seedlings during space shuttle missions to see how seeds respond to changes in gravity. So far, there are no definite answers from the results of these experiments.

## All Matter Is Affected by Gravity

All matter has mass. Gravity is a result of mass. Therefore, all matter experiences gravity. That is, all objects experience an attraction toward all other objects. This gravitational force "pulls" objects toward each other. Right now, because of gravity, you are being pulled toward this book, your pencil, and every other object around you.

These objects are also being pulled toward you and toward each other because of gravity. So why don't you see the effects of this attraction? In other words, why don't you notice objects moving toward each other? The reason is that the mass of most objects is too small to cause an attraction large enough to move objects toward each other. However, you are familiar with one object that is massive enough to cause a noticeable attraction—the Earth.

**Earth's Gravitational Force Is Large** Compared with all the objects around you, Earth has an enormous mass. Therefore, Earth's gravitational force is very large. You must apply forces to overcome Earth's gravitational force any time you lift objects or even parts of your body.

Earth's gravitational force pulls everything toward the center of Earth. Because of this, the books, tables, and chairs in the room stay in place, and dropped objects fall to Earth rather than moving together or toward you.

## ✓ Self-Check

What is gravity? *(See page 232 to check your answer.)*

## The Law of Universal Gravitation

For thousands of years, two very puzzling questions were "Why do objects fall toward Earth?" and "What keeps the planets in motion in the sky?" The two questions were treated as separate topics until a British scientist named Sir Isaac Newton (1642–1727) realized that they were two parts of the same question.

**The Core of an Idea** Legend has it that Newton made the connection when he observed a falling apple during a summer night, as shown in **Figure 19.** He knew that unbalanced forces are necessary to move or change the motion of objects. He concluded that there had to be an unbalanced force on the apple to make it fall, just as there had to be an unbalanced force on the moon to keep it moving around Earth. He realized that these two forces are actually the same force—a force of attraction called gravity.

**A Law Is Born** Newton generalized his observations on gravity in a law now known as the *law of universal gravitation.* This law describes the relationships between gravitational force, mass, and distance. It is called universal because it applies to all objects in the universe.

**Figure 19**
**Newton Makes the Connection**

The law of universal gravitation states the following: All objects in the universe attract each other through gravitational force. The size of the force depends on the masses of the objects and the distance between them. The examples in **Figure 20** show the effects of the law of universal gravitation. It is easier to understand the law if you consider it in two parts.

**a** Gravitational force is small between objects with small masses.

**b** Gravitational force is larger between objects with larger masses.

**Figure 20** *The arrows indicate the gravitational force between the objects. The width of the arrows indicates the strength of the force.*

**c** If the distance between two objects is increased, the gravitational force pulling them together is reduced.

## Part 1: Gravitational Force Increases as Mass Increases

Imagine an elephant and a cat. Because an elephant has a larger mass than a cat, the amount of gravity between an elephant and Earth is greater than the amount of gravity between a cat and Earth. That is why a cat is much easier to pick up than an elephant! There is gravity between the cat and the elephant, but it is very small because the cat's mass and the elephant's mass are so much smaller than Earth's mass.

The moon has less mass than Earth. Therefore, the moon's gravitational force is less than Earth's. Remember the astronauts on the moon? They bounced around as they walked because they were not being pulled down with as much force as they would have been on Earth.

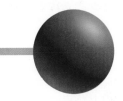

**Astronomy CONNECTION**

Black holes are formed when massive stars collapse. Black holes are 10 times to 1 billion times more massive than our sun. Thus, their gravitational force is incredibly large. The gravity of a black hole is so large that an object that enters a black hole can never get out. Even light cannot escape from a black hole. Because black holes do not emit light, they cannot be seen—hence their name.

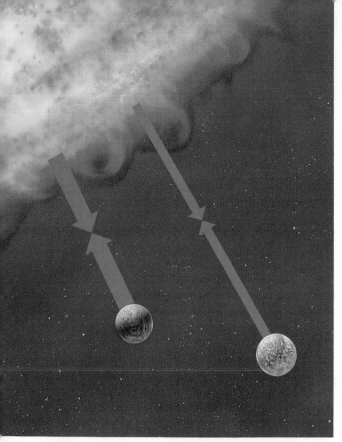

**Figure 21** *Venus and Earth have approximately the same mass. However, Venus is closer to the sun. Thus, the gravity between Venus and the sun is greater than the gravity between Earth and the sun.*

**Part 2: Gravitational Force Decreases as Distance Increases** The gravity between you and Earth is large. Whenever you jump up, you are pulled back down by Earth's gravitational force. On the other hand, the sun is more than 300,000 times more massive than Earth. So why doesn't the sun's gravitational force affect you more than Earth's does? The reason is that the sun is so far away.

You are approximately 150 million kilometers away from the sun. At this distance, the gravity between you and the sun is very small. If there were some way you could stand on the sun (and not burn up), you would find it impossible to jump or even walk. The gravitational force acting on you would be so great that your muscles could not lift any part of your body!

Although the sun's gravitational force does not have much of an effect on your body here, it does have a big effect on Earth itself and the other planets, as shown in **Figure 21.** The gravity between the sun and the planets is large because the objects have large masses. If the sun's gravitational force did not have such an effect on the planets, the planets would not stay in orbit around the sun.

## Weight Is a Measure of Gravitational Force

You have learned that gravity is a force of attraction between objects that is due to their masses. **Weight** is a measure of the gravitational force exerted on an object. When you see or hear the word *weight,* it usually refers to Earth's gravitational force on an object. But weight can also be a measure of the gravitational force exerted on objects by the moon or other planets.

You have learned that the unit of force is a newton. Because gravity is a force and weight is a measure of gravity, weight is also expressed in newtons (N). On Earth, a 100 g object, such as a medium-sized apple, weighs approximately 1 N.

**Weight and Mass Are Different**  Weight is related to mass, but the two are not the same. Weight changes when gravitational force changes. **Mass** is the amount of matter in an object, and its value does not change. If an object is moved to a place with a greater gravitational force—like Jupiter—its weight will increase, but its mass will remain the same. **Figure 22** shows the weight and mass of an object on Earth and a place with about one-sixth the gravitational force—the moon.

Gravitational force is about the same everywhere on Earth, so the weight of any object is about the same everywhere. Because mass and weight are constant on Earth, the terms are often used to mean the same thing. This can lead to confusion. Be sure you understand the difference!

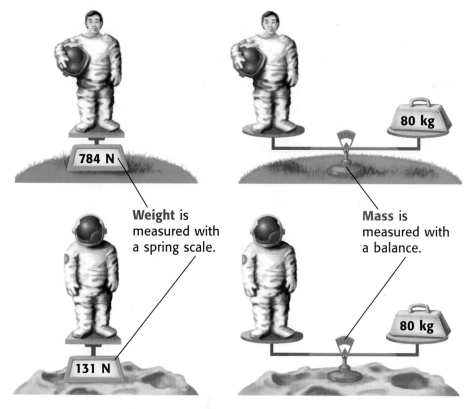

**Figure 22** *The astronaut's weight on the moon is about one-sixth of his weight on Earth, but his mass remains constant.*

784 N

80 kg

**Weight** is measured with a spring scale.

**Mass** is measured with a balance.

131 N

80 kg

## SECTION REVIEW

1. How does the mass of an object relate to the gravitational force the object exerts on other objects?

2. How does the distance between objects affect the gravity between them?

3. **Comparing Concepts**  Explain why your weight would change if you orbited Earth in the space shuttle but your mass would not.

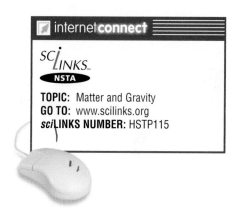

internet**connect**

SC*i*LINKS.
NSTA

**TOPIC:** Matter and Gravity
**GO TO:** www.scilinks.org
*sci*LINKS **NUMBER:** HSTP115

# Detecting Acceleration

Have you ever noticed that you can "feel" acceleration? In a car or in an elevator, you notice the change in speed or direction—even with your eyes closed! Inside your ears are tiny hair cells. These cells can detect the movement of fluid in your inner ear. When you accelerate, the fluid does, too. The hair cells detect this acceleration in the fluid and send a message to your brain. This message allows you to sense acceleration. In this activity you will build a device that detects acceleration.

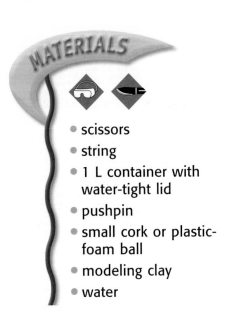

## MATERIALS

- scissors
- string
- 1 L container with water-tight lid
- pushpin
- small cork or plastic-foam ball
- modeling clay
- water

## Procedure

**1** Cut a piece of string that is just long enough to reach three-quarters of the way inside the container.

**2** Use a pushpin to attach one end of the string to the cork or plastic-foam ball.

**3** Use modeling clay to attach the other end of the string to the center of the inside of the container lid. Be careful not to use too much string—the cork (or ball) should hang no farther than three-quarters of the way into the container.

**4** Fill the container to the top with water.

**5** Put the lid tightly on the container with the string and cork (or ball) on the inside.

**6** Turn the container upside down (lid on the bottom). The cork should float about three-quarters of the way up inside the container, as shown at right. You are now ready to use your accelerometer to detect acceleration by following the steps on the next page.

**7** Put the accelerometer lid side down on a tabletop. Notice that the cork floats straight up in the water.

**8** Now gently start pushing the accelerometer across the table at a constant speed. Notice that the cork quickly moves in the direction you are pushing and then swings backward. If you did not see this motion, try the same thing again until you are sure you can see the first movement of the cork.

**9** Once you are familiar with how to use your accelerometer, try the following changes in motion. Record your observations of the cork's first motion for each change in your ScienceLog.

   **a.** While moving the device across the table, push a little faster.

   **b.** While moving the device across the table, slow down.

   **c.** While moving the device across the table, change the direction that you are pushing. (Try changing both to the left and to the right.)

   **d.** Make any other changes in motion you can think of. You should only change one part of the motion at a time.

## Analysis

**10** The cork moves forward (in the direction you were pushing the bottle) when you speed up but backward when you slow down. Explain why. (Hint: Think about the direction of acceleration.)

**11** When you push the bottle at a constant speed, why does the cork quickly swing back after it shows you the direction of acceleration?

**12** Imagine you are standing on a corner and watching a car that is waiting at a stoplight. A passenger inside the car is holding some helium balloons. Based on what you observed with your accelerometer, what do you think will happen to the balloons when the car begins moving?

### Going Further
If you move the bottle in a circle at a constant speed, what do you predict the cork will do? Try it, and check your answer.

# Chapter Highlights

## SECTION 1

### Vocabulary

**motion** *(p. 4)*

**speed** *(p. 5)*

**velocity** *(p. 6)*

**acceleration** *(p. 8)*

### Section Notes

- An object is in motion if it changes position over time when compared with a reference point.

- The speed of a moving object depends on the distance traveled by the object and the time taken to travel that distance.

- Speed and velocity are not the same thing. Velocity is speed in a given direction.

- Acceleration is the rate at which velocity changes.

- An object can accelerate by changing speed, changing direction, or both.

- Acceleration is calculated by subtracting starting velocity from final velocity, then dividing by the time required to change velocity.

### Labs

**Built for Speed** *(p. 186)*

## SECTION 2

### Vocabulary

**force** *(p. 11)*

**newton** *(p. 11)*

**net force** *(p. 12)*

### Section Notes

- A force is a push or a pull.

- Forces are expressed in newtons.

- Force is always exerted by one object on another object.

- Net force is determined by combining forces.

- Unbalanced forces produce a change in motion. Balanced forces produce no change in motion.

# ☑ Skills Check

## Math Concepts

**ACCELERATION** An object's acceleration can be determined using the following equation:

$$\text{Acceleration} = \frac{\text{final velocity} - \text{starting velocity}}{\text{time it takes to change velocity}}$$

For example, suppose a cheetah running at a velocity of 27 m/s east slows down. After 15 seconds, the cheetah has stopped.

$$\frac{0 \text{ m/s} - 27 \text{ m/s}}{15 \text{ s}} = -1.8 \text{ m/s/s east}$$

## Visual Understanding

**THE SOURCE OF FRICTION** Even surfaces that look or feel very smooth are actually rough at the microscopic level. To understand how this roughness causes friction, review Figure 11 on page 15.

**THE LAW OF UNIVERSAL GRAVITATION** This law explains that the gravity between objects depends on their masses and the distance between them. Review the effects of this law by looking at Figure 20 on page 23.

## SECTION 3

### Vocabulary

**friction** (p. 15)

### Section Notes

- Friction is a force that opposes motion.

- Friction is caused by "hills and valleys" touching on the surfaces of two objects.

- The amount of friction depends on factors such as the roughness of the surfaces and the force pushing the surfaces together.

- Four kinds of friction that affect your life are sliding friction, rolling friction, fluid friction, and static friction.

- Friction can be harmful or helpful.

## SECTION 4

### Vocabulary

**gravity** (p. 21)

**weight** (p. 24)

**mass** (p. 25)

### Section Notes

- Gravity is a force of attraction between objects that is due to their masses.

- The law of universal gravitation states that all objects in the universe attract each other through gravitational force. The size of the force depends on the masses of the objects and the distance between them.

- Weight and mass are not the same. Mass is the amount of matter in an object; weight is a measure of the gravitational force on an object.

### Labs

**Relating Mass and Weight** (p. 187)

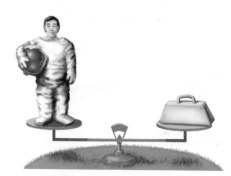

# Chapter Review

## USING VOCABULARY

To complete the following sentences, choose the correct term from each pair of terms listed below:

1. ___?___ opposes motion between surfaces that are touching. *(Friction or Gravity)*

2. Forces are expressed in ___?___. *(newtons or mass)*

3. A ___?___ is determined by combining forces. *(net force or newton)*

4. ___?___ is the rate at which ___?___ changes. *(Velocity or Acceleration/velocity or acceleration)*

## UNDERSTANDING CONCEPTS

### Multiple Choice

5. A student riding her bicycle on a straight, flat road covers one block every 7 seconds. If each block is 100 m long, she is traveling at
   a. constant speed.
   b. constant velocity.
   c. 10 m/s.
   d. Both (a) and (b)

6. Friction is a force that
   a. opposes an object's motion.
   b. does not exist when surfaces are very smooth.
   c. decreases with larger mass.
   d. All of the above

7. Rolling friction
   a. is usually less than sliding friction.
   b. makes it difficult to move objects on wheels.
   c. is usually greater than sliding friction.
   d. is the same as fluid friction.

8. If Earth's mass doubled, your weight would
   a. increase because gravity increases.
   b. decrease because gravity increases.
   c. increase because gravity decreases.
   d. not change because you are still on Earth.

9. A force
   a. is expressed in newtons.
   b. can cause an object to speed up, slow down, or change direction.
   c. is a push or a pull.
   d. All of the above

10. The amount of gravity between 1 kg of lead and Earth is _____ the amount of gravity between 1 kg of marshmallows and Earth.
    a. greater than        c. the same as
    b. less than           d. none of the above

### Short Answer

11. Describe the relationship between motion and a reference point.

12. How is it possible to be accelerating and traveling at a constant speed?

13. Explain the difference between mass and weight.

## Concept Mapping

**14.** Use the following terms to create a concept map: speed, velocity, acceleration, force, direction, motion.

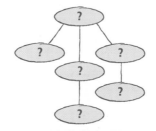

**19.** Is this a graph of positive or negative acceleration? How can you tell?

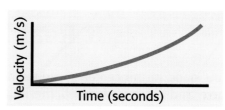

## CRITICAL THINKING AND PROBLEM SOLVING

**15.** Your family is moving, and you are asked to help move some boxes. One box is so heavy that you must push it across the room rather than lift it. What are some ways you could reduce friction to make moving the box easier?

**16.** Explain how using the term *accelerator* when talking about a car's gas pedal can lead to confusion, considering the scientific meaning of the word *acceleration*.

**17.** Explain why it is important for airplane pilots to know wind velocity, not just wind speed, during a flight.

**20.** You know how to combine two forces that act in one or two directions. The same method you learned can be used to combine several forces acting in several directions. Examine the diagrams below, and predict with how much force and in what direction the object will move.

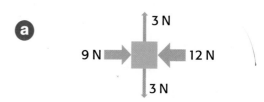

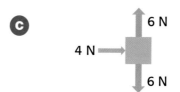

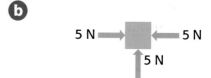

## MATH IN SCIENCE

**18.** A kangaroo hops 60 m to the east in 5 seconds.
  **a.** What is the kangaroo's speed?
  **b.** What is the kangaroo's velocity?
  **c.** The kangaroo stops at a lake for a drink of water, then starts hopping again to the south. Every second, the kangaroo's velocity increases 2.5 m/s. What is the kangaroo's acceleration after 5 seconds?

**Reading Check-up**

Take a minute to review your answers to the Pre-Reading Questions found at the bottom of page 2. Have your answers changed? If necessary, revise your answers based on what you have learned since you began this chapter.

# Science, Technology, and Society

## Is It Real . . . or Is It Virtual?

You stand in the center of a darkened room and put on a helmet. The helmet covers your head and face, making it impossible for you to see or hear anything from outside. Wires run from the helmet to a series of computers, carrying information about how your head is positioned and where you are looking. Other wires carry back to you the sights and sounds the computer wants you to "see" and "hear." All of a sudden you find your-self driving a race car around a tricky course at 300 km/h. Then in another instant, you are in the middle of a rain forest staring at a live snake!

### It's All an Illusion

Such simulated-reality experiences were once thought the stuff of science fiction alone. But today devices called motion simulators can stimulate the senses of sight and sound to create illusions of movement.

Virtual-reality devices, as these motion simu-lators are called, were first used during World War II to train pilots. Mock-ups of fighter-plane cockpits, films of simulated terrain, and a joy-stick that manipulated large hydraulic arms simulated the plane in "virtual flight." Today's jet pilots train with similar equipment, except the simulators use extremely sophisticated computer graphics instead of films.

### Fooled You!

Virtual-reality hoods and gloves take people into a variety of "realities." Inside the hood, two small television cameras or computer-graphic images fool the wearer's sense of vision. The brain perceives the image as three-dimensional because one image is placed in front of each eye. As the images change, the computer adjusts the scene's perspective so that it appears to the viewer as though he or she is moving through the scene. When the position of the head changes, the computer adjusts the scene to account for the movement. All the while, sounds coming through the headphones trick the wearer's ears into thinking he or she is moving too.

In addition to hoods, gloves, and images, virtual-reality devices may have other types of sensors. Driving simulators, for instance, often have a steering wheel, a gas pedal, and a brake so that the participant has the sensation of driving. So whether you want spine-tingling excitement or on-the-job training, virtual reality could very well take *you* places!

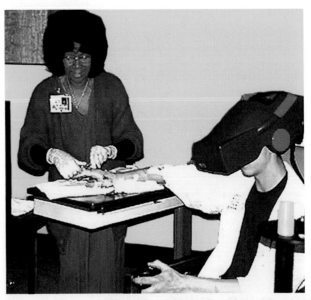

▲ *Wearing a virtual-reality helmet helps to lessen the pain this burn patient feels while his dressings are changed.*

### Explore New Realities

▶ What other activities or skills could be learned or practiced with virtual reality? What are some problems with relying on this tech-nology? Record your ideas in your ScienceLog.

# The Golden Gate Bridge

Have you ever relaxed in a hammock? If so, you may have noticed how tense the strings got when the hammock supported your weight. Now imagine a hammock 1,965 m long supporting a 20-ton roadway with more than 100,000 cars traveling along its length each day. That describes the Golden Gate Bridge! Because of the way the bridge is built, it is very much like a giant hammock.

## Tug of War

The bridge's roadway is suspended from main cables 2.33 km long that sweep from one end of the bridge to the other and that are anchored at each end. Smaller cables called *hangers* connect the main cables to the roadway. Tension, the force of being pulled apart, is created as the cables are pulled down by the weight of the roadway while being pulled up by their attachment to the top of each tower.

▲ *The Golden Gate Bridge spans the San Francisco Bay.*

## Towering Above

Towers 227 m tall support the cables over the long distance across San Francisco Bay, making the Golden Gate the tallest bridge in the world. The towers receive a force that is the exact opposite of tension—compression. Compression is the force of being pushed together. The main cables holding the weight of the roadway push down on the top of the towers while Earth pushes up on the bottom.

## Stretching the Limits

Tension and compression are elastic forces, which means they are dependent on elasticity, the ability of an object to return to its original shape after being stretched or compressed. If an object is not very elastic, it breaks easily or becomes permanently deformed when subjected to an elastic force. The cables and towers of the Golden Gate Bridge are made of steel, a material with great elastic strength. A single steel wire 2.54 mm thick can support over half a ton without breaking!

## On the Road

The roadway of the Golden Gate Bridge is subjected to multiple forces at the same time, including friction, gravity, and elastic forces. Rolling friction is caused by the wheels of each vehicle moving across the roadway's surface. Gravity pulls down on the roadway but is counteracted by the support of the towers and cables. This causes each roadway span to bend slightly and experience both tension and compression. The bottom of each span is under tension because the cables and towers pull up along the road's sides, while gravity pulls down at its center. These same forces cause compression of the top of each span. Did you ever imagine that so many forces were at work on a bridge?

## Bridge the Gap

▶ Find out more about another type of bridge, such as an arch, a beam, or a cable-stayed bridge. How do forces such as friction, gravity, tension, and compression affect these types of bridges?

# CHAPTER 2

# Forces in Motion

Pre-Reading
Questions

1. How does the force of gravity affect falling objects?
2. What is projectile motion?
3. What are Newton's laws of motion?
4. What is momentum?

## VOMIT COMET

Have you ever wondered what it would be like to move around without gravity? To help train astronauts for space flight, scientists have designed a special airplane called the KC-135 that simulates what it feels like to move with reduced gravity. The KC-135 first flies upward at a steep angle. When the airplane flies downward at a 45° angle, the effect of reduced gravity is produced inside. Then, the astronaut trainees in the plane can "float." Because the floating often makes passengers queasy, the KC-135 has earned a nickname—the Vomit Comet. In this chapter, you will learn how gravity affects the motion of objects and how the laws of motion apply to your life.

## FALLING WATER

Gravity is one of the most important forces in your life. In this activity, you will observe the effect of gravity on a falling object.

### Procedure

1. Place a **wide plastic tub** on the floor. Punch a small hole in the side of a **paper cup,** near the bottom.

2. Hold your finger over the hole, and fill the cup with **water.** Keeping your finger over the hole, hold the cup about waist high above the tub.

3. Uncover the hole. Describe your observations in your ScienceLog.

4. Next, predict what will happen to the water if you drop the cup at the same time you uncover the hole. Write your prediction in your ScienceLog.

5. Cover the hole with your finger again, and refill the cup.

6. Uncover the hole, and drop the cup at the same time. Record your observations.

7. Clean up any spilled water with **paper towels.**

### Analysis

8. What differences did you observe in the behavior of the water during the two trials?

9. In the second trial, how fast did the cup fall compared with the water?

**Terms to Learn**

terminal velocity
free fall
projectile motion

**What You'll Do**

◆ Explain how gravity and air resistance affect the acceleration of falling objects.
◆ Explain why objects in orbit appear to be weightless.
◆ Describe how an orbit is formed.
◆ Describe projectile motion.

# Gravity and Motion

Suppose you drop a baseball and a marble at the same time from the same height. Which do you think would land first? In ancient Greece around 400 B.C., an important philosopher named Aristotle (ER is TAWT uhl) believed that the rate at which an object falls depends on the object's mass. Imagine that you could ask Aristotle which object would land first. He would predict that the baseball would land first.

## All Objects Fall with the Same Acceleration

In the late 1500s, a young Italian scientist named Galileo questioned Aristotle's idea about falling objects. Galileo proved that the mass of an object does not affect the rate at which it falls. According to one story, Galileo did this by dropping two cannonballs of different masses from the top of the Leaning Tower of Pisa. The crowd watching from the ground was amazed to see the two cannonballs land at the same time. Whether or not this story is true, Galileo's idea changed people's understanding of gravity and falling objects.

**Acceleration Due to Gravity** Objects fall to the ground at the same rate because the acceleration due to gravity is the same for all objects. Does that seem odd? The force of gravity is greater between Earth and an object with a large mass than between Earth and a less massive object, so you may think that the acceleration due to gravity should be greater too. But a greater force must be applied to a large mass than to a small mass to produce the same acceleration. Thus, the difference in force is canceled by the difference in mass. **Figure 1** shows objects with different masses falling with the same acceleration.

**Figure 1** *A table tennis ball and a golf ball fall with the same acceleration even though they have different masses.*

**Accelerating at a Constant Rate** All objects accelerate toward Earth at a rate of 9.8 meters per second per second, which is expressed as 9.8 m/s/s. This means that for every second that an object falls, the object's downward velocity increases by 9.8 m/s, as shown in **Figure 2.** Remember, this acceleration is the same for all objects regardless of their mass. Do the MathBreak at right to learn how to calculate the velocity of a falling object.

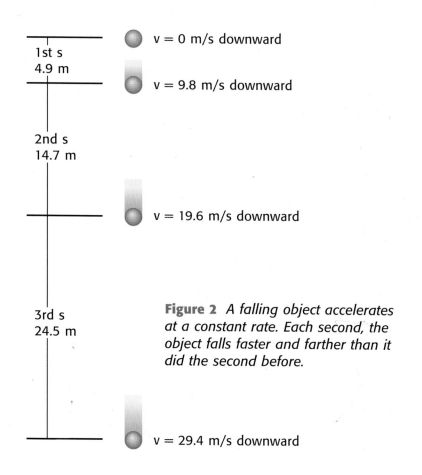

1st s
4.9 m

v = 0 m/s downward

v = 9.8 m/s downward

2nd s
14.7 m

v = 19.6 m/s downward

3rd s
24.5 m

**Figure 2** *A falling object accelerates at a constant rate. Each second, the object falls faster and farther than it did the second before.*

v = 29.4 m/s downward

## MATH BREAK

### Velocity of Falling Objects

To find the change in velocity ($\Delta v$) of a falling object, multiply the acceleration due to gravity ($g$) by the time it takes for the object to fall in seconds ($t$):

$$\Delta v = g \times t$$

For example, a stone at rest is dropped from a cliff, and it takes 3 seconds to hit the ground. Its downward velocity when it hits the ground is as follows:

$$\Delta v = 9.8 \ \frac{m/s}{\cancel{s}} \times 3 \ \cancel{s}$$
$$= 29.4 \ m/s$$

### Now It's Your Turn

A penny at rest is dropped from the top of a tall stairwell.

1. What is the penny's velocity after it has fallen for 2 seconds?

2. The penny hits the ground in 4.5 seconds. What is its final velocity?

## Air Resistance Slows Down Acceleration

Try this simple experiment. Drop two sheets of paper—one crumpled in a tight ball and the other kept flat. Did your results contradict what you just learned about falling objects? The flat paper fell more slowly because of fluid friction that opposes the motion of objects through air. This fluid friction is also known as *air resistance*. Air resistance occurs between the surface of the falling object and the air that surrounds it.

Gravity helps make roller coasters thrilling to ride. Read about a roller coaster designer on page 59.

## Self-Check

Which is more affected by air resistance—a leaf or an acorn? *(See page 232 to check your answer.)*

### Air Resistance Affects Some Objects More than Others

The amount of air resistance acting on an object depends on the size and shape of the object. Air resistance affects the flat sheet of paper more than the crumpled one, causing the flat sheet to fall more slowly than the crumpled one. Because air is all around you, any falling object you see is affected by air resistance. **Figure 3** shows the effect of air resistance on the downward acceleration of a falling object.

*Figure 3  The force of gravity pulls the object downward as the force of air resistance pushes it upward.*

This arrow represents **the force of air resistance** pushing up on the object. This force is subtracted from the force of gravity to produce the net force.

This arrow represents **the net force** on the object. Because the net force is not zero, the object still accelerates downward, but not as fast as it would without air resistance.

This arrow represents **the force of gravity** on the object. If this were the only force acting on the object, it would accelerate at a rate of 9.8 m/s/s.

### Acceleration Stops at the Terminal Velocity

As long as the net force on a falling object is not zero, the object accelerates downward. But the amount of air resistance on an object increases as the speed of the object increases. As an object falls, the upward force of air resistance continues to increase until it exactly matches the downward force of gravity. When this happens, the net force is zero, and the object stops accelerating. The object then falls at a constant velocity, which is called the **terminal velocity.**

Sometimes the fact that falling objects have a terminal velocity is a good thing. The terminal velocity of hailstones is between 5 and 40 m/s, depending on the size of the stones. Every year cars, buildings, and vegetation are all severely damaged in hail storms. Imagine how much more destructive hail would be if there were no air resistance—hailstones would hit the Earth at velocities near 350 m/s! **Figure 4** shows another situation in which terminal velocity is helpful.

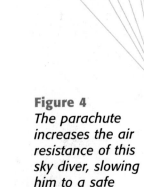

**Figure 4**
*The parachute increases the air resistance of this sky diver, slowing him to a safe terminal velocity.*

**Free Fall Occurs When There Is No Air Resistance** Sky divers are often described as being in free fall before they open their parachutes. However, that is an incorrect description, because air resistance is always acting on the sky diver.

An object is in **free fall** only if gravity is pulling it down and no other forces are acting on it. Because air resistance is a force (fluid friction), free fall can occur only where there is no air—in a vacuum (a place in which there is no matter) or in space. **Figure 5** shows objects falling in a vacuum. Because there is no air resistance, the two objects are in free fall.

**Figure 5** *Air resistance normally causes a feather to fall more slowly than an apple. But in a vacuum, the feather and the apple fall with the same acceleration because both are in free fall.*

## Orbiting Objects Are in Free Fall

Look at the astronaut in **Figure 6.** Why is the astronaut floating inside the space shuttle? It might be tempting to say it is because she is "weightless" in space. In fact, you may have read or heard that objects are weightless in space. However, it is impossible to be weightless anywhere in the universe.

Weight is a measure of gravitational force. The size of the force depends on the masses of objects and the distances between them. If you traveled in space far away from all the stars and planets, the gravitational force acting on you would be almost undetectable because the distance between you and other objects would be great. But you would still have mass, and so would all the other objects in the universe. Therefore, gravity would still attract you to other objects—even if just slightly—so you would still have weight.

Astronauts "float" in orbiting spaceships because of free fall. To understand this better, you need to understand what *orbiting* means and then consider the astronauts inside the ship.

**Figure 6** *Astronauts appear to be weightless while floating inside the space shuttle—but they're not!*

**Two Motions Combine to Cause Orbiting** An object is said to be orbiting when it is traveling in a circular or nearly circular path around another object. When a spaceship orbits Earth, it is moving forward, but it is also in free fall toward Earth. **Figure 7** shows how these two motions occur together to cause orbiting.

**Figure 7 How an Orbit Is Formed**

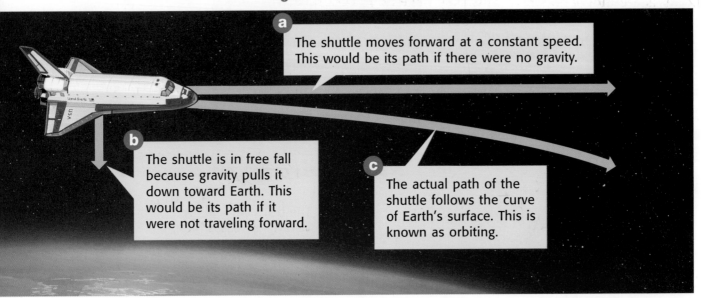

**a** The shuttle moves forward at a constant speed. This would be its path if there were no gravity.

**b** The shuttle is in free fall because gravity pulls it down toward Earth. This would be its path if it were not traveling forward.

**c** The actual path of the shuttle follows the curve of Earth's surface. This is known as orbiting.

As you can see in the illustration above, the space shuttle is always falling while it is in orbit. So why don't astronauts hit their heads on the ceiling of the falling shuttle? Because they are also in free fall—they are always falling, too. Because the astronaut in Figure 6 is in free fall, she appears to be floating.

**The Role of Gravity in Orbiting** Besides spaceships and satellites, many other objects in the universe are in orbit. The moon orbits the Earth, Earth and the other planets orbit the sun, and many stars orbit large masses in the center of galaxies. All of these objects are traveling in a circular or nearly circular path. Remember, any object in circular motion is constantly changing direction. Because an unbalanced force is necessary to change the motion of any object, there must be an unbalanced force working on any object in circular motion.

The unbalanced force that causes objects to move in a circular path is called a *centripetal force*. Gravity provides the centripetal force that keeps objects in orbit. The word *centripetal* means "toward the center." As you can see in **Figure 8,** the centripetal force on the moon points toward the center of the circle traced by the moon's orbit.

**Path of moon**

**Centripetal force on the moon**

**Figure 8** *The moon stays in orbit around the Earth because Earth's gravitational force provides a centripetal force on the moon.*

# Projectile Motion and Gravity

The orbit of the space shuttle around the Earth is an example of projectile (proh JEK tuhl) motion. **Projectile motion** is the curved path an object follows when thrown or propelled near the surface of the Earth. The motions of leaping dancers, thrown balls, hopping grasshoppers, and arrows shot from a bow are all examples of projectile motion. Projectile motion has two components—horizontal and vertical. The two components are independent; that is, they have no effect on each other. When the two motions are combined, they form a curved path, as shown in **Figure 9.**

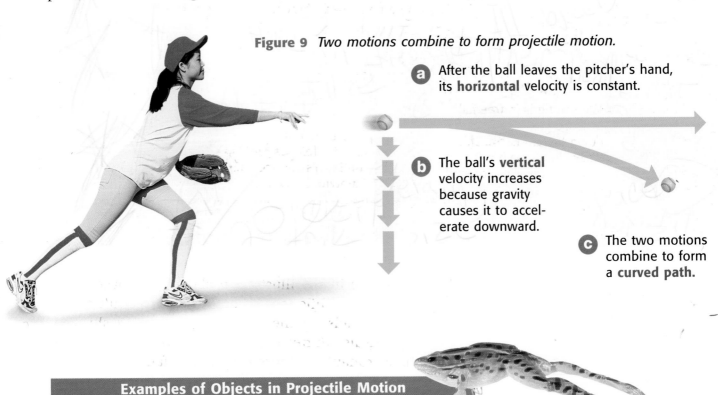

**Figure 9** *Two motions combine to form projectile motion.*

**a** After the ball leaves the pitcher's hand, its **horizontal** velocity is constant.

**b** The ball's **vertical** velocity increases because gravity causes it to accelerate downward.

**c** The two motions combine to form a **curved path.**

| Examples of Objects in Projectile Motion | |
|---|---|
| ■ A football being passed | ■ Water sprayed by a sprinkler |
| ■ Balls being juggled | ■ A swimmer diving into water |
| ■ An athlete doing a high jump | ■ A leaping frog |

**Horizontal Motion**  When you throw a ball, your hand exerts a force on the ball that makes the ball move forward. This force gives the ball its horizontal motion. Horizontal motion is motion that is parallel to the ground.

After you let go of the ball, there are no horizontal forces acting on the ball (if you ignore air resistance). Therefore, there are no forces to change the ball's horizontal motion. Thus, the horizontal velocity of the ball is constant after the ball leaves your hand, as shown in Figure 9.

**Vertical Motion** After you throw a ball, gravity pulls it downward, giving the ball vertical motion. Vertical motion is motion that is perpendicular to the ground. Because objects in projectile motion accelerate downward, you always have to aim above a target if you want to hit it with a thrown or propelled object. That's why when you aim an arrow directly at a bull's-eye, your arrow strikes the bottom of the target rather than the middle.

Gravity pulls objects in projectile motion down with an acceleration of 9.8 m/s/s (if air resistance is ignored), just as it does all falling objects. **Figure 10** shows that the downward acceleration of a thrown object and a falling object are the same.

**Figure 10  Projectile Motion and Acceleration Due to Gravity**

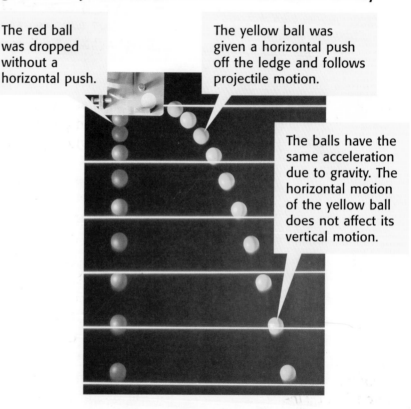

The red ball was dropped without a horizontal push.

The yellow ball was given a horizontal push off the ledge and follows projectile motion.

The balls have the same acceleration due to gravity. The horizontal motion of the yellow ball does not affect its vertical motion.

## SECTION REVIEW

1. How does air resistance affect the acceleration of falling objects?

2. Explain why an astronaut in an orbiting spaceship floats.

3. How is an orbit formed?

4. **Applying Concepts** Think about a sport you play that involves a ball. Identify at least four different instances in which an object is in projectile motion.

*Terms to Learn*

inertia                    momentum

*What You'll Do*

◆ State and apply Newton's laws of motion.
◆ Compare the momentum of different objects.
◆ State and apply the law of conservation of momentum.

# Newton's Laws of Motion

In 1686, Sir Isaac Newton published his book *Principia*. In it, he described three laws that relate forces to the motion of objects. Although he did not discover all three of the laws, he explained them in a way that helped many people understand them. Thus, the three laws are commonly known as Newton's laws of motion. In this section, you will learn about these laws and how they influence the motion of objects.

## Newton's First Law of Motion

*An object at rest remains at rest and an object in motion remains in motion at constant speed and in a straight line unless acted on by an unbalanced force.*

Newton's first law of motion describes the motion of an object that has a net force of zero acting on it. This law may seem complicated when you first read it, but it's easy to understand when you consider its two parts separately.

**Part 1: Objects at Rest**  What does it mean for an object to be at rest? Objects don't get tired! An object that is not moving is said to be at rest. Objects are at rest all around you. A plane parked on a runway, a chair on the floor, and a golf ball balanced on a tee are all examples of objects at rest.

Newton's first law says that objects at rest will remain at rest unless they are acted on by an unbalanced force. That means that objects will not start moving until a push or a pull is exerted on them. A plane won't soar in the air unless it is pushed by the exhaust from its jet engines, a chair won't slide across the room unless you push it, and a golf ball won't move off the tee unless struck by a golf club, as shown in **Figure 11**.

**Figure 11** *A golf ball will remain at rest on a tee until it is acted on by the unbalanced force of a moving club.*

Unbalanced force

Object at rest

Object in motion

**a** An unbalanced force from another car acts on your car, changing its motion.

**b** The collision changes your car's motion, but not yours. Your motion continues with the same velocity.

**c** Another unbalanced force, from your seat belt, changes your motion.

**Figure 12** *Bumper cars let you have fun with Newton's first law.*

## Part 2: Objects in Motion

Think about riding in a bumper car at an amusement park. Your ride is pleasant as long as you are driving in an open space. But the name of the game is bumper cars, so sooner or later you are likely to run into another car, as shown in **Figure 12.**

The second part of Newton's first law explains that an object moving at a certain velocity will continue to move *forever* at the same speed and in the same direction unless some unbalanced force acts on it. Thus, your bumper car stops, but you continue to move forward until your seat belt stops you.

**Friction and Newton's First Law** Because an object in motion will stay in motion forever unless it is acted on by an unbalanced force, you should be able to give your desk a small push and send it sailing across the floor. If you try it, you will find that the desk quickly comes to a stop. What does this tell you?

There must be an unbalanced force that acts on the desk to stop its motion. That unbalanced force is friction. The friction between the desk and the floor works against the motion of the desk. Because of friction, it is often difficult to observe the effects of Newton's first law on the motion of everyday objects. For example, friction will cause a ball rolling on grass to slow down and stop. Friction will also make a car decelerate on a flat surface if the driver lets up on the gas pedal. Because of friction, the motion of these objects changes.

### Stopping Motion

The dummy in this crash test is wearing a seat belt, but the car does not have an air bag. Explain why Newton's first law of motion could lead to serious injuries in accidents involving cars without air bags.

**Inertia Is Related to Mass** Newton's first law of motion is sometimes called the law of inertia. **Inertia** (in UHR shuh) is the tendency of all objects to resist any change in motion. Due to inertia, an object at rest will remain at rest until something makes it move. Likewise, inertia is why a moving object stays in motion with the same velocity unless a force acts on it to change its speed or direction. Inertia causes you to slide toward the side of a car when the driver makes a sharp turn. Inertia is also why it is impossible for a plane, car, or bicycle to stop instantaneously.

**Mass Is a Measure of Inertia** An object with a small mass has less inertia than an object with a large mass. Therefore, it is easier to start and to change the motion of an object with a small mass. For example, a softball has less mass and therefore less inertia than a bowling ball. Because the softball has a small amount of inertia, it is easy to pitch a softball and to change its motion by hitting it with a bat. Imagine how difficult it would be to play softball with a bowling ball! **Figure 13** further illustrates the relationship between mass and inertia. Try the QuickLab at right to test the relationship yourself.

*Figure 13 Inertia makes it harder to push a car than to push a bicycle. Inertia also makes it easier to stop a moving bicycle than a car moving at the same speed.*

**First-Law Magic**

1. On a table or desk, place a **large, empty plastic cup** on top of a **paper towel.**

2. Without touching the cup or tipping it over, remove the paper towel from under the cup. What did you do to accomplish this?

3. Repeat the first two steps a few times until you are comfortable with the procedure.

4. Fill the cup half full with **water,** and place the cup on the paper towel.

5. Once again, remove the paper towel from under the cup. Was it easier or harder to do this? Explain your answer in terms of mass and inertia.

## Self-Check

When you stand while riding a bus, why do you tend to fall backward when the bus starts moving?
*(See page 232 to check your answer.)*

# Environment
## C O N N E C T I O N

Modern cars pollute the air less than older cars. One reason for this is that modern cars are less massive than older models and have considerably smaller engines. According to Newton's second law, a less massive object requires less force to achieve the same acceleration as a more massive object. This is why a smaller car can have a smaller engine and still have acceptable acceleration. And because smaller engines use less fuel, they pollute less.

## Newton's Second Law of Motion

*The acceleration of an object depends on the mass of the object and the amount of force applied.*

Newton's second law describes the motion of an object when an unbalanced force is acting on it. As with Newton's first law, it is easier to consider the parts of this law separately.

**Part 1: Acceleration Depends on Mass** Suppose you are pushing a shopping cart at the grocery store. At the beginning of your shopping trip, you have to exert only a small force on the cart to accelerate it. But when the cart is full, the same amount of force will not accelerate the cart as much as before, as shown in **Figure 14.** This example illustrates that for the same force, an object's acceleration *decreases* as its mass *increases* and its acceleration *increases* as its mass *decreases*.

**Figure 14** *If the force applied is the same, the acceleration of the empty cart is greater than the acceleration of the full cart.*

**Part 2: Acceleration Depends on Force** Now suppose you give the shopping cart a hard push, as shown in **Figure 15.** The cart will start moving faster than if you only gave it a soft push. This illustrates that an object's acceleration *increases* as the force on it *increases*. Conversely, an object's acceleration *decreases* as the force on it *decreases*.

The acceleration of an object is always in the same direction as the force applied. The shopping cart moved forward because the push was in the forward direction. To change the direction of an object, you must exert a force in the direction you want the object to go.

**Figure 15** *Acceleration will increase when a larger force is exerted.*

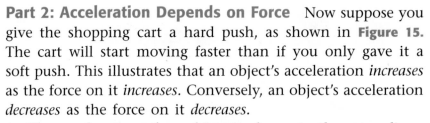

**Expressing Newton's Second Law Mathematically** The relationship of acceleration (*a*) to mass (*m*) and force (*F*) can be expressed mathematically with the following equation:

$$a = \frac{F}{m}$$

This equation is often rearranged to the following form:

$$F = m \times a$$

Both forms of the equation can be used to solve problems. Try the MathBreak at right to practice using the equations. Newton's second law explains why objects fall to Earth with the same acceleration. In **Figure 16,** you can see how the larger weight of the watermelon is offset by its greater inertia. Thus, the accelerations of the watermelon and the apple are the same when you put the numbers into the equation for acceleration.

÷ 5 ÷   Ω   ∞   +Ω  √  9  ≤  Σ 2
+           ≤       ∞

## MATH BREAK

### Second-Law Problems

You can rearrange the equation $F = m \times a$ to find acceleration and mass as shown below.

$$a = \frac{F}{m} \qquad m = \frac{F}{a}$$

1. What is the acceleration of a 7 kg mass if a force of 68.6 N is used to move it toward Earth? (Hint: 1 N is equal to 1 kg•m/s/s.)

2. What force is necessary to accelerate a 1,250 kg car at a rate of 40 m/s/s?

3. What is the mass of an object if a force of 34 N produces an acceleration of 4 m/s/s?

**Figure 16   Newton's Second Law and Acceleration Due to Gravity**

The **apple** has less mass, so the gravitational force on it is smaller. However, the apple also has less inertia and is easier to move.

$m = 0.102$ kg

$F = 1$ N

1 N = 1 kg•m/s/s

$$a = \frac{1 \text{ kg•m/s/s}}{0.102 \text{ kg}} = 9.8 \text{ m/s/s}$$

The **watermelon** has more mass and therefore more inertia, so it is harder to move.

$m = 1.02$ kg

$F = 10$ N

10 N = 10 kg•m/s/s

$$a = \frac{10 \text{ kg•m/s/s}}{1.02 \text{ kg}} = 9.8 \text{ m/s/s}$$

## SECTION REVIEW

1. How is inertia related to Newton's first law of motion?

2. Name two ways to increase the acceleration of an object.

3. **Making Predictions**   If the acceleration due to gravity were somehow doubled to 19.6 m/s/s, what would happen to your weight?

**internetconnect**

SC*i*LINKS.
**NSTA**

**TOPIC:** Newton's Laws of Motion
**GO TO:** www.scilinks.org
*sci*LINKS NUMBER: HSTP145

# Newton's Third Law of Motion

*Whenever one object exerts a force on a second object, the second object exerts an equal and opposite force on the first.*

Newton's third law can be simply stated as follows: All forces act in pairs. If a force is exerted, another force occurs that is equal in size and opposite in direction. The law itself addresses only forces. But the way that force pairs interact affects the motion of objects.

What is meant by "forces act in pairs"? Study **Figure 17** to learn how one force pair helps propel a swimmer through water.

**Figure 17** *The action force and reaction force are a pair. The two forces are equal in size but opposite in direction.*

The **action force** is the swimmer's hands and feet pushing on the water.

The **reaction force** is the water pushing on the hands and feet. The reaction force moves the swimmer forward.

Action and reaction force pairs occur even when there is no motion. For example, you exert a force on a chair when you sit on it. Your weight pushing down on the chair is the action force. The reaction force is the force exerted by the chair that pushes up on your body and is equal to your weight.

**Force Pairs Do Not Act on the Same Object** You know that a force is always exerted by one object on another object. This is true for all forces, including action and reaction forces. However, it is important to remember that action and reaction forces in a pair do not act on the same object. If they did, the net force would always be zero and nothing would ever move! To understand this better, look back at Figure 17. In this example, the action force was exerted on the water by the swimmer's hands and feet. But the reaction force was exerted on the swimmer's hands and feet by the water. The forces did not act on the same object.

## Activity

Choose a sport that you enjoy playing or watching. In your ScienceLog, list five ways that Newton's laws of motion are involved in the game you selected.

*TRY at HOME*

**The Effect of a Reaction Can Be Difficult to See** Another example of a force pair is shown in **Figure 18.** Remember, gravity is a force of attraction between objects that is due to their masses. If you drop a ball off a ledge, the force of gravity pulls the ball toward Earth. This is the action force exerted by Earth on the ball. But the force of gravity also pulls Earth toward the ball. That is the reaction force exerted by the ball on Earth.

It's easy to see the effect of the action force—the ball falls to Earth. Why don't you notice the effect of the reaction force—Earth being pulled upward? To find the answer to this question, think back to Newton's second law. It states that the acceleration of an object depends on the force applied to it and on the mass of the object. The force on Earth is equal to the force on the ball, but the mass of Earth is much *larger* than the mass of the ball. Therefore, the acceleration of Earth is much *smaller* than the acceleration of the ball. The acceleration is so small that you can't even see it or feel it. Thus, it is difficult to observe the effect of Newton's third law on falling objects.

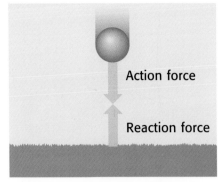

**Figure 18** *The force of gravity between Earth and a falling object is a force pair.*

**More Examples of Action and Reaction Force Pairs** The examples below illustrate a variety of action and reaction force pairs. In each example, notice which object exerts the action force and which object exerts the reaction force.

The rabbit's legs exert a force on Earth. Earth exerts an equal force on the rabbit's legs, causing the rabbit to accelerate upward.

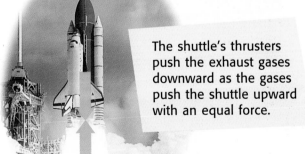

The bat exerts a force on the ball, sending the ball into the outfield. The ball exerts an equal force on the bat, but the bat does not fly toward the catcher because the batter is exerting another force on the bat.

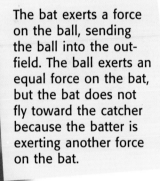

The shuttle's thrusters push the exhaust gases downward as the gases push the shuttle upward with an equal force.

When you hit a table with your hand, your hand will hurt. This is because the table meets your hand with a force equal in size to the force you exerted.

## Momentum Is a Property of Moving Objects

If a compact car and a large truck are traveling with the same velocity, it takes longer for the truck to stop than it does for the car if the same braking force is applied. Likewise, it takes longer for a fast moving car to stop than it does for a slow moving car with the same mass. The truck and the fast moving car have more momentum than the compact car and the slow moving car.

**Momentum** is a property of a moving object that depends on the object's mass and velocity. The more momentum an object has, the harder it is to stop the object or change its direction. Although the compact car and the truck are traveling with the same velocity, the truck has more mass and therefore more momentum, so it is harder to stop than the car. Similarly, the fast moving car has a greater velocity and thus more momentum than the slow moving car.

**Momentum Is Conserved**  When a moving object hits another object, some or all of the momentum of the first object is transferred to the other object. If only some of the momentum is transferred, the rest of the momentum stays with the first object.

Imagine you hit a billiard ball with a cue ball so that the billiard ball starts moving and the cue ball stops, as shown in **Figure 19.** The cue ball had a certain amount of momentum before the collision. During the collision, all of the cue ball's momentum was transferred to the billiard ball. After the collision, the billiard ball moved away with the same amount of momentum the cue ball had. This example illustrates the *law of conservation of momentum.* Any time two or more objects interact, they may exchange momentum, but the total amount of momentum stays the same.

**Figure 19** *The momentum before a collision is equal to the momentum after the collision.*

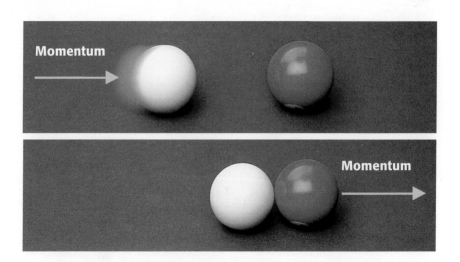

Momentum

Momentum

Bowling is another example of how conservation of momentum is used in a game. The bowling ball rolls down the lane with a certain amount of momentum. When the ball hits the pins, some of the ball's momentum is transferred to the pins and the pins move off in different directions. Furthermore, some of the pins that were hit by the ball go on to hit other pins, transferring the momentum again.

### Conservation of Momentum and Newton's Third Law

Conservation of momentum can be explained by Newton's third law. In the example with the billiard ball, the cue ball hit the billiard ball with a certain amount of force. This was the action force. The reaction force was the equal but opposite force exerted by the billiard ball on the cue ball. The action force made the billiard ball start moving, and the reaction force made the cue ball stop moving, as shown in **Figure 20.** Because the action and reaction forces are equal and opposite, momentum is conserved.

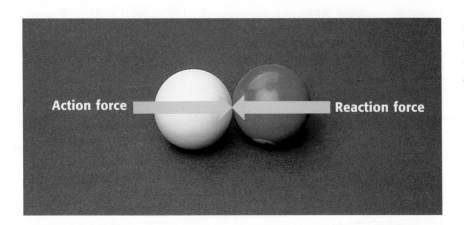

**Action force** → ← **Reaction force**

**Figure 20** *The action force makes the billiard ball begin moving, and the reaction force stops the cue ball's motion.*

## SECTION REVIEW

1. Name three action and reaction force pairs involved in doing your homework. Name what object is exerting and what object is receiving the forces.

2. Which has more momentum, a mouse running at 1 m/s north or an elephant walking at 3 m/s east? Explain your answer.

3. **Applying Concepts** When a truck pulls a trailer, the trailer and truck accelerate forward even though the action and reaction forces are the same size but in opposite directions. Why don't these forces balance each other out?

Catapult forward! Or is it backward? Find out on page 188 of the LabBook.

# Skill Builder Lab

## Inertia-Rama!

Inertia is a property of all matter, from small particles of dust to enormous planets and stars. In this lab, you will investigate the inertia of various shapes and types of matter. Keep in mind that each investigation requires you to either overcome or use the object's inertia.

### MATERIALS

Be sure to wear safety goggles while doing this lab and to handle sharp objects with care.

**Station 1**
- hard-boiled egg
- raw egg

**Station 2**
- coin
- index card
- cup

**Station 3**
- spool of thread
- suspended mass
- scissors
- meterstick

## Station 1: Magic Eggs
### Procedure

1. There are two eggs at this station—one is hard-boiled (solid all the way through) and the other is raw (liquid inside). The masses of the two eggs are about the same. The eggs are not marked. You should not be able to tell them apart by their appearance. Without breaking them open, how can you tell which egg is which?

2. Before you do anything to either egg, make some predictions. Will there be any difference in the way the two eggs spin? Which egg will be easier to stop?

3. First, spin one egg. Then gently place your finger on it to make it stop spinning. Record your observations in your ScienceLog.

4. Repeat step 3 with the second egg.

5. Compare your predictions with your observations. (Repeat steps 3 and 4 if necessary.)

6. Identify which egg is hard-boiled and which one is raw. Explain your choices.

### Analysis

7. Explain why the eggs behave differently when you spin them even though they should have the same inertia. (Hint: Think about what happens to the liquid inside the raw egg.)

8. In terms of inertia, explain why the eggs react differently when you try to stop them.

## Station 2: Coin in a Cup
## Procedure

**9** At this station, you will find a coin, an index card, and a cup. Place the card over the cup. Then place the coin on the card over the center of the cup, as shown below.

**10** In your ScienceLog, write a method for getting the coin into the cup without touching the coin and without lifting the card.

**11** Try your method. If it doesn't work, try again until you find a method that does work. When you are done, place the card and coin on the table for the next group.

## Analysis

**12** Use Newton's first law of motion to explain why the coin falls into the cup if you remove the card quickly.

**13** Explain why pulling on the card slowly will not work even though the coin has inertia. (Hint: Friction is a force.)

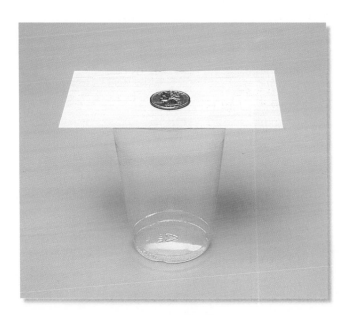

## Station 3: The Magic Thread
## Procedure

**14** At this station, you will find a spool of thread and a mass hanging from a strong string. Cut a piece of thread about 40 cm long. Tie the thread around the bottom of the mass, as shown at right.

**15** Pull gently on the end of the thread. Observe what happens, and record your observations in your ScienceLog.

**16** Stop the mass from moving. Now hold the end of the thread so that there is a lot of slack between your fingers and the mass.

**17** Give the thread a quick, hard pull. You should observe a very different event. Record your observations in your ScienceLog. Throw away the thread.

## Analysis

**18** Use Newton's first law of motion to explain why the results of a gentle pull are so different from the results of a hard pull.

## Draw Conclusions

Remember that both moving and nonmoving objects have inertia. Explain why throwing a bowling ball and catching a thrown bowling ball are hard.

Why is it harder to run with a backpack full of books than to run with an empty backpack?

# Chapter Highlights

## Vocabulary

**terminal velocity** (p. 38)

**free fall** (p. 39)

**projectile motion** (p. 41)

## Section Notes

- All objects accelerate toward Earth at 9.8 m/s/s.

- Air resistance slows the acceleration of falling objects.

- An object is in free fall if gravity is the only force acting on it.

  - An orbit is formed by combining forward motion and free fall.

  - Objects in orbit appear to be weightless because they are in free fall.

- A centripetal force is needed to keep objects in circular motion. Gravity acts as a centripetal force to keep objects in orbit.

- Projectile motion is the curved path an object follows when thrown or propelled near the surface of Earth.

- Projectile motion has two components—horizontal and vertical. Gravity affects only the vertical motion of projectile motion.

## Labs

**A Marshmallow Catapult** (p. 188)

# ☑ Skills Check

## Math Concepts

**NEWTON'S SECOND LAW** The equation $a = F/m$ on page 47 summarizes Newton's second law of motion. The equation shows the relationship between the acceleration of an object, the force causing the acceleration, and the object's mass. For example, if you apply a force of 18 N to a 6 kg object, the object's acceleration is

$$a = \frac{F}{m} = \frac{18\,\text{N}}{6\,\text{kg}} = \frac{18\,\text{kg} \cdot \text{m/s/s}}{6\,\text{kg}} = 3\,\text{m/s/s}$$

## Visual Understanding

**HOW AN ORBIT IS FORMED** An orbit is a combination of two motions—forward motion and free fall. Figure 7 on page 40 shows how the two motions combine to form an orbit.

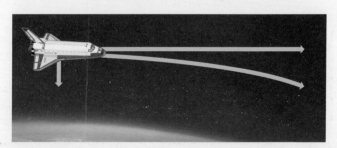

## Vocabulary

**inertia** *(p. 45)*

**momentum** *(p. 50)*

## Section Notes

- Newton's first law of motion states that the motion of an object will not change if no unbalanced forces act on it.

- Inertia is the tendency of matter to resist a change in motion. Mass is a measure of inertia.

- Newton's second law of motion states that the acceleration of an object depends on its mass and on the force exerted on it.

- Newton's third law of motion states that whenever one object exerts a force on a second object, the second object exerts an equal and opposite force on the first.

- Momentum is the property of a moving object that depends on its mass and velocity.

- When two or more objects interact, momentum may be exchanged, but the total amount of momentum does not change. This is the law of conservation of momentum.

## Labs

**Blast Off!** *(p. 189)*

**Quite a Reaction** *(p. 190)*

### internet**connect**

**GO TO:** go.hrw.com

**GO TO:** www.scilinks.org

Visit the **HRW** Web site for a variety of learning tools related to this chapter. Just type in the keyword:

**KEYWORD:** HSTFOR

Visit the **National Science Teachers Association** on-line Web site for Internet resources related to this chapter. Just type in the *sci*LINKS number for more information about the topic:

| TOPIC: The Force of Gravity | *sci*LINKS NUMBER: HSTP130 |
| TOPIC: Gravity and Orbiting Objects | *sci*LINKS NUMBER: HSTP135 |
| TOPIC: Projectile Motion | *sci*LINKS NUMBER: HSTP140 |
| TOPIC: Newton's Laws of Motion | *sci*LINKS NUMBER: HSTP145 |

# Chapter Review

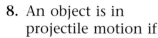

## USING VOCABULARY

To complete the following sentences, choose the correct term from each pair of terms listed below:

1. An object in motion tends to stay in motion because it has ___?___. (*inertia* or *terminal velocity*)

2. Falling objects stop accelerating at ___?___. (*free fall* or *terminal velocity*)

3. ___?___ is the path that a thrown object follows. (*Free fall* or *Projectile motion*)

4. A property of moving objects that depends on mass and velocity is ___?___. (*inertia* or *momentum*)

5. ___?___ only occurs when there is no air resistance. (*Momentum* or *Free fall*)

## UNDERSTANDING CONCEPTS

### Multiple Choice

6. A feather and a rock dropped at the same time from the same height would land at the same time when dropped by
   a. Galileo in Italy.
   b. Newton in England.
   c. an astronaut on the moon.
   d. an astronaut on the space shuttle.

7. When a soccer ball is kicked, the action and reaction forces do not cancel each other out because
   a. the force of the foot on the ball is bigger than the force of the ball on the foot.
   b. the forces act on two different objects.
   c. the forces act at different times.
   d. All of the above

8. An object is in projectile motion if
   a. it is thrown with a horizontal push.
   b. it is accelerated downward by gravity.
   c. it does not accelerate horizontally.
   d. All of the above

9. Newton's first law of motion applies
   a. to moving objects.
   b. to objects that are not moving.
   c. to objects that are accelerating.
   d. Both (a) and (b)

10. Acceleration of an object
    a. decreases as the mass of the object increases.
    b. increases as the force on the object increases.
    c. is in the same direction as the force on the object.
    d. All of the above

11. A golf ball and a bowling ball are moving at the same velocity. Which has more momentum?
    a. the golf ball, because it has less mass
    b. the bowling ball, because it has more mass
    c. They both have the same momentum because they have the same velocity.
    d. There is no way to know without additional information.

### Short Answer

12. Explain how an orbit is formed.

13. Describe how gravity and air resistance combine when an object reaches terminal velocity.

14. Explain why friction can make observing Newton's first law of motion difficult.

## Concept Mapping

**15.** Use the following terms to create a concept map: gravity, free fall, terminal velocity, projectile motion, air resistance.

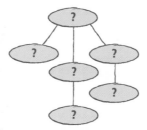

## CRITICAL THINKING AND PROBLEM SOLVING

**16.** During a shuttle launch, about 830,000 kg of fuel is burned in 8 minutes. The fuel provides the shuttle with a constant thrust, or push off the ground. How does Newton's second law of motion explain why the shuttle's acceleration increases during takeoff?

**17.** When using a hammer to drive a nail into wood, you have to swing the hammer through the air with a certain velocity. Because the hammer has both mass and velocity, it has momentum. Describe what happens to the hammer's momentum after the hammer hits the nail.

**18.** Suppose you are standing on a skateboard or on in-line skates and you toss a backpack full of heavy books toward your friend. What do you think will happen to you and why? Explain your answer in terms of Newton's third law of motion.

## MATH IN SCIENCE

**19.** A 12 kg rock falls from rest off a cliff and hits the ground in 1.5 seconds.

  **a.** Ignoring air resistance, what is the rock's velocity just before it hits the ground?

  **b.** What is the rock's weight after it hits the ground? (Hint: Weight is a measure of the gravitational force on an object.)

## INTERPRETING GRAPHICS

**20.** The picture below shows a common desk toy. If you pull one ball up and release it, it hits the balls at the bottom and comes to a stop. In the same instant, the ball on the other side swings up and repeats the cycle. How does conservation of momentum explain how this toy works?

**Reading Check-up** Take a minute to review your answers to the Pre-Reading Questions found at the bottom of page 34. Have your answers changed? If necessary, revise your answers based on what you have learned since you began this chapter.

# Eureka!

## A Bat with Dimples

**W**ouldn't it be nice to hit a home run every time? Jeff DiTullio, a teacher at MIT, in Cambridge, Massachusetts, has found a way for you to get more bang from your bat. Would you believe *dimples*?

### Building a Better Bat

If you look closely at the surface of a golf ball, you'll see dozens of tiny craterlike dimples. When air flows past these dimples, it gets stirred up. By keeping air moving near the surface of the ball, the dimples help the golf ball move faster and farther through the air.

DiTullio decided to apply this same idea to a baseball bat. His hypothesis was that dimples would allow a bat to move more easily through the air. This would help batters swing the bat faster and hit the ball harder. To test his hypothesis, DiTullio pressed hundreds of little dimples about 1 mm deep and 2 mm across into the surface of a bat.

When DiTullio tested his dimpled bat in a wind tunnel, he found that it could be swung 3 to 5 percent faster. That may not sound like much, but it could add about 5 m to a fly ball!

### Safe . . . or Out?

As you might imagine, many baseball players would love to have a bat that could turn a long fly ball into a home run. But are dimpled baseball bats legal?

The size and shape of every piece of equipment used in Major League Baseball games are regulated. A baseball bat, for instance, must be no more than 107 cm long and no more than 7 cm across at its widest point. When DiTullio

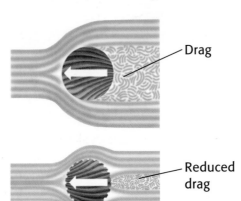

**Drag**

**Reduced drag**

▲ *By reducing the amount of drag behind the bat, dimples help the bat move faster through the air.*

designed his dimpled bat, there was no rule stating that bats had to be smooth. But when Major League Baseball found out about the new bat, they changed the rules! Today official rules require that all bats be smooth, and they prohibit any type of "experimental" bat. Someday the rules may be revised to allow DiTullio's dimpled bat. When that happens, fans of the dimpled baseball bat will all shout, "Play ball!"

### Dimple Madness

▶ Now that you know how dimples can improve baseball bats, think of other uses for dimples. How might dimples improve the way other objects move through the air? Draw a sketch of a dimpled object, and describe how the dimples improve the design.

▶ *Jeff DiTullio, pictured with his dimpled baseball bat, is an aeronautical engineer— someone who studies both the way air moves and the way things move through air.*

# CAREERS

## ROLLER COASTER DESIGNER

Roller coasters have fascinated **Steve Okamoto** ever since his first ride on one. "I remember going to Disneyland as a kid. My mother was always upset with me because I kept looking over the sides of the rides, trying to figure out how they worked," he laughs. To satisfy his curiosity, Okamoto became a mechanical engineer. Today he uses his scientific knowledge to design and build machines, systems, and buildings. But his specialty is roller coasters.

**H**is West Coaster, which sits on the Santa Monica pier in Santa Monica, California, towers five stories above the Pacific Ocean. The cars on the Steel Force, at Dorney Park, in Pennsylvania, reach speeds of over 120 km/h and drop more than 60 m to disappear into a 37 m long tunnel. The Mamba, at Worlds of Fun, in Missouri, sends cars flying along as high and as fast as the Steel Force does, but it also has two giant back-to-back hills, a fast spiral, and five "camelback" humps. The camelbacks are designed to pull riders' seats out from under them, giving the riders "air time."

## Coaster Motion

Roller-coaster cars really do coast along the track. A motor pulls the cars up a high hill to start the ride. After that, the cars are powered by gravity alone. As the cars roll downhill, they pick up enough speed to whiz through the rest of the curves, loops, twists, and bumps in the track.

Designing a successful coaster is no simple task. Steve Okamoto has to calculate the cars' speed and acceleration on each part of the track. "The coaster has to go fast enough to make it up the next hill," he explains. Okamoto uses his knowledge of geometry and physics to create safe but scary curves, loops, humps, and dips. Okamoto must also keep in mind that the ride's towers and structures need to be strong enough to support both the track and

the speeding cars full of people. The cars themselves need special wheels to keep them locked onto the track and seat belts or bars to keep passengers safely inside. "It's like putting together a puzzle, except the pieces haven't been cut out yet," says Okamoto.

## Take the Challenge

▶ Step outside for a moment. Gather some rope and a medium-sized plastic bucket half-full of water. Can you get the bucket over your head and upside down without any water escaping? How does this relate to roller coasters?

▲ *The Wild Thing, in Shakopee, Minnesota, was designed by Steve Okamoto.*

# Forces in Fluids

## Sections

Pre-Reading Questions

1. What is a fluid?
2. How is fluid pressure exerted?
3. Do moving fluids exert different forces than nonmoving fluids?

## A NEED FOR SPEED

Even when you are racing downhill on your bicycle, a fluid force slows you down. "What a drag!" you say. Well, actually, it is a drag. When designing bicycle gear and clothing, manufacturers consider more than just looks and comfort. They also try to decrease drag, a fluid force that opposes motion. Here a cyclist rides a bike in a wind tunnel in a study of how a fluid—air—affects his ride. In this chapter, you'll learn more about forces that fluids exert on objects in your everyday life.

## Activity

## TAKING FLIGHT

In this activity, you will build a model airplane to help you identify how wing size affects flight.

### Procedure

1. Fold a **sheet of paper** in half lengthwise. Then open it. Fold the top corners toward the center crease. Then fold the entire sheet in half along the center crease.

2. With the plane on its side, fold the top front edge down so that it meets the bottom edge. Fold the top edge down again so that it meets the bottom edge.

3. Turn the plane over. Repeat step 2.

4. Raise both wings so that they are perpendicular to the body.

5. Point the plane slightly upward, and gently throw it. Repeat several times. Describe what you see.

6. Make the wings smaller by folding them one more time. Gently throw the plane. Repeat several times. Describe what you see.

7. Try to achieve the same flight path you saw when the wings were bigger. Record your technique.

### Analysis

8. What happened to the plane's flight when you reduced the size of its wings? Explain.

9. What gave your plane its forward motion?

## Terms to Learn

fluid
pressure
pascal
atmospheric pressure
density
Pascal's principle

## What You'll Do

◆ Describe how fluids exert pressure.
◆ Analyze how fluid depth affects pressure.
◆ Give examples of fluids flowing from high to low pressure.
◆ State and apply Pascal's principle.

÷ 5 ÷ $\Omega$ ∞ +$\Omega$ √ 9 ∞ ≤ Σ 2
+ ≤ ∞

## MATH BREAK

**Pressure, Force, and Area**

The equation on this page can be used to find pressure or rearranged to find force or area.

$$Force = Pressure \times Area$$
$$Area = \frac{Force}{Pressure}$$

1. Find the pressure exerted by a 3,000 N crate with an area of 2 m².

2. Find the weight of a rock with an area of 10 m² that exerts a pressure of 250 Pa.

(Be sure to express your answers in the correct SI unit.)

# Fluids and Pressure

What does a dolphin have in common with a sea gull? What does a dog have in common with a fly? What do you have in common with all these living things? The answer is that you and all these other living things spend a lifetime moving through and even breathing fluids. A **fluid** is any material that can flow and that takes the shape of its container. Fluids include liquids (such as water and oil) and gases (such as oxygen and carbon dioxide). Fluids are able to flow because the particles in fluids, unlike the particles in solids, can move easily past each other. As you will find out, the remarkable properties of fluids allow huge ships to float, divers to explore the ocean depths, and jumbo jets to soar across the skies.

## All Fluids Exert Pressure

You probably have heard the terms *air pressure, water pressure,* and *blood pressure.* Air, water, and blood are all fluids, and all fluids exert pressure. So what's pressure? Well, think about this example. When you pump up a bicycle tire, you push air into the tire. And like all matter, air is made of tiny particles that are constantly moving. Inside the tire, the air particles push against each other and against the walls of the tire, as shown in **Figure 1.** The more air you pump into the tire, the more the air particles push against the inside of your tire. Together, these pushes create a force against the tire. The amount of force exerted on a given area is **pressure.** Pressure can be calculated by dividing the force that a fluid exerts by the area over which the force is exerted:

$$Pressure = \frac{Force}{Area}$$

The SI unit for pressure is the **pascal.** One pascal (1 Pa) is the force of one newton exerted over an area of one square meter (1 N/m²). Try the MathBreak at left to practice calculating pressure.

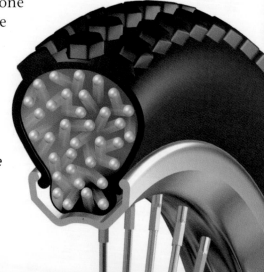

**Figure 1** *The force of the air particles hitting the inner surface of the tire creates pressure, which keeps the tire inflated.*

**Why Are Bubbles Round?** When you blow a soap bubble, you blow in only one direction. So why doesn't the bubble get longer and longer as you blow instead of rounder and rounder? The shape of the bubble is due in part to an important property of fluids: Fluids exert pressure evenly in all directions. The air you blow into the bubble exerts pressure evenly in every direction, so the bubble expands in every direction, helping to create a sphere, as shown in **Figure 2.** This property also explains why tires inflate evenly (unless there is a weak spot in the tire).

## Atmospheric Pressure

The *atmosphere* is the layer of nitrogen, oxygen, and other gases that surrounds the Earth. The atmosphere stretches about 150 km above us. If you could stack 500 Eiffel Towers on top of each other, they would come close to reaching the top of the atmosphere. However, approximately 80 percent of the gases in the atmosphere are found within 10 km of the Earth's surface. Earth's atmosphere is held in place by gravity, which pulls the gases toward Earth. The pressure caused by the weight of the atmosphere is called **atmospheric pressure.**

Atmospheric pressure is exerted on everything on Earth, including you. The atmosphere exerts a pressure of approximately 101,300 N on every square meter, or 101,300 Pa. This means that there is a weight of about 10 N (roughly the weight of a pineapple) on every square centimeter (roughly the area of the tip of your little finger) of your body. Ouch!

Why don't you feel this crushing pressure? The fluids inside your body also exert pressure, just like the air inside a balloon exerts pressure. **Figure 3** can help you understand.

**Figure 2** *You can't blow a square bubble, because fluids exert pressure equally in every direction.*

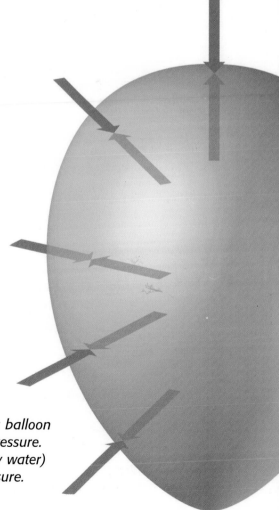

**Figure 3** *The pressure exerted by the air inside a balloon keeps the balloon inflated against atmospheric pressure. Similarly, the pressure exerted by the fluid (mostly water) inside your body works against atmospheric pressure.*

## Figure 4 Differences in Atmospheric Pressure

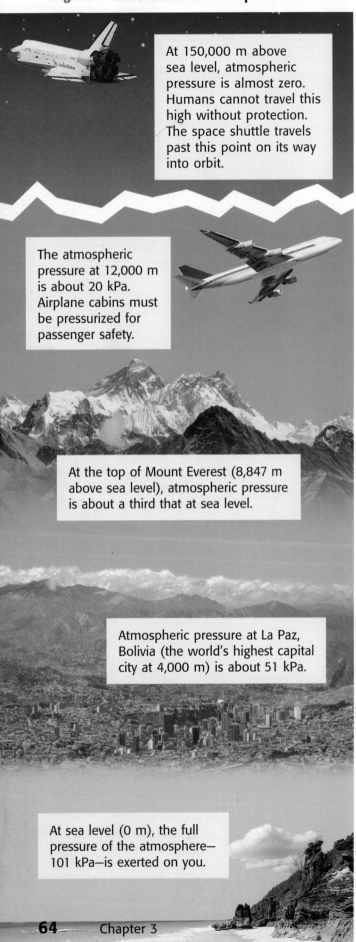

At 150,000 m above sea level, atmospheric pressure is almost zero. Humans cannot travel this high without protection. The space shuttle travels past this point on its way into orbit.

The atmospheric pressure at 12,000 m is about 20 kPa. Airplane cabins must be pressurized for passenger safety.

At the top of Mount Everest (8,847 m above sea level), atmospheric pressure is about a third that at sea level.

Atmospheric pressure at La Paz, Bolivia (the world's highest capital city at 4,000 m) is about 51 kPa.

At sea level (0 m), the full pressure of the atmosphere— 101 kPa—is exerted on you.

**Atmospheric Pressure Varies** At the top of the atmosphere, pressure is almost non-existent because there is no atmosphere pressing down. At the top of Mount Everest in south-central Asia (which is the highest point on Earth), atmospheric pressure is about 33,000 Pa, or 33 kilopascals (kPa). At sea level, atmospheric pressure is about 101 kPa.

**Pressure Depends on Depth** As shown in **Figure 4,** pressure increases as you descend through the atmosphere. In other words, the pressure increases as the atmosphere gets "deeper." This is an important point about fluids: Pressure depends on the depth of the fluid. At lower levels of the atmosphere, there is more fluid above you being pulled by Earth's gravitational force, so there is more pressure.

If you travel to higher or lower points in the atmosphere, the fluids in your body have to adjust to maintain equal pressure. You may have experienced this if your ears have "popped" when you were in a plane taking off or a car traveling down a steep mountain road. Small pockets of air behind your eardrums contract or expand as atmospheric pressure increases or decreases. The "pop" occurs when air is released due to these pressure changes.

## SECTION REVIEW

1. How do particles in a fluid exert pressure on a container?

2. Why are you not crushed by atmospheric pressure?

3. **Applying Concepts** Explain why dams on deep lakes should be thicker at the bottom than near the top.

## Water Pressure

Water is a fluid; therefore, it exerts pressure, just like the atmosphere does. Water pressure also increases with depth because of gravity. Take a look at **Figure 5.** The deeper a diver goes in the water, the greater the pressure becomes because more water above the diver is being pulled by Earth's gravitational force. In addition, the atmosphere presses down on the water, so the total pressure on the diver includes water pressure as well as atmospheric pressure.

But pressure does not depend on the total amount of fluid present, only on the depth of the fluid. A swimmer would feel the same pressure swimming at 5 m below the surface of a small pond as at 5 m below the surface of an ocean, even though there is more water in the ocean.

**Density Makes a Difference** Water is about 1,000 times more dense than air. (Remember, **density** is the amount of matter in a certain volume, or mass per unit volume.) Because water is more dense than air, a certain volume of water has more mass—and therefore weighs more—than the same volume of air. Therefore, water exerts greater pressure than air.

For example, if you climb a 10 m tree, the decrease in atmospheric pressure is too small to notice. But if you dive 10 m underwater, the pressure on you increases to 201 kPa, which is almost twice the atmospheric pressure at the surface!

**Figure 5  Differences in Water Pressure**

Pressure exerted on a diver 10 m below the water's surface is twice the pressure at the surface.

At 500 m below the surface, pressure is about 5,000 kPa. Divers at or below this level must wear special suits to survive the pressure.

The wreck of the *Titanic* rests 3,660 m below sea level. The water pressure at this depth is 36,600 kPa.

The viper fish lives 8,000 m below the ocean's surface. No fish are found below this level. The water pressure at this depth is 80,000 kPa.

In 1960, the *Trieste* descended to the deepest part of the ocean (11,000 m), where the pressure is 110,000 kPa.

Figure 6 *Atmospheric pressure helps you sip through a straw!*

# Fluids Flow from High Pressure to Low Pressure

Look at **Figure 6.** When you drink through a straw, you remove some of the air in the straw. Because there is less air, the pressure in the straw is reduced. But the atmospheric pressure on the surface of the liquid remains the same. This creates a difference between the pressure inside the straw and the pressure outside the straw. The outside pressure forces the liquid up into the straw and into your mouth. So just by sipping your drink through a straw, you can observe another important property of fluids: Fluids flow from regions of high pressure to regions of low pressure.

**Go with the Flow** Take a deep breath—that's fluid flowing from high to low pressure! When you inhale, a muscle increases the space in your chest, giving your lungs room to expand. This expansion lowers the pressure in your lungs so that it becomes lower than the outside air pressure. Air then flows into your lungs—from higher to lower pressure. This air carries oxygen that you need to live. **Figure 7** shows how exhaling also causes fluids to flow from higher to lower pressure. You can see this same exchange when you open a carbonated beverage or squeeze toothpaste onto your toothbrush.

## Quick Lab

### Blown Away

1. Lay an **empty plastic soda bottle** on its side.
2. Wad **a small piece of paper** (about 4 × 4 cm) into a ball.
3. Place the paper ball just inside the bottle's opening.
4. Blow straight into the opening.
5. Record your observations in your ScienceLog.
6. Explain your results in terms of high and low fluid pressures.

*TRY at HOME*

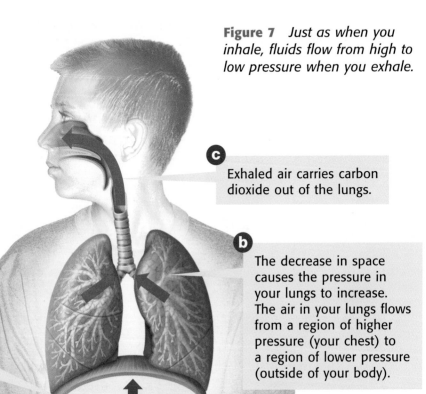

Figure 7 *Just as when you inhale, fluids flow from high to low pressure when you exhale.*

**c** Exhaled air carries carbon dioxide out of the lungs.

**b** The decrease in space causes the pressure in your lungs to increase. The air in your lungs flows from a region of higher pressure (your chest) to a region of lower pressure (outside of your body).

**a** When you exhale, a muscle in your chest moves upward, decreasing the space in your chest.

# Pascal's Principle

Imagine that the water-pumping station in your town can now increase the water pressure by 20 Pa. Will the water pressure be increased more at a supermarket two blocks away or at a home 2 km away?

Believe it or not, the increase in water pressure will be transmitted through all of the water and will be the same—20 Pa—at both locations. This is explained by Pascal's principle, named for Blaise Pascal, the seventeenth-century French scientist who discovered it. **Pascal's principle** states that a change in pressure at any point in an enclosed fluid will be transmitted equally to all parts of that fluid.

*Figure 8 Thanks to Pascal's principle, the touch of a foot can stop tons of moving metal.*

### Putting Pascal's Principle to Work

Devices that use liquids to transmit pressure from one point to another are called *hydraulic* (hie DRAW lik) devices. Hydraulic devices use liquids because they cannot be compressed, or squeezed, into a smaller space very much. This property allows liquids to transmit pressure more efficiently than gases, which can be compressed a great deal.

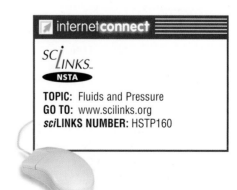

Hydraulic devices can multiply forces. The brakes of a typical car are a good example. In **Figure 8,** a driver's foot exerts pressure on a cylinder of liquid. Pascal's principle tells you that this pressure is transmitted equally to all parts of the liquid-filled brake system. This liquid presses a brake pad against each wheel, and friction brings the car to a stop. The force is multiplied because the pistons that push the brake pads on each wheel are much larger than the piston that is pushed by the brake pedal.

## SECTION REVIEW

1. Explain how atmospheric pressure helps you drink through a straw.

2. What does Pascal's principle state?

3. **Making Predictions** When you squeeze a balloon, where is the pressure inside the balloon increased the most? Explain your answer in terms of Pascal's principle.

**internet connect**

SCi LINKS
NSTA

**TOPIC:** Fluids and Pressure
**GO TO:** www.scilinks.org
**sciLINKS NUMBER:** HSTP160

*Terms to Learn*

buoyant force
Archimedes' principle

*What You'll Do*

◆ Explain the relationship between fluid pressure and buoyant force.
◆ Predict whether an object will float or sink in a fluid.
◆ Analyze the role of density in an object's ability to float.

# Buoyant Force

Why does a rubber duck float on water? Why doesn't it sink to the bottom of your bathtub? Even if you pushed the rubber duck to the bottom, it would pop back to the surface when you released it. Some force pushes the rubber duck to the top of the water. That force is **buoyant force,** the upward force that fluids exert on all matter.

Air is a fluid, so it exerts a buoyant force. But why don't you ever see rubber ducks floating in air? Read on to find out!

## Buoyant Force Is Caused by Differences in Fluid Pressure

Look at **Figure 9.** Water exerts fluid pressure on all sides of an object. The pressure exerted horizontally on one side of the object is equal to the pressure exerted horizontally on the opposite side. These equal pressures cancel one another. Thus, the only fluid pressures affecting the object are at the top and at the bottom. Because pressure increases with depth, the pressure on the bottom of the object is greater than the pressure at the top, as shown by the width of the arrows. Therefore, the water exerts a net upward force on the object. This upward force is buoyant force.

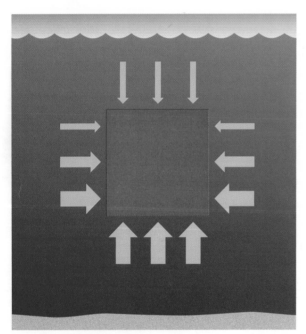

**Figure 9** *There is more fluid pressure on the bottom of an object because pressure increases with depth. This results in an upward force on the object—buoyant force.*

**Determining Buoyant Force** Archimedes (ahr kuh MEE deez), a Greek mathematician who lived in the third century B.C., discovered how to determine buoyant force. **Archimedes' principle** states that the buoyant force on an object in a fluid is an upward force equal to the weight of the volume of fluid that the object displaces. (*Displace* means "to take the place of.") For example, suppose the object in Figure 9 displaces 250 mL of water. The weight of that volume of displaced water is about 2.5 N. Therefore, the buoyant force on the object is 2.5 N. Notice that the weight of the object has nothing to do with the buoyant force. Only the weight of the displaced fluid determines the buoyant force on an object.

# Weight Vs. Buoyant Force

An object in a fluid will sink if it has a weight greater than the weight of the fluid that is displaced. In other words, an object will sink if its weight is greater than the buoyant force acting on it. An object floats only when it displaces a volume of fluid that has a weight equal to the object's weight—that is, if the buoyant force on the object is equal to the object's weight.

**Sinking** The lake scene in **Figure 10** looks quite peaceful, but there are forces being exerted! The rock weighs 75 N. It displaces 5 L of water. According to Archimedes' principle, the buoyant force is equal to the weight of the displaced water—about 50 N. Because the rock's weight is greater than the buoyant force, the rock sinks.

**Floating** The fish weighs 12 N. It displaces a volume of water that has a weight of 12 N. Because the fish's weight is equal to the buoyant force, the fish floats in the water. Now look at the duck. The duck weighs 9 N. The duck does not sink. What does that tell you? The buoyant force on the duck must be equal to the duck's weight. But the duck isn't even all the way underwater! Only the duck's feet, legs, and stomach have to be underwater in order to displace enough water to equal 9 N. Thus, the duck floats.

**Buoying Up** If the duck dove underwater, it would then displace more water, and the buoyant force would therefore be greater. When the buoyant force on an object is greater than the object's weight, the object is *buoyed up* (pushed up) out of the water until what's left underwater displaces an amount of water that equals the object's entire weight. That's why a rubber duck pops to the surface when it is pushed to the bottom of a filled bathtub.

## Activity

Find five things that float in water and five things that sink in water. What do the floating objects have in common? What do the sinking objects have in common?

*TRY at HOME*

**Figure 10** *Will an object sink or float? It depends on whether the buoyant force is less than or equal to the object's weight.*

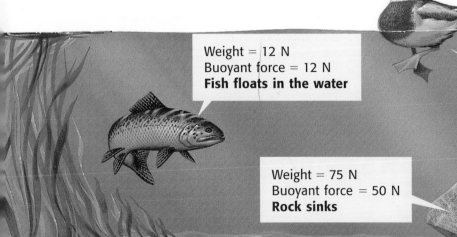

Weight = 12 N
Buoyant force = 12 N
**Fish floats in the water**

Weight = 9 N
Buoyant force = 9 N
**Duck floats on the surface**

Weight = 75 N
Buoyant force = 50 N
**Rock sinks**

## An Object Will Float or Sink Based on Its Density

### How to Calculate Density

The volume of any sample of matter, no matter what state or shape, can be calculated using this equation:

$$\text{Density} = \frac{\text{Mass}}{\text{Volume}}$$

1. What is the density of a 20 cm³ sample of liquid with a mass of 25 g?
2. A 546 g fish displaces 420 cm³ of water. What is the density of the fish?

Think again about the rock at the bottom of the lake. The rock displaces 5 L of water, which means that the volume of the rock is 5,000 cm³. (Remember that liters are used only for fluid volumes.) But 5,000 cm³ of rock weighs more than an equal volume of water. This is why the rock sinks. Because mass is proportional to weight on Earth, you can say that the rock has more mass per volume than water. Remember, mass per unit volume is *density*. The rock sinks because it is more dense than water. The duck floats because it is less dense than water. In Figure 10, the density of the fish is exactly equal to the density of the water.

**More Dense Than Air** Think back to the question about the rubber duck: "Why does it float on water but not in air?" The rubber duck floats because it is less dense than water. However, most substances are *more* dense than air. Therefore, there are few substances that float in air. The plastic that makes up the rubber duck is more dense than air, so the rubber duck doesn't float in air.

**Less Dense Than Air** One substance that is less dense than air is helium, a gas. In fact, helium is over 70 times less dense than air. A volume of helium displaces a volume of air that is much heavier than itself, so helium floats. That's why helium is used in airships and parade balloons, like the one shown in **Figure 11.**

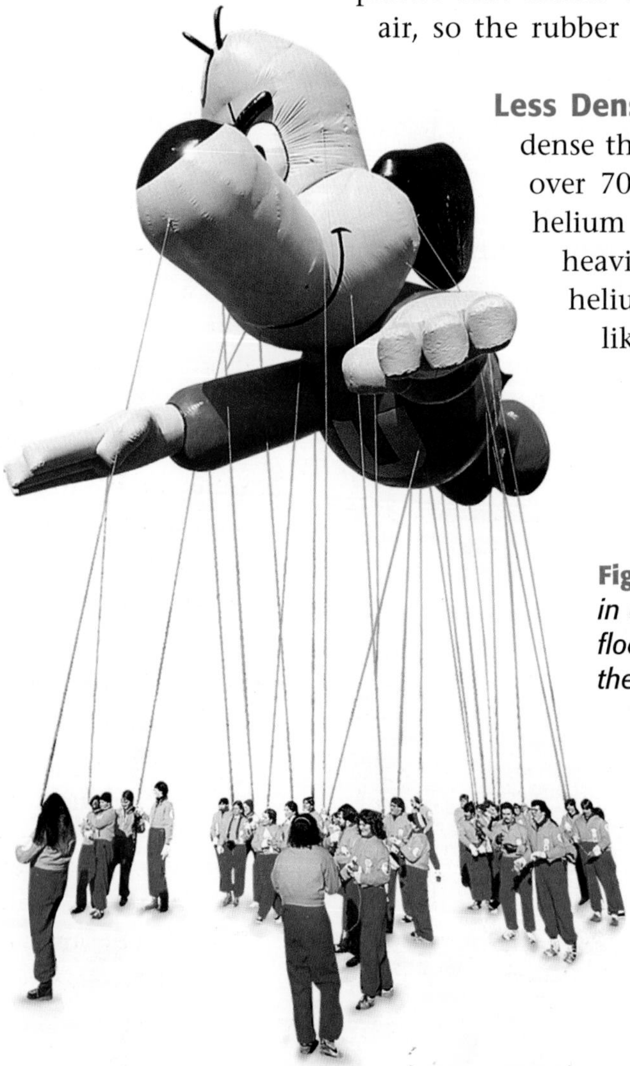

**Figure 11** *Helium in a balloon floats in air for the same reason a duck floats in water—it is less dense than the surrounding fluid.*

# The Mystery of Floating Steel

Steel is almost eight times more dense than water. And yet huge steel ships cruise the oceans with ease, even while carrying enormous loads. But hold on! Didn't you just learn that substances that are more dense than water will sink in water? You bet! So how does a steel ship float?

The secret is in the shape of the ship. What if a ship were just a big block of steel, as shown in **Figure 12**? If you put that steel block into water, the block would sink because it is more dense than water. For this reason, ships are built with a hollow shape, as shown below. The amount of steel in the ship is the same as in the block, but the hollow shape increases the volume of the ship. Because density is mass per volume, an increase in the ship's volume leads to a decrease in its density. Therefore, ships made of steel float because their *overall density* is less than the density of water. This is true of boats of any size, made of any material. Most ships are actually built to displace even more water than is necessary for the ship to float so that the ship won't sink when people and cargo are loaded onboard.

**BRAIN FOOD**

The *Seawise Giant* is the largest ship in the world. It is so large that crew members often use bicycles to travel around the ship.

**Figure 12  A Ship's Shape Makes the Difference**

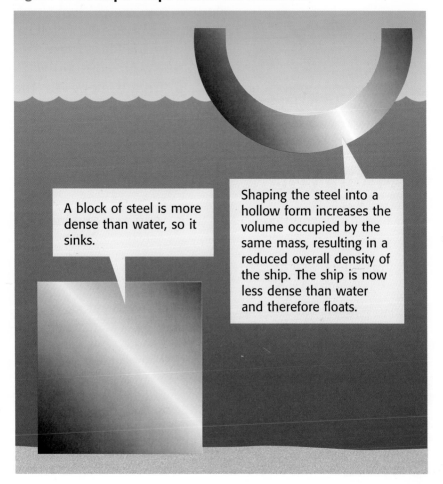

A block of steel is more dense than water, so it sinks.

Shaping the steel into a hollow form increases the volume occupied by the same mass, resulting in a reduced overall density of the ship. The ship is now less dense than water and therefore floats.

**QuickLab**

**Ship-Shape**

1. Roll a **piece of clay** into a ball the size of a golf ball, and drop it into a **container of water**. Record your observations in your ScienceLog.

2. With your hands, flatten the ball of clay until it is a bit thinner than your little finger, and press it into the shape of a bowl or canoe.

3. Place the clay boat gently in the water. How does the change of shape affect the buoyant force on the clay? How is that change related to the average density of the clay boat? Record your answers in your ScienceLog.

**Density on the Move**   A submarine is a special kind of ship that can travel on the surface of the water and underwater. Submarines have special tanks that can be opened to allow sea water to flow in. This water adds mass, thus increasing the submarine's overall density so it can descend into the ocean. Crew members can control the amount of water taken in, thereby controlling the submarine's change in density and thus its depth in the ocean. Compressed air is used to blow the water out of the tanks so the submarine can rise through the water. Most submarines are built of high-strength metals that withstand water pressure. Still, most submarines can go no deeper than 400 m below the surface of the ocean.

**How Is a Fish Like a Submarine?**   No, this is not a trick question! Like a submarine, some fish adjust their overall density in order to stay at a certain depth in the water. Most bony fish have an organ called a *swim bladder,* shown in **Figure 13.** This swim bladder is filled with gases produced in the fish's blood. The inflated swim bladder increases the fish's volume, thereby decreasing the fish's overall density and keeping it from sinking in the water. The fish's nervous system controls the amount of gas in the bladder according to the fish's depth in the water. Some fish, such as sharks, do not have a swim bladder. These fish must swim constantly to keep from sinking to the bottom of the water.

**Figure 13** *Most bony fish have an organ called a swim bladder that allows the fish to adjust its overall density.*

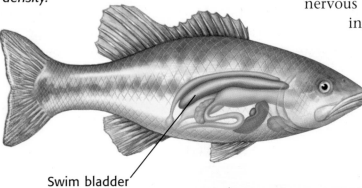

Swim bladder

## SECTION REVIEW

1. Explain how differences in fluid pressure create buoyant force on an object.

2. An object weighs 20 N. It displaces a volume of water that weighs 15 N.
   a. What is the buoyant force on the object?
   b. Will this object float or sink? Explain your answer.

3. Iron has a density of 7.9 g/cm$^3$. Mercury has a density of 13.6 g/cm$^3$. Will iron float or sink in mercury? Explain your answer.

4. **Applying Concepts**   Why is it inaccurate to say that all heavy objects will sink in water?

**What You'll Do**

◆ Describe the relationship between pressure and fluid speed.
◆ Analyze the roles of lift, thrust, and drag in flight.
◆ Give examples of Bernoulli's principle in real-life situations.

# Bernoulli's Principle

Has this ever happened to you? You've just turned on the shower. Upon stepping into the water stream, you decide that the water pressure is not strong enough. You turn the faucet to provide more water, and all of a sudden the bottom edge of the shower curtain starts swirling around your legs. What's going on? It might surprise you that the explanation for this unusual occurrence also explains how wings help birds and planes fly and how pitchers throw curve balls.

## Fluid Pressure Decreases as Speed Increases

The strange reaction of the shower curtain is caused by a property of moving fluids that was first described in the eighteenth century by Daniel Bernoulli (buhr NOO lee), a Swiss mathematician. **Bernoulli's principle** states that as the speed of a moving fluid increases, its pressure decreases. In the case of the shower curtain, the faster the water moves, the less pressure it exerts. This creates an imbalance between the pressure inside the shower curtain and the pressure outside it. Because the pressure outside is now greater than the pressure inside, the shower curtain is pushed toward the water stream.

**Science in a Sink** You can see Bernoulli's principle at work in **Figure 14.** A table-tennis ball is attached to a string and swung gently into a moving stream of water. Instead of being pushed back out, the ball is actually held in the moving water when the string is given a tug. Why does the ball do that? The water is moving, so it has a lower pressure than the surrounding air. The higher air pressure then pushes the ball into the area of lower pressure—the water stream. Try this at home to see for yourself!

**Figure 14** *This ball is pushed by the higher pressure of the air into an area of reduced pressure—the water stream.*

**QuickLab**

**Breathing Bernoulli-Style**

1. Hold **two pieces of paper** by their top edges, one in each hand, so that they hang next to one another about 5 cm apart.

2. Blow a steady stream of air between the two sheets of paper.

3. Record your observations in your ScienceLog. Explain the results according to Bernoulli's principle.

*TRY at HOME*

**73**

## It's a Bird! It's a Plane! It's Bernoulli's Principle!

The most common commercial airplane in the skies today is the Boeing 737 jet. A 737 jet is almost 37 m long and has a wingspan of 30 m. Even without passengers, the plane weighs 350,000 N. That's more than 35 times heavier than an average car! How can something so big and heavy get off the ground, much less fly 10,000 m into the sky? Wing design plays a role in helping these big planes—as well as smaller planes and even birds—achieve flight, as shown in **Figure 15.**

According to Bernoulli's principle, the faster-moving air above the wing exerts less pressure than the slower-moving air below the wing. The increased pressure that results below the wing exerts an upward force. This upward force contributes to lift. **Lift** is an upward force that opposes the downward pull of gravity.

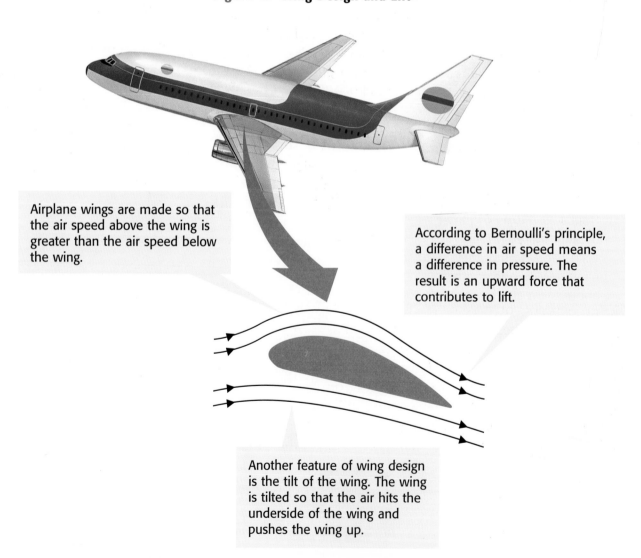

**Figure 15  Wing Design and Lift**

Airplane wings are made so that the air speed above the wing is greater than the air speed below the wing.

According to Bernoulli's principle, a difference in air speed means a difference in pressure. The result is an upward force that contributes to lift.

Another feature of wing design is the tilt of the wing. The wing is tilted so that the air hits the underside of the wing and pushes the wing up.

## Thrust and Wing Size Determine Lift

The amount of lift created by a plane's wing is determined in part by the size of the wing and the speed at which air travels around the wing. The speed of an airplane is in large part determined by its **thrust**—the forward force produced by the plane's engine. In general, a plane with a greater amount of thrust moves faster than a plane with less thrust. This faster speed means air travels around the wing at a greater speed, which increases lift.

You can understand the relationship between wing size, thrust, and speed by thinking about a jet plane, like the one in **Figure 16.** This plane is able to fly with a relatively small wing size because its engine creates an enormous amount of thrust. This thrust pushes the plane through the sky at tremendous speeds. Therefore, the jet generates sufficient lift with small wings by moving very quickly through the air. Smaller wings keep a plane's weight low, which also contributes to speed.

Compared with the jet, a glider, like the one in **Figure 17,** has a large wing area. A glider is an engineless plane that rides rising air currents to stay in flight. Without engines, gliders produce no thrust and move more slowly than many other kinds of planes. Thus, a glider must have large wings to create the lift necessary to keep it in the air.

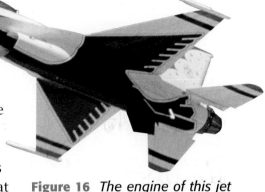

**Figure 16** *The engine of this jet creates a great deal of thrust, so the wings don't have to be very big.*

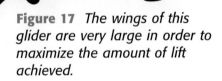

**Figure 17** *The wings of this glider are very large in order to maximize the amount of lift achieved.*

### ✓ Self-Check

Does air travel faster or slower over the top of a wing? *(See page 232 to check your answer.)*

**Bernoulli's Principle Is for the Birds** Birds don't have engines, of course, so they must flap their wings to push themselves through the air. The hawk shown at left uses its large wing size to fly with a minimum of effort. By extending its large wings to their full length and gliding on wind currents, a hawk can achieve enough lift to stay in the air while flapping only occasionally. Smaller birds must flap their wings more often to stay in the air.

**Lift and Spoilers**

At high speeds, air moving around the body of this race car could lift the car just as it lifts a plane's wing. This could cause the wheels to lose contact with the ground, sending the car out of control. To prevent this situation, an upside-down wing, or spoiler, is mounted on the rear of the car. How do spoilers help reduce the danger of accidents?

## Drag Opposes Motion in Fluids

Have you ever walked into a strong wind and noticed that the wind seemed to slow you down? Fluids exert a force that opposes motion. The force that opposes or restricts motion in a fluid is called **drag.** In a strong wind, air "drags" on your clothes and body, making it difficult for you to move forward. Drag forces in flight work against the forward motion of a plane or bird and are usually caused by an irregular flow of air around the wings. An irregular or unpredictable flow of fluids is known as *turbulence.*

Lift is often reduced when turbulence causes drag. At faster speeds, drag can become a serious problem, so airplanes are equipped with ways to reduce turbulence as much as possible when in flight. For example, flaps like those shown in **Figure 18** can be used to change the shape or area of a wing, thereby reducing drag and increasing lift. Similarly, birds can adjust their wing feathers in response to turbulence to achieve greater lift.

**Figure 18** *During flight, the pilot of this airplane can adjust these flaps to help increase lift.*

# Wings Are Not Always Required

You don't have to look up at a bird or a plane flying through the sky to see Bernoulli's principle in your world. In fact, you've already learned how Bernoulli's principle can affect such things as shower curtains and race cars. Any time fluids are moving, Bernoulli's principle is at work. In **Figure 19,** you can see how Bernoulli's principle can mean the difference between a home run and a strike during a baseball game.

Bernoulli's principle at play— read how Frisbees® were invented on page 84.

**Figure 19** *A pitcher can take advantage of Bernoulli's principle to produce a confusing curveball that is difficult for the batter to hit.*

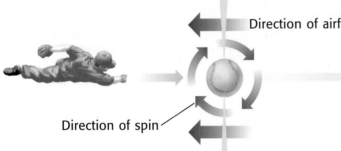

**a** Air speed on the left side of the ball is decreased because air being dragged around the ball moves in the opposite direction of the airflow. This results in a region of increased pressure on the left side of the ball.

Direction of airflow

Direction of spin

**b** Air speed on the right side of the ball is increased because air being dragged around the ball moves in the same direction as the airflow. This results in a region of decreased pressure on the right side of the ball.

**c** Because air pressure on the left side is greater than that on the right side, the ball is pushed toward the right in a curved path.

## SECTION REVIEW

1. Does fluid pressure increase or decrease as fluid speed increases?

2. Explain how wing design can contribute to lift during flight.

3. What force opposes motion through a fluid?

4. **Interpreting Graphics** When the space through which a fluid flows becomes narrow, fluid speed increases. Explain how this could lead to a collision for the two boats shown at right.

# Skill Builder Lab

## Fluids, Force, and Floating

Why do some objects sink in fluids but others float? In this lab, you'll get a sinking feeling as you determine that an object floats when its weight is less than the buoyant force exerted by the surrounding fluid.

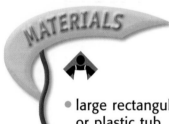

### MATERIALS

- large rectangular tank or plastic tub
- water
- metric ruler
- small rectangular baking pan
- labeled masses
- metric balance
- paper towels

### Procedure

1. Copy the table on the next page into your ScienceLog.

2. Fill the tank or tub half full with water. Measure (in centimeters) the length, width, and initial height of the water. Record your measurements in the table.

3. Using the equation given in the table, determine the initial volume of water in the tank. Record your results in the table.

4. Place the pan in the water, and place masses in the pan, as shown on the next page. Keep adding masses until the pan sinks to about three-quarters of its height. Record the new height of the water in the table. Then use this value to determine and record the new volume of water.

5. Determine the volume of the water that was displaced by the pan and masses, and record this value in the table. The displaced volume is equal to the new volume minus the initial volume.

6. Determine the mass of the displaced water by multiplying the displaced volume by its density (1 g/cm$^3$). Record the mass in the table.

7. Divide the mass by 100. The value you get is the weight of the displaced water in newtons (N). This weight is equal to the buoyant force. Record the weight of the displaced water in the table.

8. Remove the pan and masses, and determine their total mass (in grams), using the balance. Convert the mass to weight (N), as you did in step 7. Record the weight of the masses and pan in the table.

| Measurement | Trial 1 | Trial 2 |
|---|---|---|
| Length ($l$), cm | | |
| Width ($w$), cm | | |
| Initial height ($h_1$), cm | | |
| Initial volume ($V_1$), cm$^3$ $V_1 = l \times w \times h_1$ | | |
| New height ($h_2$), cm | | |
| New volume ($V_2$), cm$^3$ $V_2 = l \times w \times h_2$ | | |
| Displaced volume ($\Delta V$), cm$^3$ $\Delta V = V_2 - V_1$ | | |
| Mass of displaced water, g $m = \Delta V \times 1$ g/cm$^3$ | | |
| Weight of displaced water, N (buoyant force) | | |
| Weight of pan and masses, N | | |

*DO NOT WRITE IN BOOK*

**9** Place the empty pan back in the tank. Perform a second trial by repeating steps 4–8. This time, add masses until the pan is just about to sink.

## Analysis

**10** In your ScienceLog, compare the buoyant force (the weight of the displaced water) with the weight of the pan and masses for both trials.

**11** How did the buoyant force differ between the two trials? Explain.

**12** Based on your observations, what would happen if you were to add even more mass to the pan than you did in the second trial? Explain your answer in terms of the buoyant force, balanced forces, and unbalanced forces.

**13** What would happen if you put the masses in the water without the pan? What difference does the pan's shape make?

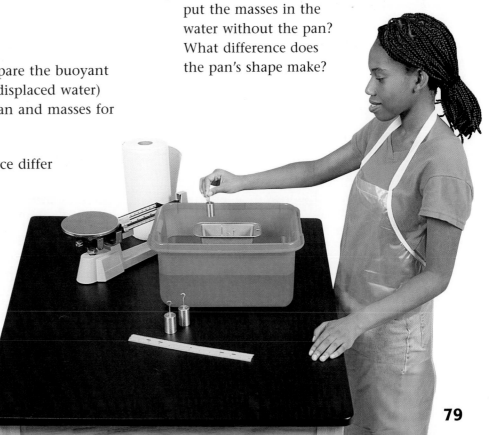

# Chapter Highlights

## Vocabulary

**fluid** (*p. 62*)

**pressure** (*p. 62*)

**pascal** (*p. 62*)

**atmospheric pressure** (*p. 63*)

**density** (*p. 65*)

**Pascal's principle** (*p. 67*)

## Section Notes

- A fluid is any material that flows and that takes the shape of its container.

- Pressure is force exerted on a given area.

- Moving particles of matter create pressure by colliding with one another and with the walls of their container.

- Fluids exert pressure equally in all directions.

- The pressure caused by the weight of Earth's atmosphere is called atmospheric pressure.

- Fluid pressure increases as depth increases.

- Fluids flow from areas of high pressure to areas of low pressure.

- Pascal's principle states that a change in pressure at any point in an enclosed fluid will be transmitted equally to all parts of the fluid.

- Hydraulic devices transmit changes of pressure through liquids.

## Labs

**Out the Spouts** (*p. 193*)

## Vocabulary

**buoyant force** (*p. 68*)

**Archimedes' principle** (*p. 68*)

## Section Notes

- All fluids exert an upward force called buoyant force.

- Buoyant force is caused by differences in fluid pressure.

- Archimedes' principle states that the buoyant force on an object is equal to the weight of the fluid displaced by the object.

# ☑ Skills Check

## Math Concepts

**PRESSURE** If an object exerts a force of 10 N over an area of 2 m², the pressure exerted can be calculated as follows:

$$\text{Pressure} = \frac{\text{Force}}{\text{Area}}$$

$$= \frac{10 \text{ N}}{2 \text{ m}^2}$$

$$= \frac{5 \text{ N}}{1 \text{ m}^2} \text{, or } 5 \text{ Pa}$$

## Visual Understanding

**ATMOSPHERIC PRESSURE** Why aren't you crushed by atmospheric pressure? Figure 3 on page 63 can help you understand.

**BUOYANT FORCE** To understand how differences in fluid pressure cause buoyant force, review Figure 9 on page 68.

**BERNOULLI'S PRINCIPLE AND WING DESIGN** Turn to page 74 to review how a wing is often designed to take advantage of Bernoulli's principle in creating lift.

- Any object that is more dense than the surrounding fluid will sink; any object that is less dense than the surrounding fluid will float.

## Labs

**Density Diver** (*p. 192*)

## Vocabulary

**Bernoulli's principle** (*p. 73*)

**lift** (*p. 74*)

**thrust** (*p. 75*)

**drag** (*p. 76*)

## Section Notes

- Bernoulli's principle states that fluid pressure decreases as the speed of a moving fluid increases.

- Wings are often designed to allow airplanes to take advantage of decreased pressure in moving air in order to achieve flight.

- Lift is an upward force that acts against gravity.

- Lift on an airplane is determined by wing size and thrust (the forward force produced by the engine).

- Drag opposes motion through fluids.

## internet**connect**

**GO TO:** go.hrw.com

Visit the **HRW** Web site for a variety of learning tools related to this chapter. Just type in the keyword:

**KEYWORD:** HSTFLU

*SCiLINKS*.SM

**N S T A**

**GO TO:** www.scilinks.org

Visit the **National Science Teachers Association** on-line Web site for Internet resources related to this chapter. Just type in the *sci*LINKS number for more information about the topic:

**TOPIC:** Submarines and Undersea Technology    *sci*LINKS NUMBER: HSTP155

**TOPIC:** Fluids and Pressure    *sci*LINKS NUMBER: HSTP160

**TOPIC:** The Buoyant Force    *sci*LINKS NUMBER: HSTP165

**TOPIC:** Bernoulli's Principle    *sci*LINKS NUMBER: HSTP170

# Chapter Review

## USING VOCABULARY

To complete the following sentences, choose the correct term from each of the pair of terms listed below:

1. __?__ increases with the depth of a fluid. *(Pressure* or *Lift)*

2. A plane's engine produces __?__ to push the plane forward. *(thrust* or *drag)*

3. Force divided by area is known as __?__. *(density* or *pressure)*

4. The hydraulic brakes of a car transmit pressure through fluid. This is an example of __?__. *(Archimedes' principle* or *Pascal's principle)*

5. Bernoulli's principle states that the pressure exerted by a moving fluid is __?__ *(greater than* or *less than)* the pressure of the fluid when it is not moving.

## UNDERSTANDING CONCEPTS

### Multiple Choice

6. The design of a wing
   a. causes the air above the wing to travel faster than the air below the wing.
   b. helps create lift.
   c. creates a low-pressure zone above the wing.
   d. All of the above

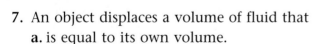

7. An object displaces a volume of fluid that
   a. is equal to its own volume.
   b. is less than its own volume.
   c. is greater than its own volume.
   d. is more dense than itself.

8. Fluid pressure is always directed
   a. up.                c. sideways.
   b. down.              d. in all directions.

9. If an object weighing 50 N displaces a volume of water with a weight of 10 N, what is the buoyant force on the object?
   a. 60 N
   b. 50 N
   c. 40 N
   d. 10 N

10. A helium-filled balloon will float in air because
    a. there is more air than helium.
    b. helium is less dense than air.
    c. helium is as dense as air.
    d. helium is more dense than air.

11. Materials that can flow to fit their containers include
    a. gases.
    b. liquids.
    c. both gases and liquids.
    d. neither gases nor liquids.

### Short Answer

12. What two factors determine the amount of lift achieved by an airplane?

13. Where is water pressure greater, at a depth of 1 m in a large lake or at a depth of 2 m in a small pond? Explain.

14. Is there buoyant force on an object at the bottom of an ocean? Explain your reasoning.

15. Why are liquids used in hydraulic brakes instead of gases?

**16.** Use the following terms to create a concept map: fluid, pressure, depth, buoyant force, density.

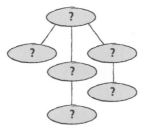

## CRITICAL THINKING AND PROBLEM SOLVING

**17.** Compared with an empty ship, will a ship loaded with plastic-foam balls float higher or lower in the water? Explain your reasoning.

**18.** Inside all vacuum cleaners is a high-speed fan. Explain how this fan causes dirt to be picked up by the vacuum cleaner.

**19.** A 600 N clown on stilts says to two 600 N clowns sitting on the ground, "I am exerting twice as much pressure as the two of you together!" Could this statement be true? Explain your reasoning.

## MATH IN SCIENCE

**20.** Calculate the area of a 1,500 N object that exerts a pressure of 500 Pa (N/m²). Then calculate the pressure exerted by the same object over twice that area. Be sure to express your answers in the correct SI unit.

## INTERPRETING GRAPHICS

Examine the illustration of an iceberg below, and answer the questions that follow.

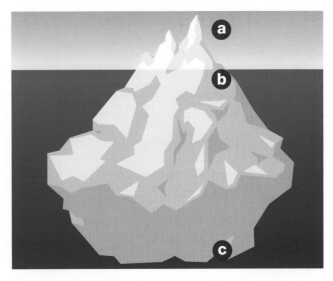

**21.** At what point (*a*, *b*, or *c*) is water pressure greatest on the iceberg?

**22.** How much of the iceberg has a weight equal to the buoyant force?
**a.** all of it
**b.** the section from *a* to *b*
**c.** the section from *b* to *c*

**23.** How does the density of ice compare with the density of water?

**24.** Why do you think icebergs are so dangerous to passing ships?

**Reading Check-up**

Take a minute to review your answers to the Pre-Reading Questions found at the bottom of page 60. Have your answers changed? If necessary, revise your answers based on what you have learned since you began this chapter.

# Eureka!

## Stayin' Aloft—The Story of the Frisbee®

Whoa! Nice catch! Your friend 30 m away just sent a disk spinning toward you. As you reached for it, a gust of wind floated it up over your head. With a quick jump, you snagged it. A snap of your wrist sends the disk soaring back. You are "Frisbee-ing," a game more than 100 years old. But back then, there were no plastic disks, only pie plates.

### From Pie Plate...

In the late 1800s, ready-made pies baked in tin plates began to appear in stores and restaurants. A bakery near Yale University, in New Haven, Connecticut, embossed its name, Frisbie's Pies, on its pie plates. When a few fun-loving college students tossed empty pie plates, they found that the metal plates had a marvelous ability to stay in the air. Soon the students began alerting their companions of an incoming pie plate by shouting "Frisbie!" So tossing pie plates became known as Frisbie-ing. By the late 1940s, the game was played across the country.

### ...to Plastic

In 1947, California businessmen Fred Morrison and Warren Franscioni needed to make a little extra money. They were familiar with pie-plate tossing, and they knew the plates often cracked when they landed and developed sharp edges that caused injuries.

At the time, plastic was becoming widely available. Plastic is more durable and flexible than metal, and it isn't as likely to injure fingers. Why not make a "pie plate" out of plastic, thought Morrison and Franscioni? They did, and their idea was a huge success.

Years later, a toy company bought the rights to make the toy. One day the president of the company heard someone yelling "Frisbie!" while tossing a disk and decided to use that name, changing the spelling to "Frisbee."

### Saucer Science

It looks simple, but Frisbee flight is quite complicated. It involves *thrust,* the force you give the disk to move it through the air; *angle of attack,* the slight upward tilt you give the disk when you throw it; and *lift,* the upward forces (explained in part by Bernoulli's principle) acting on the Frisbee to counteract gravity. But perhaps the most important aspect of Frisbee physics is *spin,* which gives the Frisbee stability as it flies. The faster a Frisbee spins, the more stable it is and the farther it can fly.

### What Do You Think?

▶ From what you've learned in class, why do you think the Frisbee has a curved lip? Would a completely flat Frisbee fly as well? Why or why not? Find out more about the interesting aerodynamics of Frisbee flight. Fly a Frisbee for the class, and explain what you've learned.

# Science Fiction

## "Wet Behind the Ears"

### by Jack C. Haldeman II

**W**illie Joe Thomas is a college student who lied to get into college and cheated to get a swimming scholarship. Now he is faced with a major swim meet, and his coach has told him that he has to swim or be kicked off the team. Willie Joe could lose his scholarship. What's worse, he would have to get a *job*.

"Wet Behind the Ears" is Willie Joe's story. It's the story of someone who has always taken the easy way (even if it takes more work), of someone who lies and cheats as easily as he breathes. Willie Joe could probably do things the right way, but it never even occurred to him to try it!

So when Willie Joe's roommate, Frank Emerson, announces that he has made an amazing discovery in the chemistry lab, Willie Joe doesn't much care. Frank works too hard. Frank follows the rules. Willie Joe isn't impressed.

But when he is running late for the all-important swim meet, Willie Joe remembers what Frank's new compound does. Frank said it was a "sliding compound." Willie Joe may not know chemistry, but "slippery" he understands. And Frank also said something about selling the stuff to the Navy to make its ships go faster. Hey, if it works for ships . . .

See what happens when Willie Joe tries to save his scholarship. Go to the *Holt Anthology of Science Fiction,* and read "Wet Behind the Ears," by Jack C. Haldeman II.

# Work and Machines

Pre-Reading
Questions

1. What does it mean to do work?

2. How are machines helpful when doing work?

3. What are some examples of simple machines?

## "ONE, TWO, STROKE!" . . .

. . . shouts the coach as the team races to the finish line. This paddling team is competing in Hong Kong's annual Dragon Boat Races. The Dragon Boat Festival is a 2,000-year-old Chinese tradition that commemorates the death of the national hero, Qu Yuan. The paddlers you see here are using the paddles to move the boat forward. Even though they are celebrating by racing their dragon boat, in scientific terms this team is doing *work*. How is this possible? Read on to find out!

## C'MON, LEVER A LITTLE!

In this activity, you will use a simple machine, a lever, to make your task a little easier.

### Procedure

1. Gather a few **books** and stack them on a table, one on top of the other.

2. Slide your index finger underneath the edge of the bottom book. Using only the force of your finger, try to lift one side of the books 2 or 3 cm off the table. Is it difficult? Write your observations in your ScienceLog.

3. Slide the end of a **wooden ruler** underneath the edge of the bottom book. Then slip a **large pencil eraser** under the ruler.

4. Again using only your index finger, push down on the edge of the ruler and try to lift the books. Record your observations.

   **Caution:** Push down slowly to keep the ruler and eraser from flipping.

### Analysis

5. Which was easier, lifting the books with your finger or with the ruler? Explain.

6. What was different about the direction of the force your finger applied on the books compared with the direction of the force you applied on the ruler?

**What You'll Do**

◆ Determine when work is being done on an object.
◆ Calculate the amount of work done on an object.
◆ Explain the difference between work and power.

# Work and Power

Suppose your science teacher has just given you a homework assignment. You have to read an entire chapter by tomorrow! Wow, that's a lot of work, isn't it? Actually, in the scientific sense, you won't be doing any work at all! How can that be?

## The Scientific Meaning of *Work*

In science, **work** occurs when a force causes an object to move in the direction of the force. In the example above, you may put a lot of mental effort into doing your homework, but you won't be using a force to move an object. Therefore, in the scientific sense, you will not be doing work.

Now think about the example shown in **Figure 1.** This student is having a lot of fun, isn't she? But she is doing work, even though she is having fun. That's because she's applying a force to the bowling ball to make it move through a distance. However, it's important to understand that she is doing work on the ball only as long as she is touching it. The ball will continue to move away from her after she releases it, but she will no longer be doing work on the ball because she will no longer be applying a force to it.

**Figure 1** *You might be surprised to find out that bowling is doing work!*

**Working Hard or Hardly Working?**   You should understand that applying a force doesn't always result in work being done. Suppose your neighbor asks you to help push his stalled car. You push and push, but the car doesn't budge. Even though you may be exhausted and sweaty, you haven't done any work on the car. Why? Because the car hasn't moved. Remember, work is done on an object only when a force makes that object move. In this case, your pushing doesn't make the car move. You only do work on the car if it starts to move.

**Force and Motion in the Same Direction** Suppose you're in the airport and you're late for a flight. You have to run through the airport carrying a heavy suitcase. Because you're making the suitcase move, you're doing work on it, right? Wrong! For work to be done, the object must move in the same direction as the force. In this case, the motion is in a different direction than the force, as shown in **Figure 2.** So no work is done on the suitcase. However, work *is* done on the suitcase when you lift it off the ground.

You'll know that work is done on an object if two things occur: (1) the object moves as a force is applied and (2) the direction of the object's motion is the same as the direction of the force applied. The pictures and the arrows in the chart below will help you understand how to determine when work is being done on an object.

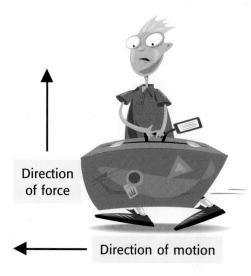

Direction of force

Direction of motion

**Figure 2** *You exert an upward force on the suitcase. But the motion of the suitcase is forward. Therefore, you are not doing work on the suitcase.*

| Work or Not Work? | | | |
|---|---|---|---|
| **Example** | **Direction of force** | **Direction of motion** | **Doing work?** |
| | → | → | Yes |
| | ↑ | → | No |
| | ↑ | ↑ | Yes |
| | ↑ | → | No |

> ✓ **Self-Check**
>
> If you pulled a wheeled suitcase instead of carrying it, would you be doing work on the suitcase? Why or why not? *(See page 232 to check your answer.)*

## MATH BREAK

### Working It Out

Use the equation for work shown on this page to solve the following problems:

1. A man applies a force of 500 N to push a truck 100 m down the street. How much work does he do?

2. In which situation do you do more work?
   a. You lift a 75 N bowling ball 2 m off the floor.
   b. You lift two 50 N bowling balls 1 m off the floor.

# Calculating Work

Do you do more work when you lift an 80 N barbell or a 160 N barbell? It would be tempting to say that you do more work when you lift the 160 N barbell because it weighs more. But actually, you can't answer this question with the information given. You also need to know how high each barbell is being lifted. Remember, work is a force applied through a distance. The greater the distance through which you exert a given force, the more work you do. Similarly, the greater the force you exert through a given distance, the more work you do.

The amount of work ($W$) done in moving an object can be calculated by multiplying the force ($F$) applied to the object by the distance ($d$) through which the force is applied, as shown in the following equation:

$$W = F \times d$$

Recall that force is expressed in newtons, and the meter is the basic SI unit for length or distance. Therefore, the unit used to express work is the newton-meter (N•m), which is more simply called the **joule (J).** Look at **Figure 3** to learn more about calculating work. You can also practice calculating work yourself by doing the MathBreak on this page.

**Figure 3  Work Depends on Force and Distance**

$W = 80 \text{ N} \times 1 \text{ m} = 80 \text{ J}$

The force needed to lift an object is equal to the gravitational force on the object—in other words, the object's weight.

$W = 160 \text{ N} \times 1 \text{ m} = 160 \text{ J}$

Increasing the amount of force increases the amount of work done.

$W = 80 \text{ N} \times 2 \text{ m} = 160 \text{ J}$

Increasing the distance also increases the amount of work done.

## Power—How Fast Work Is Done

Like *work*, the term *power* is used a lot in everyday language but has a very specific meaning in science. **Power** is the rate at which work is done. To calculate power (*P*), you divide the amount of work done (*W*) by the time (*t*) it takes to do that work, as shown in the following equation:

$$P = \frac{W}{t}$$

You just learned that the unit for work is the joule, and the basic unit for time is the second. Therefore, the unit used to express power is joules per second (J/s), which is more simply called the **watt (W).** So if you do 50 J of work in 5 seconds, your power is 10 J/s, or 10 W. You can calculate your own power in the QuickLab at right.

**Increasing Power**   Power is how fast work happens. Power is increased when more work is done in a given amount of time. Power is also increased when the time it takes to do a certain amount of work is decreased, as shown in **Figure 4.**

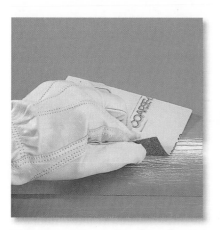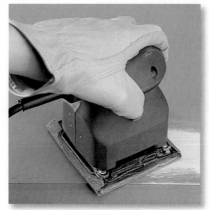

**Figure 4** *No matter how fast you can sand with sandpaper, an electric sander can do the same amount of work faster. Therefore, the electric sander has more power.*

## QuickLab

### More Power to You

1. Use a loop of **string** to attach a **spring scale** to a **book.**

2. Slowly pull the book across a table by the spring scale. Use a **stopwatch** to determine the time this takes. In your ScienceLog, record the amount of time it took and the force used as the book reached the edge of the table.

3. With a **metric ruler,** measure the distance you pulled the book.

4. Now quickly pull the book across the same distance. Again record the time and force.

5. Calculate work and power for both trials.

6. How were the amounts of work and power affected by your pulling the book faster? Record your answers in your ScienceLog.

## SECTION REVIEW

1. Work is done on a ball when a pitcher throws it. Is the pitcher still doing work on the ball as it flies through the air? Explain.

2. Explain the difference between work and power.

3. **Doing Calculations**   You lift a chair that weighs 50 N to a height of 0.5 m and carry it 10 m across the room. How much work do you do on the chair?

**internet** connect

*sci*LINKS
NSTA

**TOPIC:** Work and Power
**GO TO:** www.scilinks.org
*sci*LINKS NUMBER: HSTP180

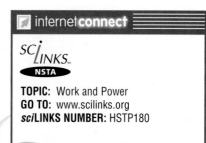

# What Is a Machine?

Imagine you're in the car with your mom on the way to a party when suddenly—*KABLOOM hisssss*—a tire blows out. "Now I'm going to be late!" you think as your mom pulls over to the side of the road. You watch as she opens the trunk and gets out a jack and a tire iron. Using the tire iron, she pries the hubcap off and begins to unscrew the lug nuts from the wheel. She then puts the jack under the car and turns the handle several times until the flat tire no longer touches the ground. After exchanging the flat tire with the spare, she lowers the jack and puts the lug nuts and hubcap back on the wheel. "Wow!" you think, "That wasn't as hard as I thought it would be." As your mom drops you off at the party, you think how lucky it was that she had the right equipment to change the tire.

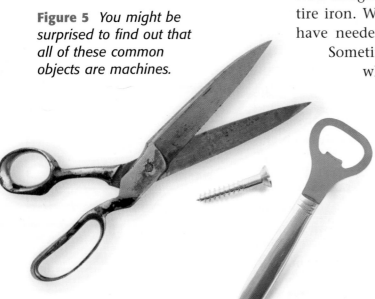

**Figure 5** *You might be surprised to find out that all of these common objects are machines.*

## Machines—Making Work Easier

Now imagine changing a tire without the jack and the tire iron. Would it have been so easy? No, you would have needed several people just to hold up the car! Sometimes you need a little help to do work. That's where machines come in. A **machine** is a device that helps make work easier by changing the size or direction of a force.

When you think of machines, you might think of things like cars, big construction equipment, or even computers. But not all machines are complicated or even have moving parts. In fact, the tire iron, jack, and lug nut shown above are all machines. Even the items shown in **Figure 5** are machines.

**Work In, Work Out** Suppose you need to get the lid off a can of paint. What do you do? Well, one way to pry the lid off is to use the flat end of a common machine known as a screwdriver, as shown in **Figure 6.** You place the tip of the screwdriver under the edge of the lid and then push down on the handle. The other end of the screwdriver lifts the lid as you push down. In other words, you do work on the screwdriver, and the screwdriver does work on the lid. This example illustrates that two kinds of work are always involved when a machine is used—the work done on the machine and the work the machine does on another object.

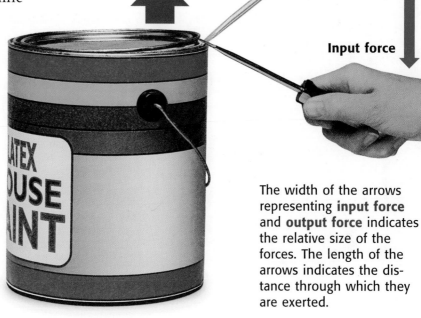

**Output force**

**Input force**

The width of the arrows representing **input force** and **output force** indicates the relative size of the forces. The length of the arrows indicates the distance through which they are exerted.

**Figure 6** *When you use a machine, you do work on the machine, and the machine does work on something else.*

Remember that work is a force applied through a distance. Look again at Figure 6. The work you do on a machine is called **work input.** You apply a force, called the *input force,* to the machine and move it through a distance. The work done by the machine is called **work output.** The machine applies a force, called the *output force,* through a distance. The output force opposes the forces you and the machine are working against—in this case, the weight of the lid and the friction between the can and the lid.

**How Machines Help** You might think that machines help you because they increase the amount of work done. But that's not true. If you multiplied the forces by the distances through which they are applied in Figure 6 (remember, $W = F \times d$), you would find that the screwdriver does *not* do more work on the lid than you do on the screwdriver. Work output can *never* be greater than work input.

**Machines Do Not Save Work** Machines make work easier because they change the size or direction of the input force. And using a screwdriver to open a paint can changes *both* the size and direction of the input force. Just remember that using a machine does not mean that you do less work. As you can see in **Figure 7,** the same amount of work is involved with or without the ramp. The ramp decreases the amount of input force necessary to do the work of lifting the box. But the distance over which the force is exerted increases. In other words, the machine allows a smaller force to be applied over a longer distance.

**Figure 7** *A simple plank of wood acts as a machine when it is used to help raise a load.*

Force: 450 N          Distance: 1 m

$$W = 450 \text{ N} \times 1 \text{ m} = 450 \text{ J}$$

Lifting this box straight up requires an input force equal to the weight of the box.

Force: 150 N          Distance: 3 m

$$W = 150 \text{ N} \times 3 \text{ m} = 450 \text{ J}$$

Using a ramp to lift the box requires an input force less than the weight of the box, but the input force must be exerted over a greater distance.

**The Force-Distance Trade-off** When a machine changes the size of the force, the distance through which the force is exerted must also change. Force or distance can increase, but not together. When one increases, the other must decrease. This is because the work output is never greater than the work input.

The diagram on the next page will help you better understand this force-distance trade-off. It also shows that some machines affect only the direction of the force, not the size of the force or the distance through which it is exerted.

# Machines Change the Size or Direction (or Both) of a Force

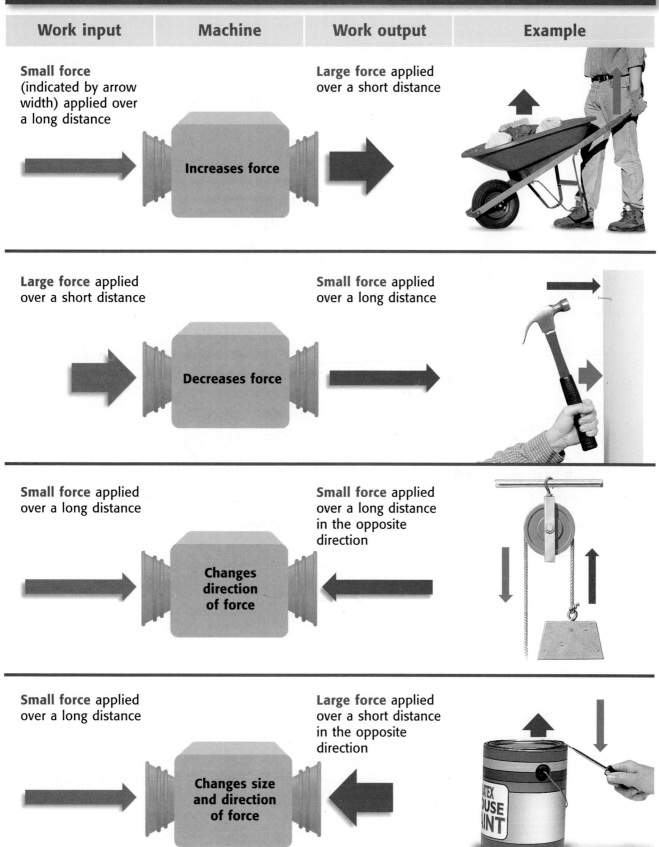

| Work input | Machine | Work output | Example |
|---|---|---|---|
| **Small force** (indicated by arrow width) applied over a long distance | **Increases force** | **Large force** applied over a short distance | |
| **Large force** applied over a short distance | **Decreases force** | **Small force** applied over a long distance | |
| **Small force** applied over a long distance | **Changes direction of force** | **Small force** applied over a long distance in the opposite direction | |
| **Small force** applied over a long distance | **Changes size and direction of force** | **Large force** applied over a short distance in the opposite direction | |

## MATH BREAK

### Finding the Advantage

1. You apply 200 N to a machine, and the machine applies 2,000 N to an object. What is the mechanical advantage?

2. You apply 10 N to a machine, and the machine applies 10 N to another object. What is the mechanical advantage? Can such a machine be useful? Why or why not?

3. Which of the following makes work easier to do?
   **a.** a machine with a mechanical advantage of 15
   **b.** a machine to which you apply 15 N and that exerts 255 N

**Figure 8** *A machine that has a large mechanical advantage can make lifting a heavy load a whole lot easier.*

**Figure 9** *With chopsticks you can pick up a big bite of food with just a little wiggle of your fingers.*

# Mechanical Advantage

Do some machines make work easier than others? Yes, because some machines can increase force more than others. A machine's **mechanical advantage** tells you how many times the machine multiplies force. In other words, it compares the input force with the output force. You can find mechanical advantage by using the following equation:

$$\text{Mechanical advantage } (MA) = \frac{\text{output force}}{\text{input force}}$$

Take a look at **Figure 8**. In this example, the output force is greater than the input force. Using the equation above, you can find the mechanical advantage of the handcart:

$$MA = \frac{500 \text{ N}}{50 \text{ N}} = 10$$

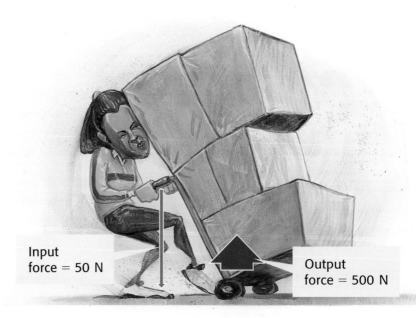

Input force = 50 N

Output force = 500 N

Because the mechanical advantage of the handcart is 10, the output force is 10 times bigger than the input force. The larger the mechanical advantage, the easier a machine makes your work. But as mechanical advantage increases, the distance that the output force moves the object decreases.

Remember that some machines only change the direction of the force. In such cases, the output force is equal to the input force, and the mechanical advantage is 1. Other machines have a mechanical advantage that is less than 1. That means that the input force is greater than the output force. Although such a machine actually decreases your force, it does allow you to exert the force over a longer distance, as shown in **Figure 9**.

## Mechanical Efficiency

As mentioned earlier, the work output of a machine can never be greater than the work input. In fact, the work output of a machine is always *less* than the work input. Why? Because some of the work done by the machine is used to overcome the friction created by the use of the machine. But keep in mind that no work is *lost*. The work output plus the work done to overcome friction equals the work input.

The less work a machine has to do to overcome friction, the more *efficient* it is. **Mechanical efficiency** (e FISH uhn see) is a comparison of a machine's work output with the work input. A machine's mechanical efficiency is calculated using the following equation:

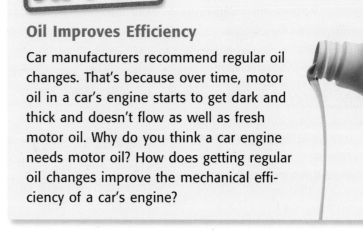

$$\text{Mechanical efficiency} = \frac{\text{work output}}{\text{work input}} \times 100$$

The 100 in this equation means that mechanical efficiency is expressed as a percentage. Mechanical efficiency tells you what percentage of the work input gets converted into work output. No machine is 100 percent efficient, but reducing the amount of friction in a machine is a way to increase its mechanical efficiency. Inventors have tried for many years to create a machine that has no friction to overcome, but so far they have been unsuccessful. If a machine could be made that had 100 percent mechanical efficiency, it would be called an *ideal machine*.

## SECTION REVIEW

1. Explain how using a ramp makes work easier.

2. Why can't a machine be 100 percent efficient?

3. Suppose you exert 15 N on a machine, and the machine exerts 300 N on another object. What is the machine's mechanical advantage?

4. **Comparing Concepts** For the machine described in question 3, how does the distance through which the output force is exerted differ from the distance through which the input force is exerted?

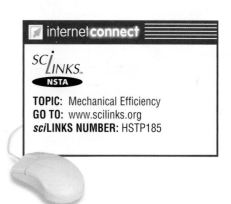

**internet connect**

SCiLINKS.
NSTA

**TOPIC:** Mechanical Efficiency
**GO TO:** www.scilinks.org
*sci*LINKS **NUMBER:** HSTP185

## *Terms to Learn*

| | |
|---|---|
| lever | wheel and axle |
| inclined plane | pulley |
| wedge | compound |
| screw | machine |

## *What You'll Do*

- ◆ Identify and give examples of the six types of simple machines.
- ◆ Analyze the mechanical advantage provided by each simple machine.
- ◆ Identify the simple machines that make up a compound machine.

# Types of Machines

All machines are constructed from these six simple machines: *lever, inclined plane, wedge, screw, wheel and axle,* and *pulley.* You've seen a couple of these machines already—a screwdriver can be used as a lever, and a ramp is an inclined plane. In the next few pages, each of the six simple machines will be discussed separately. Then you'll learn how compound machines are formed from combining simple machines.

## Levers

Have you ever used the claw end of a hammer to remove a nail from a piece of wood? If so, you were using the hammer as a lever. A **lever** is a simple machine consisting of a bar that pivots at a fixed point, called a *fulcrum.* Levers are used to apply a force to a load. There are three classes of levers, based on the locations of the fulcrum, the load, and the input force.

**First Class Levers** With a first class lever, the fulcrum is between the input force and the load, as shown in **Figure 10.** First class levers always change the direction of the input force. And depending on the location of the fulcrum, first class levers can be used to increase force or to increase distance. Some examples of first class levers are shown below.

**Figure 10** **A First Class Lever**

Input force        Output force

Load

Fulcrum

## Examples of First Class Levers

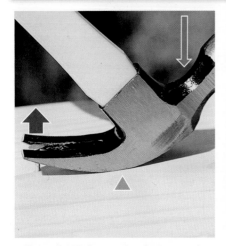

When the fulcrum is closer to the load than to the input force, a **mechanical advantage of greater than 1 results.** The output force is increased because it is exerted over a shorter distance.

When the fulcrum is exactly in the middle, a **mechanical advantage of 1 results.** The output force is not increased because the input force's distance is not increased.

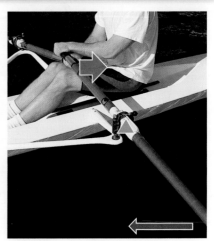

When the fulcrum is closer to the input force than to the load, a **mechanical advantage of less than 1 results.** Although the output force is less than the input force, a gain in distance occurs.

**Second Class Levers** With a second class lever, the load is between the fulcrum and the input force, as shown in **Figure 11.** Second class levers do not change the direction of the input force, but they allow you to apply less force than the force exerted by the load. Because the output force is greater than the input force, you must exert the input force over a greater distance. Some examples of second class levers are shown at right.

**Figure 11 A Second Class Lever**

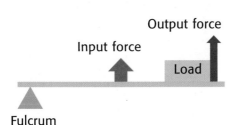

Fulcrum

## Examples of Second Class Levers

Using a second class lever results in a **mechanical advantage of greater than 1.** The closer the load is to the fulcrum, the more the force is increased and the greater the mechanical advantage.

**Third Class Levers** With a third class lever, the input force is between the fulcrum and the load, as shown in **Figure 12.** Third class levers do not change the direction of the input force. In addition, they do *not* increase the input force. Therefore, the output force is always less than the input force. Some examples of third class levers are shown at right.

**Figure 12 A Third Class Lever**

Output force

Input force

Load

Fulcrum

## Examples of Third Class Levers

Using a third class lever results in a **mechanical advantage of less than 1** because force is decreased. But third class levers are helpful because they increase the distance through which the output force is exerted.

## Inclined Planes

To build the Great Pyramid, located in Giza, Egypt, the Egyptians moved more than 2 million stone blocks, most averaging 2,000 kg. One of the machines they used was the *inclined plane*. An **inclined plane** is a simple machine that is a straight, slanted surface. A ramp is an example of an inclined plane.

Inclined planes can make work easier. Look at **Figure 13.** Using an inclined plane to load an upright piano into the back of a truck is easier than just lifting it into the truck. Rolling the piano into the truck along an inclined plane requires a smaller input force than is required to lift the piano into the truck. But remember that machines do not save work—therefore, the input force must be exerted over a longer distance.

**Figure 13** *The work you do on the piano to roll it up the ramp is the same as the work you would do to lift it straight up. An inclined plane simply allows you to apply a smaller force over a greater distance.*

Compare work done with and without an inclined plane on page 194 of the LabBook.

**Mechanical Advantage of Inclined Planes** The longer the inclined plane is compared with its height, the greater the mechanical advantage. The mechanical advantage (*MA*) of an inclined plane can be calculated by dividing the *length* of the inclined plane by the *height* to which the load is lifted, as shown below:

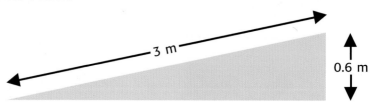

$$MA = \frac{3 \text{ m}}{0.6 \text{ m}} = 5$$

## Wedges

Imagine trying to cut a watermelon in half with a spoon. It wouldn't be easy, would it? A knife is a much more useful utensil for cutting because it's a *wedge*. A **wedge** is a double inclined plane that moves. When you move a wedge through a distance, it applies a force on an object. A wedge applies an output force that is greater than your input force, but you apply the input force over a greater distance. The greater the distance you move the wedge, the greater the force it applies on the object. For example, the deeper you move a knife into a watermelon, as shown in **Figure 14,** the more force the knife applies to the two halves. Eventually, it pushes them apart. Other useful wedges include doorstops, plows, axe heads, and chisels.

**Figure 14** *Wedges, which are often used to cut materials, allow you to exert your force over an increased distance.*

**Mechanical Advantage of Wedges** The longer and thinner the wedge is, the greater the mechanical advantage. That's why axes and knives cut better when you sharpen them—you are making the wedge thinner. Therefore, less input force is required. The mechanical advantage of a wedge can be determined by dividing the *length* of the wedge by its greatest *thickness,* as shown below.

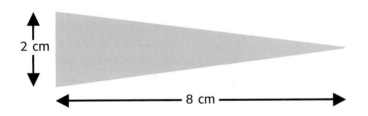

$$MA = \frac{8 \text{ cm}}{2 \text{ cm}} = 4$$

## Screws

A **screw** is an inclined plane that is wrapped in a spiral. When a screw is rotated, a small force is applied over the long distance along the inclined plane of the screw. Meanwhile, the screw applies a large force through the short distance it is pushed. In other words, you apply a small input force over a large distance, while the screw exerts a large output force over a small distance. Screws are used most commonly as fasteners. Some examples of screws are shown in **Figure 15.**

**Figure 15** *When you turn a screw, you exert a small input force over a large turning distance, but the screw itself doesn't move very far.*

**Figure 16** *The threads on the top screw are closer together and wrap more times around, so that screw has a greater mechanical advantage than the one below it.*

**Mechanical Advantage of Screws** If you could "unwind" the inclined plane of a screw, you would see that it is very long and has a gentle slope. Recall that the longer an inclined plane is compared with its height, the greater its mechanical advantage. Similarly, the longer the spiral on a screw is and the closer together the threads, the greater the screw's mechanical advantage, as shown in **Figure 16**.

## SECTION REVIEW

1. Give an example of each of the following simple machines: first class lever, second class lever, third class lever, inclined plane, wedge, and screw.

2. A third class lever has a mechanical advantage of less than 1. Explain why it is useful for some tasks.

3. **Interpreting Graphics** Look back at Figures 6, 7, and 8 in Section 2. Identify the type of simple machine shown in each case. (If a lever is shown, identify its class.)

**Figure 17**
**How a Wheel and Axle Works**

**ⓐ** When a small input force is applied to the wheel, it rotates through a circular distance.

## Wheel and Axle

Did you know that when you turn a doorknob you are using a machine? A doorknob is an example of a **wheel and axle,** a simple machine consisting of two circular objects of different sizes. A wheel can be a crank, such as the handle on a fishing reel, or it can be a knob, such as a volume knob on a radio. The axle is the smaller of the two circular objects. Doorknobs, wrenches, ferris wheels, screwdrivers, and steering wheels all use a wheel and axle. **Figure 17** shows how a wheel and axle works.

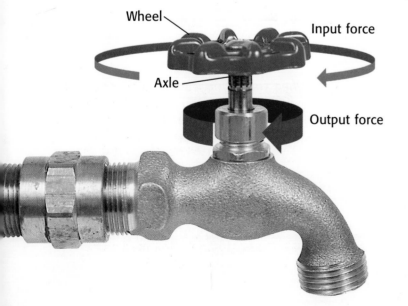

Wheel

Axle

Input force

Output force

**ⓑ** As the wheel turns, so does the axle. But because the axle is smaller than the wheel, it rotates through a smaller distance, which makes the output force larger than the input force.

## Mechanical Advantage of a Wheel and Axle

**Mechanical Advantage of a Wheel and Axle**  The mechanical advantage of a wheel and axle can be determined by dividing the *radius* (the distance from the center to the edge) of the wheel by the radius of the axle, as shown at right. Turning the wheel results in a mechanical advantage of greater than 1 because the radius of the wheel is larger than the radius of the axle.

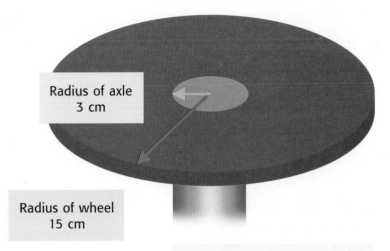

Radius of axle
3 cm

Radius of wheel
15 cm

$$MA = \frac{15 \text{ cm}}{3 \text{ cm}} = 5$$

## Pulleys

When you open window blinds by pulling on a cord, you're using a pulley. A **pulley** is a simple machine consisting of a grooved wheel that holds a rope or a cable. A load is attached to one end of the rope, and an input force is applied to the other end. There are two kinds of pulleys—*fixed* and *movable*. Fixed and movable pulleys can be combined to form a *block and tackle*.

**Fixed Pulleys**  Some pulleys only change the direction of a force. This kind of pulley is called a fixed pulley. Fixed pulleys do not increase force. A fixed pulley is attached to something that does not move. By using a fixed pulley, you can pull down on the rope in order to lift the load up. This is usually easier than trying to lift the load straight up. Elevators make use of fixed pulleys.

Input force

Output force

A **fixed pulley** only spins. So the distance through which the input force and the output force are exerted—and thus the forces themselves—are the same. Therefore, a fixed pulley provides a mechanical advantage of 1.

**Movable Pulleys**  Unlike fixed pulleys, movable pulleys are attached to the object being moved. A movable pulley does not change a force's direction. Movable pulleys do increase force, but you must exert the input force over a greater distance than the load is moved. This is because you must make *both* sides of the rope move in order to lift the load.

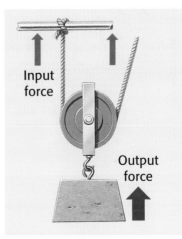

Input force

Output force

A **movable pulley** moves up with the load as it is lifted. Force is multiplied because the combined input force is exerted over twice the distance of the output force. The mechanical advantage of a movable pulley is the number of rope segments that support the load. In this example, the mechanical advantage is 2.

**Block and Tackles** When a fixed pulley and a movable pulley are used together, the pulley system is called a *block and tackle*. A block and tackle can have a large mechanical advantage if several pulleys are used. A block and tackle used within a larger pulley system is shown in **Figure 18.**

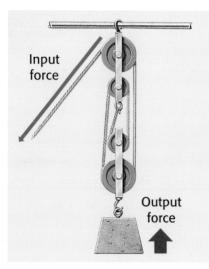

Input force

Output force

The mechanical advantage of this **block and tackle** is 4 because there are four rope segments that support the load. This block and tackle multiplies your input force four times, but you have to pull the rope 4 m just to lift the load 1 m.

**Figure 18** *The combination of pulleys used by this crane allows it to lift heavy pieces of scrap metal.*

## Compound Machines

You are surrounded by machines. As you saw earlier, you even have machines in your body! But most of the machines in your world are **compound machines,** machines that are made of two or more simple machines. You've already seen one example of a compound machine: a block and tackle. A block and tackle consists of two or more pulleys. On this page and the next, you'll see some other examples of compound machines.

**Can Opener**

The axle has gear teeth on it that grip the can and act as tiny levers to push the can along when the axle turns.

Wheel and axle

Wedge

Second class lever

**Scissors**

Each arm of the scissors is a first class lever.

Each sharpened edge of the scissors is a wedge.

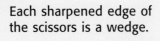

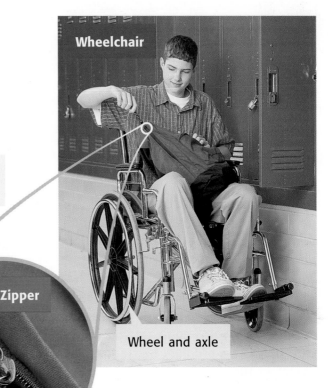

**Wheelchair**

**Zipper**

Wheel and axle

Inside the metal clasp of this zipper are three wedges. One wedge opens the zipper by splitting the teeth apart. Two other wedges close the zipper by pushing the teeth together.

**Mechanical Efficiency of Compound Machines**  In general, the more moving parts a machine has, the lower its mechanical efficiency. Thus the mechanical efficiency of compound machines is often quite low. For compound machines that involve many simple machines, such as automobiles and airplanes, it is very important that friction be reduced as much as possible through the use of lubrication and other techniques. Too much friction could cause heating and damage the simple machines involved, which could create safety problems and could be expensive to repair.

## SECTION REVIEW

1. Give an example of a wheel and axle.

2. Identify the simple machines that make up tweezers and nail clippers.

3. **Doing Calculations**  The radius of the wheel of a wheel and axle is four times greater than the radius of the axle. What is the mechanical advantage of this machine?

internet**connect**

*SCi*LINKS
**NSTA**

**TOPIC:** Simple Machines, Compound Machines
**GO TO:** www.scilinks.org
*sci*LINKS NUMBER: HSTP190, HSTP195

# Discovery Lab

## A Powerful Workout TRY at HOME

Does the amount of work you do depend on how fast you do it? No! But doing work in a shorter amount of time does affect your power—the rate at which work is done. In this lab, you'll calculate your work and power when climbing a flight of stairs at different speeds. Then you'll compare your power with that of an ordinary household object—a 100 W light bulb.

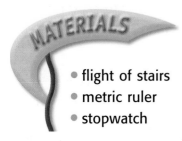

### MATERIALS

- flight of stairs
- metric ruler
- stopwatch

### Ask a Question

1. How does your power when climbing a flight of stairs compare with the power of a 100 W light bulb?

### Form a Hypothesis

2. In your ScienceLog, write a hypothesis that answers the question in step 1. Explain your reasoning.

3. Copy Table 1 into your ScienceLog, or use a computer to construct a similar one.

### Test the Hypothesis

4. Measure the height of one stair step. Record the measurement in Table 1.

5. Count the number of stairs, including the top step, and record this number in Table 1.

6. Calculate the height (in meters) of the stairs by multiplying the number of steps by the height of one step. Record your answer. (You will need to convert from centimeters to meters.)

| Table 1 Data Collection | | | | |
|---|---|---|---|---|
| Height of step (cm) | Number of steps | Height of stairs (m) | Time for slow walk (s) | Time for quick walk (s) |
| | | | | |

DO NOT WRITE IN BOOK

| Table 2  Work and Power Calculations | | | |
|---|---|---|---|
| Weight (N) | Work (J) | Power for slow walk (W) | Power for quick walk (W) |
|  | | | |

*DO NOT WRITE IN BOOK*

**7** Using a stopwatch, measure how many seconds you take to walk slowly up the flight of stairs. Record your measurement in Table 1.

**8** Now measure how many seconds you take to walk quickly up the flight of stairs. Be careful not to overexert yourself.

## Analyze the Results

**9** Copy Table 2 into your ScienceLog, or use a computer to construct a similar one.

**10** Determine your weight in newtons by multiplying your weight in pounds (lb) by 4.45 N/lb. Record your weight in Table 2.

**11** Using the following equation, calculate and record your work done to climb the stairs:

$$work = force \times distance$$

Remember that 1 N•m is 1 J. (Hint: Remember that force is expressed in newtons.)

**12** Calculate and record your power for each trial (the slow walk and the quick walk), using the following equation:

$$power = \frac{work}{time}$$

Remember that the unit for power is the watt (1 W = 1 J/s).

## Draw Conclusions

**13** In step 11 you calculated your work done in climbing the stairs. Why didn't you calculate your work for each trial?

**14** Look at your hypothesis in step 2. Was your hypothesis supported? In your ScienceLog, communicate a valid conclusion that describes how your power in each trial compares with the power of a 100 W light bulb.

**15** The work done to move one electron in a light bulb is very small. Make two inferences about why the power is large. (Hint: How many electrons are in the filament of a light bulb? Why was more power used in your second trial?)

## Communicate Results

**16** Write your average power in a class data table. Calculate the average power for the class. How many students would be needed to equal the power of a 100 W bulb?

**Where is work done in a light bulb?**
Electrons in the filament move back and forth very quickly. These moving electrons do work by heating up the filament and making it glow.

# Chapter Highlights

## SECTION 1

### Vocabulary

**work** *(p. 88)*

**joule** *(p. 90)*

**power** *(p. 91)*

**watt** *(p. 91)*

### Section Notes

- Work occurs when a force causes an object to move in the direction of the force. The unit for work is the joule (J).

- Work is done on an object only when a force makes an object move and only while that force is applied.

- For work to be done on an object, the direction of the object's motion must be in the same direction as the force applied.

- Work can be calculated by multiplying force by distance.

- Power is the rate at which work is done. The unit for power is the watt (W).

- Power can be calculated by dividing the amount of work by the time taken to do that work.

## SECTION 2

### Vocabulary

**machine** *(p. 92)*

**work input** *(p. 93)*

**work output** *(p. 93)*

**mechanical advantage** *(p. 96)*

**mechanical efficiency** *(p. 97)*

### Section Notes

- A machine makes work easier by changing the size or direction (or both) of a force.

- When a machine changes the size of a force, the distance through which the force is exerted must also change. Force or distance can increase, but not together.

# ☑ Skills Check

## Math Concepts

**WORK AND POWER** Suppose a woman raises a 65 N object 1.6 m in 4 s. The work done and her power can be calculated as follows:

$$W = F \times d \qquad\qquad P = \frac{W}{t}$$

$$= 65\ \text{N} \times 1.6\ \text{m} \qquad = \frac{104\ \text{J}}{4\ \text{s}}$$

$$= 104\ \text{J} \qquad\qquad = 26\ \text{W}$$

## Visual Understanding

**MACHINES MAKE WORK EASIER** A machine can change the size or direction (or both) of a force. Review the table on page 95 to learn more about how machines make work easier.

**COMPOUND MACHINES** A compound machine is made of two or more simple machines. Review the examples on pages 104 and 105.

## SECTION 2

- Mechanical advantage tells how many times a machine multiplies force. It can be calculated by dividing the output force by the input force.

- Mechanical efficiency is a comparison of a machine's work output with work input. Mechanical efficiency is calculated by dividing work output by work input and is expressed as a percentage.

- Machines are not 100 percent efficient because some of the work done by a machine is used to overcome friction. So work output is always less than work input.

## SECTION 3

### Vocabulary

**lever** (*p. 98*)

**inclined plane** (*p. 100*)

**wedge** (*p. 101*)

**screw** (*p. 101*)

**wheel and axle** (*p. 102*)

**pulley** (*p. 103*)

**compound machine** (*p. 104*)

### Section Notes

- All machines are constructed from these six simple machines: lever, inclined plane, wedge, screw, wheel and axle, and pulley.

- Compound machines consist of two or more simple machines.

- Compound machines have low mechanical efficiencies because they have more moving parts and thus more friction to overcome.

### Labs

**Inclined to Move** (*p. 194*)

**Building Machines** (*p. 195*)

**Wheeling and Dealing** (*p. 196*)

# Chapter Review

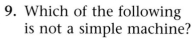

## USING VOCABULARY

For each pair of terms, explain the difference in their meanings.

1. joule/watt

2. work output/work input

3. mechanical efficiency/mechanical advantage

4. screw/inclined plane

5. simple machine/compound machine

## UNDERSTANDING CONCEPTS

### Multiple Choice

6. Work is being done when
   a. you apply a force to an object.
   b. an object is moving after you apply a force to it.
   c. you exert a force that moves an object in the direction of the force.
   d. you do something that is difficult.

7. The work output for a machine is always less than the work input because
   a. all machines have a mechanical advantage.
   b. some of the work done is used to overcome friction.
   c. some of the work done is used to overcome distance.
   d. power is the rate at which work is done.

8. The unit for work is the
   a. joule.              c. newton.
   b. joule per second.   d. watt.

9. Which of the following is not a simple machine?
   a. a faucet handle
   b. a jar lid
   c. a can opener
   d. a seesaw

10. Power is
    a. how strong someone or something is.
    b. how much force is being used.
    c. how much work is being done.
    d. how fast work is being done.

11. The unit for power is the
    a. newton.        c. watt.
    b. kilogram.      d. joule.

12. A machine can increase
    a. distance at the expense of force.
    b. force at the expense of distance.
    c. neither distance nor force.
    d. Both (a) and (b)

### Short Answer

13. Identify the simple machines that make up a pair of scissors.

14. In two or three sentences, explain the force-distance trade-off that occurs when a machine is used to make work easier.

15. Explain why you do work on a bag of groceries when you pick it up but not when you are carrying it.

## Concept Mapping

**16.** Create a concept map using the following terms: work, force, distance, machine, mechanical advantage.

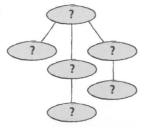

## CRITICAL THINKING AND PROBLEM SOLVING

**17.** Why do you think levers usually have a greater mechanical efficiency than other simple machines do?

**18.** The winding road shown below is actually a series of inclined planes. Describe how a winding road makes it easier for vehicles to travel up a hill.

**19.** Why do you think you would not want to reduce the friction involved in using a winding road?

## MATH IN SCIENCE

**20.** You and a friend together apply a force of 1,000 N to a 3,000 N automobile to make it roll 10 m in 1 minute and 40 seconds.
  **a.** How much work did you and your friend do together?
  **b.** What was your combined power?

## INTERPRETING GRAPHICS

For each of the images below, identify the class of lever used and calculate the mechanical advantage.

**21.**

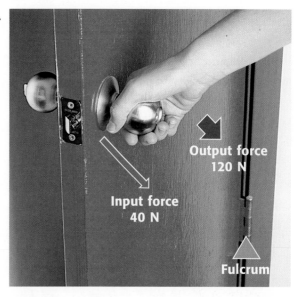

**22.**

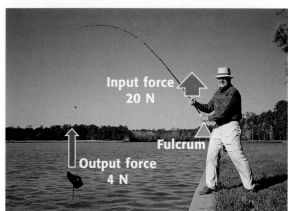

Reading Check-up

Take a minute to review your answers to the Pre-Reading Questions found at the bottom of page 86. Have your answers changed? If necessary, revise your answers based on what you have learned since you began this chapter.

# Science, Technology, and Society

## Micromachines

The technology of making things smaller and smaller keeps growing and growing. Powerful computers can now be held in the palm of your hand. But what about motors smaller than a grain of pepper? Or gnat-sized robots that can swim through the bloodstream? These are just a couple of the possibilities for micromachines.

### Microscopic Motors

Researchers have already built gears, motors, and other devices so small that you could accidentally inhale one! For example, one engineer devised a motor so small that five of the motors would fit on the period at the end of this sentence. This micromotor is powered by static electricity instead of electric current, and the motor spins at 15,000 revolutions per minute. This is about twice as fast as most automobile engines running at top speed.

### Small Sensors

So far micromachines have been most useful as sensing devices. Micromechanical sensors can be used in places too small for ordinary instruments. For example, blood-pressure sensors can fit inside blood vessels and can detect minute changes in a person's blood pressure. Each sensor has a patch so thin that it bends when the pressure changes.

### Cell-Sized Robots

Some scientists are investigating the possibility of creating cell-sized machines called nanobots. These tiny robots may have many uses in medicine. For instance, if nanobots could be injected

▲ *The earliest working micromachine had a turning central rotor.*

into a person's bloodstream, they might be used to destroy disease-causing organisms such as viruses and bacteria. Nanobots might also be used to count blood cells or to deliver medicine.

The ultimate in micromachines would be machines created from individual atoms and molecules. Although these machines do not currently exist, scientists are already able to manipulate single atoms and molecules. For example, the "molecular man" shown below is made of individual molecules. These molecules are moved by using a scanning tunneling microscope.

### A Nanobot's "Life"

▶ Imagine that you are a nanobot traveling through a person's body. What types of things do you think you would see? What type of work could you do? Write a story that describes what your experiences as a nanobot might be like.

▶ *"Molecular man" is composed of 28 carbon monoxide molecules.*

# Eureka!

## Wheelchair Innovators

Two recent inventions have dramatically improved the technology of wheelchairs. With these new inventions, some wheelchair riders can now control their chairs with voice commands and others can take a cruise over a sandy beach.

### Voice-Command Wheelchair

At age 27, Martine Kemph invented a voice-recognition system that enables people without arms or legs to use spoken commands to operate their motorized wheelchairs. Here's how it works: The voice-recognition computer translates spoken words into digital commands, which are then directed to electric motors. These commands completely control the operating speed and direction of the motors, giving the operator total control over the chair's movement.

Kemph's system can execute spoken commands almost instantly. In addition, the system is easy to program, so each user can tailor the computer's list of commands to his or her needs.

Kemph named the computer Katalvox, using the root words *katal,* which is Greek for "to understand," and *vox,* which is Latin for "voice."

### The Surf Chair

Mike Hensler was a lifeguard at Daytona Beach, Florida, when he realized that it was next to impossible for someone in a wheelchair to come onto the beach. Although he had never invented a machine before, Hensler decided to build a wheelchair that could be maneuvered across sand without getting stuck. He began spending many evenings in his driveway with a pile of lawn-chair parts, designing the chair by trial and error.

The result of Hensler's efforts looks very different from a conventional wheelchair. With huge rubber wheels and a thick frame of white PVC pipe, the Surf Chair not only moves easily over sandy terrain but also is weather resistant and easy to clean. The newest models of the Surf Chair come with optional attachments, such as a variety of umbrellas, detachable armrests and footrests, and even places to attach fishing rods.

▲ *Mike Hensler tries out his Surf Chair.*

### Design One Yourself

▶ Can you think of any other ways to improve wheelchairs? Think about it, and put your ideas down on paper. To inspire creative thinking, consider how a wheelchair could be made lighter, faster, safer, or easier to maneuver.

# CHAPTER 5

# Energy and Energy Resources

## Pre-Reading Questions

1. What is energy?
2. How is energy converted from one form to another?
3. What is an energy resource?

## THE RACE IS ON!

Imagine that you're a driver in this race. Your car will need a lot of energy to finish, so you should make sure your car is fueled up and ready. You'll probably need a lot of gasoline, right? Nope, just a lot of sunshine! The car in this photo is solar powered—energy from the sun makes it go. In this chapter, you'll learn about different types of energy. You'll also learn where the energy that runs our cars and our appliances comes from.

## ENERGY SWINGS!

All matter has energy. But what is energy? In this activity, you'll observe a moving pendulum to learn about energy.

### Procedure

1. Make a pendulum by tying a **15 cm long string** around the hook of the **100 g hooked mass.**

2. Hold the string with one hand. Pull the mass slightly to the side, and let go of the mass without pushing it. Watch at least 10 swings of the pendulum.

3. In your ScienceLog, record your observations. Be sure to note how fast and how high the pendulum swings.

4. Repeat step 2, but pull the mass farther to the side.

5. Record your observations, noting how fast and how high the pendulum swings.

### Analysis

6. Do you think the pendulum has energy? Explain your answer.

7. What causes the pendulum to move?

8. Do you think the pendulum has energy before you let go of the mass? Explain your answer.

*Terms to Learn*

energy
kinetic energy
potential energy
mechanical energy

*What You'll Do*

- ◆ Explain the relationship between energy and work.
- ◆ Compare kinetic and potential energy.
- ◆ Summarize the different forms of energy.

# What Is Energy?

It's match point. The crowd is dead silent. The tennis player steps up to serve. With a look of determination, she bounces the tennis ball several times. Next, in one fluid movement, she tosses the ball into the air and then slams it with her racket. The ball flies toward her opponent, who steps up and swings her racket at the ball. Suddenly, *THWOOSH!!* The ball goes into the net, and the net wiggles from the impact. Game, set, and match!!

## Energy and Work—Working Together

Energy is around you all the time. So what is it exactly? In science, you can think of **energy** as the ability to do work. Work occurs when a force causes an object to move in the direction of the force. How are energy and work involved in playing tennis? In this example, the tennis player does work on her racket, the racket does work on the ball, and the ball does work on the net. Each time work is done, something is given by one object to another that allows it to do work. That "something" is energy. As you can see in **Figure 1**, work is a transfer of energy.

Because work and energy are so closely related, they are expressed in the same units—joules (J). When a given amount of work is done, the same amount of energy is involved.

**Figure 1** *When one object does work on another, energy is transferred.*

**a** The tennis player can do work on her racket because she has energy.

**b** When she does work on the racket, the racket gains the ability to do work on the ball. Energy is transferred from the tennis player to the racket.

**c** When the racket does work on the ball, the ball gains the ability to do work on something else. Energy is transferred from the racket to the ball.

# Kinetic Energy Is Energy of Motion

From the tennis example on the previous page, you learned that energy is transferred from the racket to the ball. As the ball flies over the net, it has **kinetic** (ki NET ik) **energy,** the energy of motion. All moving objects have kinetic energy. Does the tennis player have kinetic energy? Definitely! She has kinetic energy when she steps up to serve and when she swings the racket. When she's standing still, she doesn't have any kinetic energy. However, the parts of her body that are moving—her eyes, her heart, and her lungs—do have some kinetic energy.

Objects with kinetic energy can do work. If you've ever gone bowling, you've done work using kinetic energy. When you throw the ball down the lane, you do work on it, transferring your kinetic energy to the ball. As a result, the bowling ball can do work on the pins. Another example of doing work with kinetic energy is shown in **Figure 2.**

Figure 2 *When you swing a hammer, you give it kinetic energy, which it uses to do work on the nail.*

**Kinetic Energy Depends on Speed and Mass** An object's kinetic energy can be determined with the following equation:

$$\text{Kinetic energy} = \frac{mv^2}{2}$$

In this equation, *m* stands for an object's mass, and *v* stands for an object's speed. The faster something is moving, the more kinetic energy it has. In addition, the more massive a moving object is, the more kinetic energy it has. But which do you think has more of an effect on an object's kinetic energy, its mass or its speed? As you can see from the equation, speed is squared, so speed has a greater effect on kinetic energy than does mass. You can see an example of how kinetic energy depends on speed and mass in **Figure 3.**

Figure 3 *The red car has more kinetic energy than the green car because the red car is moving faster. But the truck has more kinetic energy than the red car because the truck is more massive.*

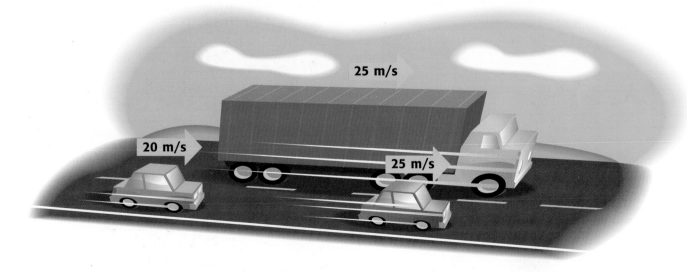

25 m/s

20 m/s

25 m/s

**Figure 4** *The stored potential energy of the bow and string allows them to do work on the arrow when the string is released.*

# Potential Energy Is Energy of Position

Not all energy involves motion. **Potential energy** is the energy an object has because of its position or shape. For example, the stretched bow shown in **Figure 4** has potential energy. The bow is not moving, but it has energy because work has been done to change its shape. A similar example of potential energy is in a stretched rubber band.

**Gravitational Potential Energy Depends on Weight and Height** When you lift an object, you do work on it by using a force that opposes gravitational force. As a result, you give that object *gravitational potential energy*. Books on a bookshelf have gravitational potential energy, as does your backpack after you lift it onto your back. As you can see in **Figure 5,** the amount of gravitational potential energy an object has depends on its weight and its distance above Earth's surface.

**Figure 5 Weight and Height Affect Gravitational Potential Energy**

**a** The diver on the left weighs less and therefore has less gravitational potential energy than the diver on the right. The diver on the left did less work to climb up the platform.

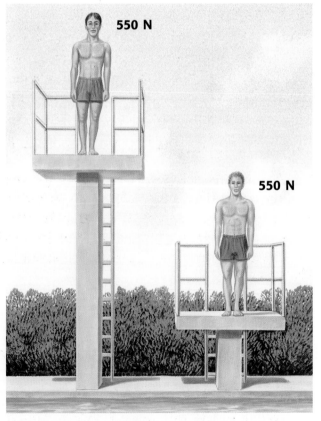

**b** The diver on the higher platform has more gravitational potential energy than the diver on the lower platform. The diver on the higher platform did more work to climb up to the platform.

**Calculating Gravitational Potential Energy** You can calculate gravitational potential energy by using the following equation:

Gravitational potential energy = weight × height

Because weight is expressed in newtons and height is expressed in meters, gravitational potential energy is expressed in newton-meters (N•m), or joules (J). So a 25 N object at a height of 3 m has 25 N × 3 m = 75 J of gravitational potential energy.

Recall that work = force × distance. Weight is the amount of force you must exert on an object in order to lift it, and height is a distance. So calculating an object's gravitational potential energy is done by calculating the amount of work done on the object to lift it to a given height. You can practice calculating gravitational potential energy as well as kinetic energy in the MathBreak at right.

**MATH BREAK**

**Calculating Energy**

1. What is the kinetic energy of a 4,000 kg elephant running at 3 m/s? at 4 m/s?

2. If you lift a 50 N watermelon to the top of a 2 m refrigerator, how much gravitational potential energy do you give the watermelon?

## Mechanical Energy Sums It All Up

How would you describe the energy of the juggler's pins in **Figure 6**? Well, to describe their total energy, you would describe their mechanical energy. **Mechanical energy** is the total energy of motion and position of an object. Mechanical energy can be all potential energy, all kinetic energy, or some of both. The following equation defines mechanical energy as the sum of kinetic and potential energy:

Mechanical energy = potential energy + kinetic energy

When potential energy increases (or decreases), kinetic energy has to decrease (or increase) in order for mechanical energy to remain constant. So the amount of an object's kinetic or potential energy may change, but its mechanical energy remains the same. You'll learn more about these changes in the next section.

**Figure 6** As a pin is juggled, its mechanical energy is the sum of its potential energy and its kinetic energy at any point.

### SECTION REVIEW

1. How are energy and work related?

2. What is the difference between kinetic and potential energy?

3. **Applying Concepts** Explain why a high-speed collision might cause more damage to vehicles than a low-speed collision.

## Forms of Energy

All energy involves either motion or position. But energy takes different forms. These forms of energy include thermal, chemical, electrical, sound, light, and nuclear energy. In the next few pages, you will learn how the different forms of energy relate to kinetic and potential energy.

**Thermal Energy** All matter is made of particles that are constantly in motion. Because the particles are in motion, they have kinetic energy. The particles also have energy because of how they are arranged. *Thermal energy* is the total energy of the particles that make up an object. At higher temperatures, particles move faster. The faster the particles move, the more kinetic energy they have and the greater the object's thermal energy is. In addition, particles of a substance that are farther apart have more energy than particles of the same substance that are closer together. Look at **Figure 7.** Thermal energy also depends on the number of particles in a substance.

**Figure 7** *The particles in steam have more energy than the particles in ice or ocean water. But the ocean has the most thermal energy because it has the most particles.*

The particles in an **ice cube** vibrate in fixed positions and therefore do not have a lot of energy.

The particles in **ocean water** are not in fixed positions and can move around. They have more energy than the particles in an ice cube.

The particles in **steam** are far apart. They move rapidly, so they have more energy than the particles in ocean water.

**Chemical Energy** What is the source of the energy in food? Food consists of chemical compounds. When compounds, such as the sugar in some foods, are formed, work is done to join, or bond, the different atoms together to form molecules. *Chemical energy* is the energy of a compound that changes as its atoms are rearranged to form new compounds. Chemical energy is a form of potential energy. Some molecules that have many atoms bonded together, such as gasoline, have a lot of chemical energy. In **Figure 8** on the next page, you can see an example of chemical energy.

**Figure 8  Examples of Chemical Energy**

When wood is burned, the chemical energy stored in the wood is used to toast your marshmallows.

When you eat a marshmallow, chemical energy stored in the sugar becomes available for you to use.

Chemical energy is stored in the marshmallow's sugar molecules.

**Electrical Energy**  The electrical outlets in your home allow you to use electrical energy. *Electrical energy* is the energy of moving electrons. Electrons are the negatively charged particles of atoms. An atom is the smallest particle into which an element can be divided.

Suppose you plug an electrical device, such as the portable stereo shown in **Figure 9,** into an outlet and turn it on. The electrons in the wires will move back and forth, changing directions 120 times per second. As they do, energy is transferred to different parts within the stereo. The electrical energy created by moving electrons is used to do work. The work of a stereo is to produce sound.

The electrical energy available to your home is produced at power plants. Huge generators rotate magnets within coils of wire to produce electrical energy. Because the electrical energy results from the changing position of the magnet, electrical energy can be considered a form of potential energy. As soon as a device is plugged into an outlet and turned on, electrons move back and forth within the wires of the cord and within parts of the device. So electrical energy can also be considered a form of kinetic energy.

**Figure 9**  *The movement of electrons produces the electrical energy that a stereo uses to produce sound.*

**Figure 10** *As the guitar strings vibrate, they cause particles in the air to vibrate. These vibrations transmit energy.*

**Sound Energy** You probably know that your vocal cords determine the sound of your voice. When you speak, air passes through your vocal cords, making them vibrate, or move back and forth. *Sound energy* is caused by an object's vibrations. **Figure 10** describes how a vibrating object transmits energy through the air around it.

Sound energy is a form of potential and kinetic energy. To make an object vibrate, work must be done to change its position. For example, when you pluck a guitar string, you stretch it and release it. The stretching changes the string's position. As a result, the string stores potential energy. In the release, the string uses its potential energy to move back to its original position. The moving guitar string has kinetic energy, which the string uses to do work on the air particles around it. The air particles vibrate and transmit this kinetic energy from particle to particle. When the vibrating air particles cause your eardrum to vibrate, you hear the sound of the guitar.

**Light Energy** Light allows us to see, but did you know that not all light can be seen? **Figure 11** shows a type of light that we use but can't see. *Light energy* is produced by the vibrations of electrically charged particles. Like sound vibrations, light vibrations cause energy to be transmitted. But unlike sound, the vibrations that transmit light energy don't cause other particles to vibrate. In fact, light energy can be transmitted through a vacuum (the absence of matter).

**Figure 11** *The energy used to cook food in a microwave is a form of light energy.*

## Quick Lab

### Hear That Energy!

1. Make a simple drum by covering the open end of an **empty coffee can** with **wax paper.** Secure the wax paper with a **rubber band.**

2. Using the eraser end of a **pencil,** tap lightly on the wax paper. In your ScienceLog, describe how the paper responds. What do you hear?

3. Repeat step 2, but tap the paper a bit harder. In your ScienceLog, compare your results with those of step 2.

4. Cover half of the wax paper with one hand. Now tap the paper. What happened? How can you describe sound energy as a form of mechanical energy?

*Try at Home*

**Nuclear Energy** What form of energy can come from a tiny amount of matter, can be used to generate electrical energy, and gives the sun its energy? It's *nuclear* (NOO klee uhr) *energy,* the energy associated with changes in the nucleus (NOO klee uhs) of an atom. Nuclear energy is produced in two ways—when two or more nuclei (NOO klee IE) join together or when the nucleus of an atom splits apart.

In the sun, shown in **Figure 12,** hydrogen nuclei join together to make a larger helium nucleus. This reaction releases a huge amount of energy, which allows the sun to light and heat the Earth.

The nuclei of some atoms, such as uranium, store a lot of potential energy. When work is done to split these nuclei apart, that energy is released. This type of nuclear energy is used to generate electrical energy at nuclear power plants, such as the one shown in **Figure 13.**

**Figure 12** *Without the nuclear energy from the sun, life on Earth would not be possible.*

**Figure 13** *In a nuclear power plant, small amounts of matter can produce large amounts of nuclear energy.*

## SECTION REVIEW

1. What determines an object's thermal energy?

2. Describe why chemical energy is a form of potential energy.

3. Explain how sound energy is produced when you beat a drum.

4. **Analyzing Relationships** When you hit a nail into a board using a hammer, the head of the nail gets warm. In terms of kinetic and thermal energy, describe why you think this happens.

*Terms to Learn*

energy conversion

*What You'll Do*

- ◆ Describe an energy conversion.
- ◆ Give examples of energy conversions among the different forms of energy.
- ◆ Explain the role of machines in energy conversions.
- ◆ Explain how energy conversions make energy useful.

# Energy Conversions

When you use a hammer to pound a nail into a board, you transfer your kinetic energy to the hammer, and the hammer transfers that kinetic energy to the nail. But energy is involved in other ways too. For example, sound energy is produced when you hit the nail. An energy transfer often leads to an **energy conversion,** a change from one form of energy into another. Any form of energy can be converted into any other form of energy, and often one form of energy is converted into more than one other form. In this section, you'll learn how energy conversions make your daily activities possible.

## From Kinetic to Potential and Back

Take a look at **Figure 14.** Have you ever jumped on a trampoline? What types of energy are involved in this bouncing activity? Because you're moving when you jump, you have kinetic energy. And each time you jump into the air, you change your position with respect to the ground, so you also have gravitational potential energy. Another kind of potential energy is involved too—that of the trampoline stretching when you jump on it.

**Figure 14** *Kinetic and potential energy are converted back and forth as you jump up and down on a trampoline.*

**1** When you jump down, your kinetic energy is converted into the potential energy of the stretched trampoline.

**2** The trampoline's potential energy is converted into kinetic energy, which is transferred to you, making you bounce up.

**3** At the top of your jump, all of your kinetic energy has been converted into potential energy.

**4** Right before you hit the trampoline, all of your potential energy has been converted back into kinetic energy.

Another example of the energy conversions between kinetic and potential energy is the motion of a pendulum (PEN dyoo luhm). Shown in **Figure 15,** a pendulum is a mass hung from a fixed point so that it can swing freely. When you lift the pendulum to one side, you do work on it, and the energy used to do that work is stored by the pendulum as potential energy. As soon as you let the pendulum go, it swings because the Earth exerts a force on it. The work the Earth does converts the pendulum's potential energy into kinetic energy.

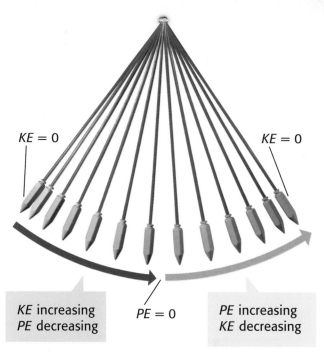

$KE = 0$

$KE = 0$

*KE* increasing
*PE* decreasing

$PE = 0$

*PE* increasing
*KE* decreasing

**Figure 15**  *A pendulum's mechanical energy is all kinetic (KE) at the bottom of its swing and all potential (PE) at the top of its swing.*

## ✔ Self-Check

At what point does a roller coaster have the greatest potential energy? the greatest kinetic energy? *(See page 232 to check your answer.)*

## Conversions Involving Chemical Energy

You've probably heard the expression "Breakfast is the most important meal of the day." What does this statement mean? Why does eating breakfast help you start the day? As your body digests food, chemical energy is released and is available to you, as discussed in **Figure 16.**

**Figure 16**  *Your body performs energy conversions.*

Chemical energy of food is converted into . . .

. . . kinetic energy when you are active and thermal energy to maintain body temperature.

Would you believe that the chemical energy in the food you eat is a result of the sun's energy? It's true! When you eat fruits, vegetables, grains, or meat from animals that ate fruits, vegetables, or grains, you are taking in chemical energy that resulted from a chemical change involving the sun's energy. As shown in **Figure 17,** photosynthesis (FOHT oh SIN thuh sis) uses light energy to produce new substances with chemical energy. In this way light energy is converted into chemical energy.

**Figure 17** *Green plants use chlorophyll and light energy from the sun to produce the chemical energy in the food you eat.*

**Photosynthesis**

$$\text{carbon dioxide} + \text{water} \xrightarrow[\text{chlorophyll}]{\text{light energy}} \text{sugar} + \text{oxygen}$$

Light energy

Chlorophyll in green leaves

Sugar in food

Carbon dioxide in the air

Water in the soil

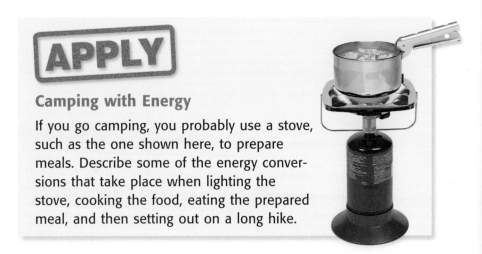

## APPLY

**Camping with Energy**

If you go camping, you probably use a stove, such as the one shown here, to prepare meals. Describe some of the energy conversions that take place when lighting the stove, cooking the food, eating the prepared meal, and then setting out on a long hike.

# Conversions Involving Electrical Energy

You use electrical energy all the time—when you listen to the radio, when you make toast, and when you take a picture with a camera. Electrical energy can be easily converted into other forms of energy. **Figure 18** shows how electrical energy is converted in a hair dryer.

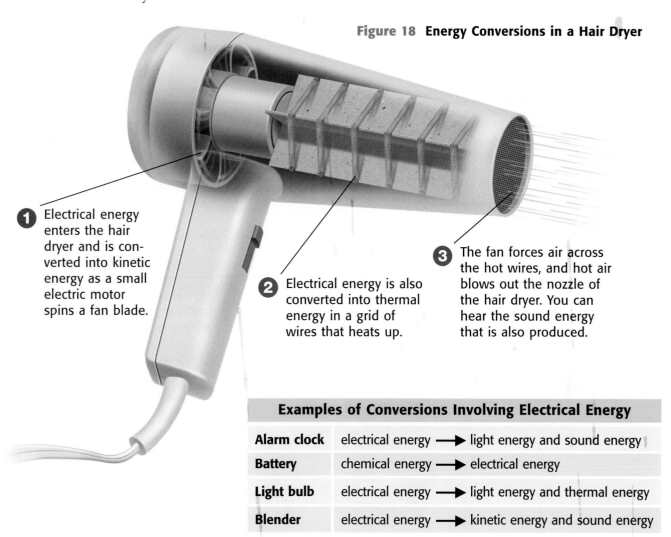

**Figure 18** **Energy Conversions in a Hair Dryer**

**1** Electrical energy enters the hair dryer and is converted into kinetic energy as a small electric motor spins a fan blade.

**2** Electrical energy is also converted into thermal energy in a grid of wires that heats up.

**3** The fan forces air across the hot wires, and hot air blows out the nozzle of the hair dryer. You can hear the sound energy that is also produced.

| Examples of Conversions Involving Electrical Energy | |
| --- | --- |
| **Alarm clock** | electrical energy ⟶ light energy and sound energy |
| **Battery** | chemical energy ⟶ electrical energy |
| **Light bulb** | electrical energy ⟶ light energy and thermal energy |
| **Blender** | electrical energy ⟶ kinetic energy and sound energy |

## SECTION REVIEW

1. What is an energy conversion?

2. Describe an example in which electrical energy is converted into thermal energy.

3. Describe an energy conversion involving chemical energy.

4. **Applying Concepts** Describe the kinetic-potential energy conversions that occur when you bounce a basketball.

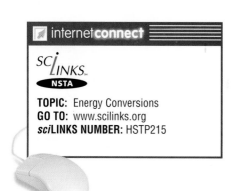

internet**connect**

SCI**LINKS**
**NSTA**

**TOPIC:** Energy Conversions
**GO TO:** www.scilinks.org
**sciLINKS NUMBER:** HSTP215

**CRR-UNCH!**

## Energy and Machines

You've been learning about energy, its different forms, and how it can undergo conversions. Another way to learn about energy is to look at how machines use energy. A machine can make work easier by changing the size or direction (or both) of the force required to do the work. Suppose you want to crack open a walnut. Using a nutcracker, like the one shown in **Figure 19,** would be much easier (and less painful) than using your fingers. You transfer your energy to the nutcracker, and it transfers energy to the nut. But the nutcracker will not transfer more energy to the nut than you transfer to the nutcracker. In addition, some of the energy you transfer to a machine can be converted by the machine into other forms of energy. Another example of how energy is used by a machine is shown in **Figure 20.**

**Figure 19** *Some of the kinetic energy you transfer to a nut-cracker is converted into sound energy as the nutcracker transfers energy to the nut.*

**Figure 20** *To start and keep your bike moving, energy must be converted and transferred.*

**1** Chemical energy in your body is converted into kinetic energy when your muscle fibers contract and relax.

**2** Your legs transfer this kinetic energy to the pedals, pushing them around in a circle.

**4** The chain moves and transfers energy to the back wheel, which gets you moving!

**3** The pedals transfer this kinetic energy to the gear wheel, which transfers kinetic energy to the chain.

**Machines Are Energy Converters**   As you saw in the examples on the previous page, when machines transfer energy, energy conversions can often result. For example, you can hear the sounds that your bike makes when you pedal it, change gears, or brake swiftly. That means that some of the kinetic energy being transferred gets converted into sound energy as the bike moves. Some machines are especially useful because they are energy converters. **Figure 21** shows an example of a machine specifically designed to convert energy from one form to another. In addition, the chart at right lists other machines that perform useful energy conversions.

| Some Machines that Convert Energy | |
|---|---|
| ▪ electric motor | ▪ microphone |
| ▪ windmill | ▪ toaster |
| ▪ doorbell | ▪ dishwasher |
| ▪ gas heater | ▪ lawn mower |
| ▪ telephone | ▪ clock |

**Figure 21**  *The continuous conversion of chemical energy into thermal energy and kinetic energy in a car's engine is necessary to make a car move.*

**1**  A mixture of gasoline and air enters the engine as the piston moves downward.

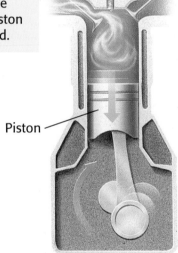

Piston

**2**  The kinetic energy of the crankshaft raises the piston, and the gasoline mixture is forced up toward the spark plug, which uses electrical energy to ignite the gasoline mixture.

Spark plug

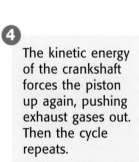

Crankshaft

**3**  As the gasoline mixture burns, chemical energy is converted into thermal energy and kinetic energy, forcing the piston back down.

**4**  The kinetic energy of the crankshaft forces the piston up again, pushing exhaust gases out. Then the cycle repeats.

Figure 22 *In a wind turbine, the kinetic energy of the wind can be collected and converted into electrical energy.*

# Science
## CONNECTION

Turn to page 146 to find out about buildings that are energy efficient as well as environmentally friendly.

# Why Energy Conversions Are Important

Everything we do is related to energy conversions. Heating our homes, obtaining energy from a meal, growing plants, and many other activities all require energy conversions.

**Making Energy Useful** You can think of energy conversions as a way of getting energy in the form that you need. Machines help harness existing energy and make that energy work for you. Did you know that the wind could help you cook a meal? A wind turbine, shown in **Figure 22,** can perform an energy conversion that would allow you to use an electric stove to do just that.

**Making Conversions Efficient** You may have heard that a car may be considered energy efficient if it gets good gas mileage, and your home may be energy efficient if it is well insulated. In terms of energy conversions, *energy efficiency* (e FISH uhn see) is a comparison of the amount of energy before a conversion with the amount of useful energy after a conversion. For example, the energy efficiency of a light bulb would be a comparison of the electrical energy going into it with the light energy coming out of it. The less electrical energy that is converted into thermal energy instead of into light energy, the more efficient the bulb.

Not all of the energy in a conversion becomes useful energy. Just as work input is always greater than work output, energy input is also always greater than energy output. But the closer the energy output is to the energy input, the more efficient the conversion is. Making energy conversions more efficient is important because greater efficiency means less waste.

## SECTION REVIEW

1. What is the role of machines in energy conversions?

2. Give an example of a machine that is an energy converter, and explain how the machine converts one form of energy to another.

3. **Applying Concepts** A car that brakes suddenly comes to a screeching halt. Is the sound energy produced in this conversion a useful form of energy? Explain your answer.

*Terms to Learn*

friction
law of conservation of energy

*What You'll Do*

◆ Explain how energy is conserved within a closed system.
◆ Explain the law of conservation of energy.
◆ Give examples of how thermal energy is always a result of energy conversion.
◆ Explain why perpetual motion is impossible.

# Conservation of Energy

Many roller coasters have a mechanism that pulls the cars up to the top of the first hill, but the cars are on their own the rest of the ride. As the cars go up and down the hills on the track, their potential energy is converted into kinetic energy and back again. But the cars never return to the same height they started from. Does that mean that energy gets *lost* somewhere along the way? Nope—it just gets converted into other forms of energy.

## Where Does the Energy Go?

In order to find out where a roller coaster's original potential energy goes, you have to consider more than just the hills of the roller coaster. You have to consider friction too. **Friction** is a force that opposes motion between two surfaces that are touching. For the roller coaster to move, work must be done to overcome the friction between the cars' wheels and the coaster track and between the cars and the surrounding air. The energy used to do this work comes from the original amount of potential energy that the cars have on the top of the first hill. The need to overcome friction affects the design of a roller coaster track. In **Figure 23,** you can see that the second hill will always be shorter than the first.

When energy is used to overcome friction, some of the energy is converted into thermal energy. Some of the cars' potential energy is converted into thermal energy on the way down the first hill, and then some of their kinetic energy is converted into thermal energy on the way up the second hill. So energy isn't lost at all—it just undergoes a conversion.

**Figure 23** *Due to friction, not all of the cars' potential energy (PE) is converted into kinetic energy (KE) as the cars go down the first hill. In addition, not all of the cars' kinetic energy is converted into potential energy as the cars go up the second hill.*

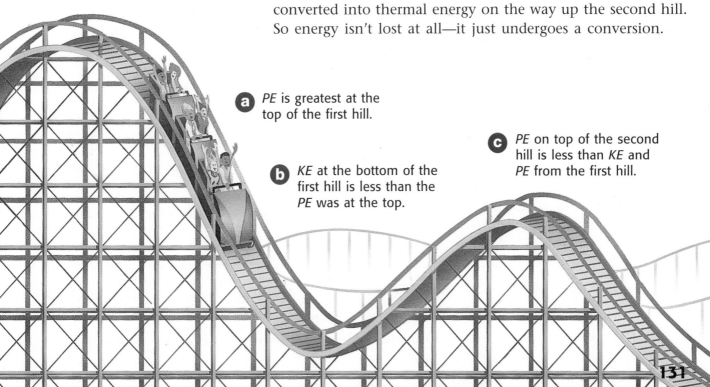

**a** *PE is greatest at the top of the first hill.*

**b** *KE at the bottom of the first hill is less than the PE was at the top.*

**c** *PE on top of the second hill is less than KE and PE from the first hill.*

# Energy Is Conserved Within a Closed System

A *closed system* is a well-defined group of objects that transfer energy between one another. For example, a closed system that involves a roller coaster consists of the track, the cars, and the surrounding air. On a roller coaster, some mechanical energy (the sum of kinetic and potential energy) is always converted into thermal energy because of friction. Sound energy is also a result of the energy conversions in a roller coaster. You can understand that energy is not lost on a roller coaster only when you consider all of the factors involved in a closed system. If you add together the cars' kinetic energy at the bottom of the first hill, the thermal energy due to overcoming friction, and the sound energy produced, you end up with the same total amount of energy as the original amount of potential energy. In other words, energy is conserved.

**Law of Conservation of Energy** No situation has been found where energy is not conserved. Because this phenomenon is always observed during energy conversions, it is described as a law. According to the **law of conservation of energy,** energy can be neither created nor destroyed. The total amount of energy in a closed system is always the same. Energy can be changed from one form to another, but all the different forms of energy in a system always add up to the same total amount of energy, no matter how many energy conversions occur.

Consider the energy conversions in a light bulb, shown in **Figure 24.** You can define the closed system to include the outlet, the wires, and the parts of the bulb. While not all of the original electrical energy is converted into light energy, no energy is lost. At any point during its use, the total amount of electrical energy entering the light bulb is equal to the total amount of light and thermal energy that leaves the bulb. Energy is conserved.

Try to keep an egg from breaking while learning more about the law of conservation of energy on page 199 in the LabBook.

**Figure 24  Energy Conservation in a Light Bulb**

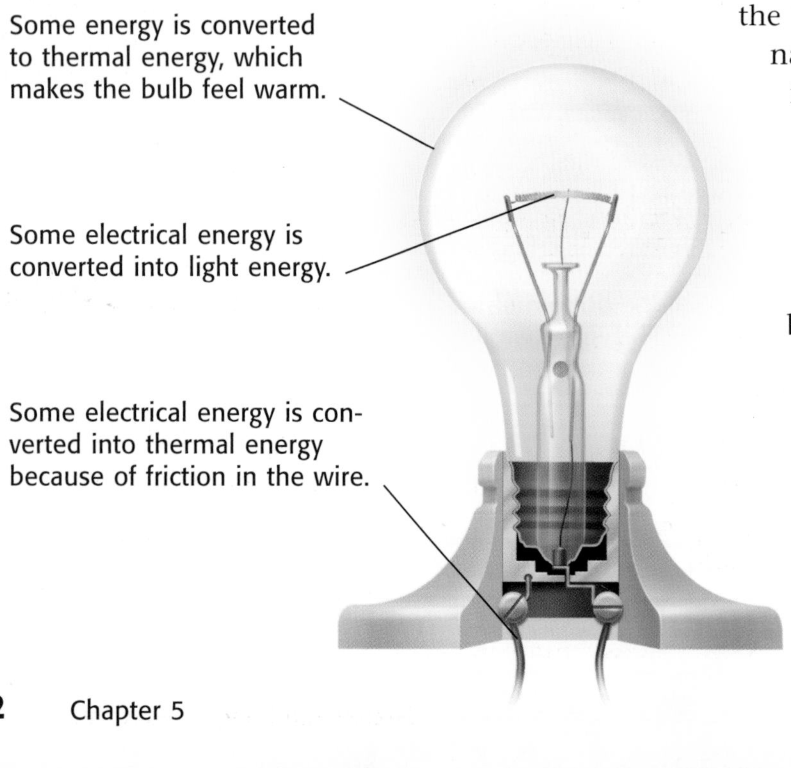

Some energy is converted to thermal energy, which makes the bulb feel warm.

Some electrical energy is converted into light energy.

Some electrical energy is converted into thermal energy because of friction in the wire.

## No Conversion Without Thermal Energy

Any time one form of energy is converted into another form, some of the original energy always gets converted into thermal energy. The thermal energy due to friction that results from energy conversions is not useful energy. That is, this thermal energy is not used to do work. Think about a car. You put gas into a car, but not all of the gasoline's chemical energy makes the car move. Some waste thermal energy will always result from the energy conversions. Much of this waste thermal energy exits a car engine through the radiator and the exhaust pipe.

**Perpetual Motion? No Way!** People have dreamed of constructing a machine that runs forever without any additional energy—a *perpetual* (puhr PECH oo uhl) *motion machine*. Such a machine would put out exactly as much energy as it takes in. But because some waste thermal energy always results from energy conversions, perpetual motion is impossible. The only way a machine can keep moving is to have a continuous supply of energy. For example, the "drinking bird" shown in **Figure 25** continually uses thermal energy from the air to evaporate the water from its head. So it is *not* a perpetual motion machine.

## Biology
### C O N N E C T I O N

Whenever you do work, you use chemical energy stored in your body that comes from food you've eaten. As you do work, some of that chemical energy is always converted into thermal energy. That's why your body heats up after performing a task, such as raking leaves, for several minutes.

**Figure 25  The "Drinking Bird"**

**a** When the bird "drinks," the felt covering its head gets wet.

**b** When the bird is upright, water evaporates from the felt, decreasing the temperature and pressure in the head. Fluid is drawn up from the tail, where pressure is higher, and the bird tips.

**c** After the bird "drinks," fluid returns to the tail, the bird flips upright, and the cycle repeats.

## SECTION REVIEW

1. Describe the energy conversions that take place in a pendulum, and explain how energy is conserved.

2. Why is perpetual motion impossible?

3. **Analyzing Viewpoints**  Imagine that you drop a ball. It bounces a few times, but then it stops. Your friend says that the ball has lost all of its energy. Using what you know about the law of conservation of energy, respond to your friend's statement.

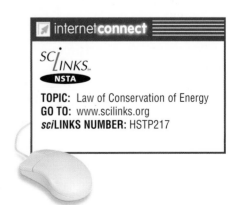

**internetconnect**

*SCI*LINKS
NSTA

**TOPIC:** Law of Conservation of Energy
**GO TO:** www.scilinks.org
***sci*LINKS NUMBER:** HSTP217

## Terms to Learn

energy resource
nonrenewable resources
fossil fuels
renewable resources

## What You'll Do

◆ Name several energy resources.
◆ Explain how the sun is the source of most energy on Earth.
◆ Evaluate the advantages and disadvantages of using various energy resources.

# Energy Resources

Energy is used to light and warm our homes; to produce food, clothing, and other products; and to transport people and products from place to place. Where does all this energy come from? An **energy resource** is a natural resource that can be converted by humans into other forms of energy in order to do useful work. In this section, you will learn about several energy resources, including the resource responsible for most other energy resources—the sun.

## Nonrenewable Resources

Some energy resources, called **nonrenewable resources,** cannot be replaced after they are used or can be replaced only over thousands or millions of years. Fossil fuels are the most important nonrenewable resources.

**Fossil Fuels**   Coal, petroleum, and natural gas, shown in **Figure 26,** are the most common fossil fuels. **Fossil fuels** are energy resources that formed from the buried remains of plants and animals that lived millions of years ago. These plants stored energy from the sun by photosynthesis. Animals used and stored this energy by eating the plants or by eating animals that ate plants. So fossil fuels are concentrated forms of the sun's energy.

This piece of coal containing a fern fossil shows that coal formed from plants that lived millions of years ago.

**Figure 26   Formation of Fossil Fuels**

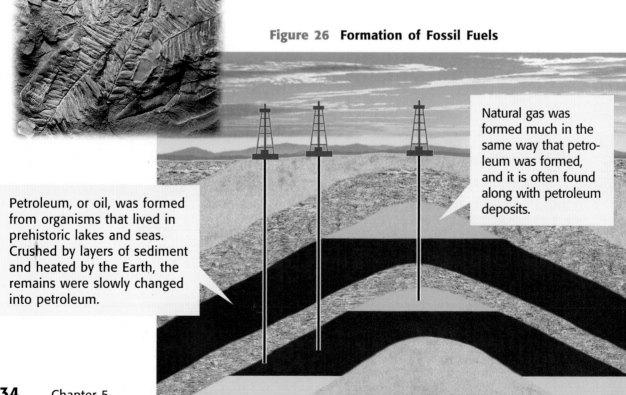

Natural gas was formed much in the same way that petroleum was formed, and it is often found along with petroleum deposits.

Petroleum, or oil, was formed from organisms that lived in prehistoric lakes and seas. Crushed by layers of sediment and heated by the Earth, the remains were slowly changed into petroleum.

Now, millions of years later, energy from the sun is released when fossil fuels are burned. Any fossil fuel contains stored energy from the sun that can be converted into other types of energy. The information below shows how important fossil fuels are to our society.

## Coal

Most coal used in the United States is burned to produce steam to run electric generators.

### Coal Use (U.S.)

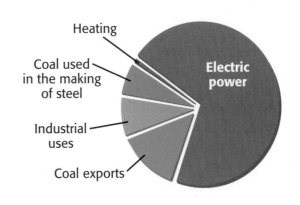

Heating

Coal used in the making of steel

Industrial uses

Coal exports

Electric power

## Petroleum

Petroleum supplies us with gasoline, kerosene, and wax as well as petrochemicals, which are used to make synthetic fibers, such as rayon.

### Annual Oil Production—Past & Predicted

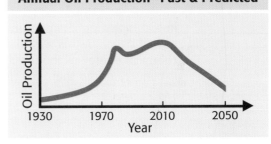

Oil Production

1930   1970   2010   2050
Year

Finding alternative energy resources will become more important in years to come.

## Natural Gas

Natural gas is used in heating systems, in stoves and ovens, and in vehicles as an alternative to gasoline.

Natural gas is the cleanest burning fossil fuel.

### Comparing Fossil Fuel Emissions

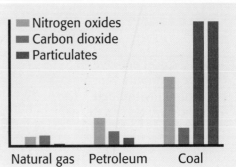

- Nitrogen oxides
- Carbon dioxide
- Particulates

Natural gas   Petroleum   Coal

Turn to page 147 to read about a day in the life of a power-plant manager.

**Electrical Energy from Fossil Fuels**  One way to generate electrical energy is to burn fossil fuels. In fact, fossil fuels are the primary source of electrical energy generated in the United States. Earlier in this chapter, you learned that electrical energy can result from energy conversions. Kinetic energy is converted into electrical energy by an *electric generator*. This energy conversion is part of a larger process, shown in **Figure 27,** of converting the chemical energy in fossil fuels into the electrical energy you use every day.

**Figure 27**
**Converting Fossil Fuels into Electrical Energy**

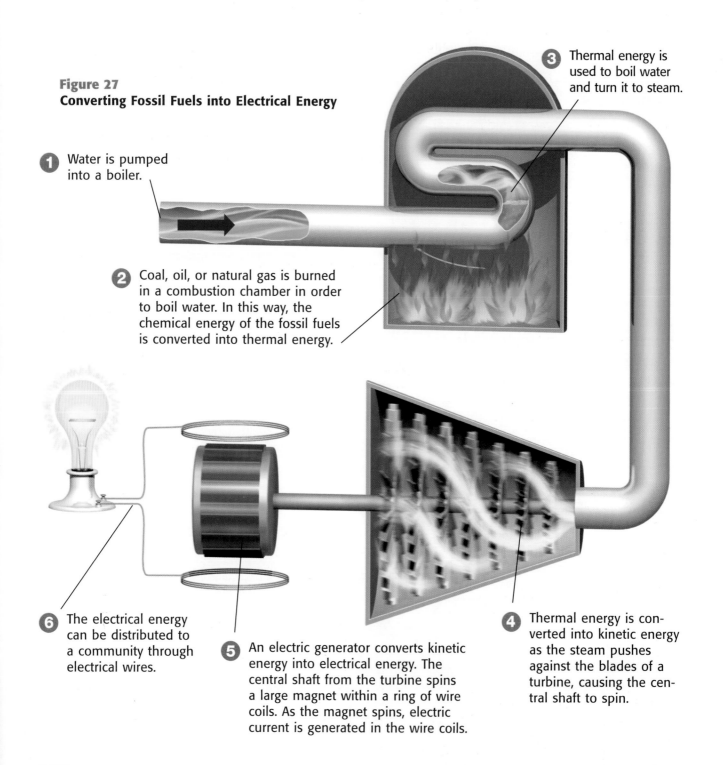

**1** Water is pumped into a boiler.

**2** Coal, oil, or natural gas is burned in a combustion chamber in order to boil water. In this way, the chemical energy of the fossil fuels is converted into thermal energy.

**3** Thermal energy is used to boil water and turn it to steam.

**4** Thermal energy is converted into kinetic energy as the steam pushes against the blades of a turbine, causing the central shaft to spin.

**5** An electric generator converts kinetic energy into electrical energy. The central shaft from the turbine spins a large magnet within a ring of wire coils. As the magnet spins, electric current is generated in the wire coils.

**6** The electrical energy can be distributed to a community through electrical wires.

**Nuclear Energy** Another way to generate electrical energy is to use nuclear energy. Like fossil-fuel power plants, a nuclear power plant generates thermal energy that boils water to produce steam. The steam then turns a turbine, which rotates a generator that converts kinetic energy into electrical energy. However, the fuels used in nuclear power plants are different from fossil fuels. Nuclear energy is generated from radioactive elements, such as uranium, shown in **Figure 28**. In a process called *nuclear fission* (FISH uhn), the nucleus of a uranium atom is split into two smaller nuclei, releasing nuclear energy. Because the supply of these elements is limited, nuclear energy can be thought of as a nonrenewable resource.

## Renewable Resources

Some energy resources, called **renewable resources,** can be used and replaced in nature over a relatively short period of time. Some renewable resources, such as solar energy and wind energy, are considered practically limitless.

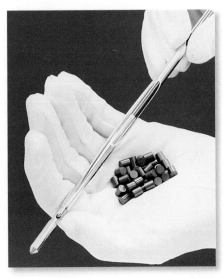

**Figure 28** *A single uranium fuel pellet contains the energy equivalent of about 1 metric ton of coal.*

### Solar Energy

Sunlight can be converted into electrical energy through solar cells, which can be used in devices such as calculators or installed in a home to provide electrical energy.

Some houses allow sunlight into the house through large windows. The sunlight is converted into thermal energy that heats the house naturally.

### Energy from Water

The sun causes water to evaporate and fall again as rain that flows through rivers. The potential energy of water in a reservoir is converted into kinetic energy as the water flows downhill through a dam.

Falling water turns a turbine in a dam, which is connected to a generator that converts kinetic energy into electrical energy. Electrical energy produced from falling water is called *hydroelectricity.*

## Wind Energy

Wind is caused by the sun's uneven heating of the Earth's surface, which creates currents of air. The kinetic energy of wind can turn the blades of a windmill. Windmills are often used to pump water from the ground.

A wind turbine converts kinetic energy into electrical energy by rotating a generator.

## Geothermal Energy

Thermal energy resulting from the heating of Earth's crust is called *geothermal energy.* Ground water that seeps into hot spots near the surface of the Earth can form geysers.

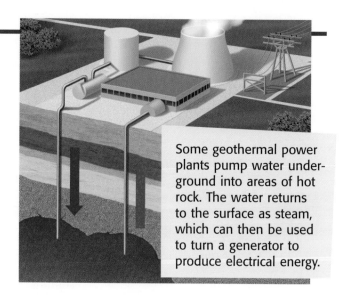

Some geothermal power plants pump water underground into areas of hot rock. The water returns to the surface as steam, which can then be used to turn a generator to produce electrical energy.

## Biomass

Plants capture and store energy from the sun. Organic matter, such as plants, wood, and waste, that can be burned to release energy is called *biomass.* Nonindustrialized countries rely heavily on biomass for energy.

Certain plants can also be converted into liquid fuel. For example, corn can be used to make ethanol, which is often mixed with gasoline to make a cleaner-burning fuel for cars.

# The Two Sides to Energy Resources

The table below compares several energy resources. Depending on where you live, what you need energy for, and how much you need, sometimes one energy resource is a better choice than another.

| Energy resource | Advantages | Disadvantages |
|---|---|---|
| **Fossil fuels** | ■ provide a large amount of thermal energy per unit of mass<br>■ easy to get and easy to transport<br>■ can be used to generate electrical energy and make products, such as plastic | ■ nonrenewable<br>■ burning produces smog<br>■ burning coal releases substances that can cause acid precipitation<br>■ risk of oil spills |
| **Nuclear** | ■ very concentrated form of energy<br>■ power plants do not produce smog | ■ produces radioactive waste<br>■ radioactive elements are nonrenewable |
| **Solar** | ■ almost limitless source of energy<br>■ does not produce pollution | ■ expensive to use for large-scale energy production<br>■ only practical in sunny areas |
| **Water** | ■ renewable<br>■ does not produce air pollution | ■ dams disrupt a river's ecosystem<br>■ available only in areas that have rivers |
| **Wind** | ■ renewable<br>■ relatively inexpensive to generate<br>■ does not produce air pollution | ■ only practical in windy areas |
| **Geothermal** | ■ almost limitless source of energy<br>■ power plants require little land | ■ only practical in locations near hot spots<br>■ waste water can damage soil |
| **Biomass** | ■ renewable | ■ requires large areas of farmland<br>■ produces smoke |

## SECTION REVIEW

1. Compare fossil fuels and biomass.

2. Why is nuclear energy a nonrenewable resource?

3. Trace electrical energy back to the sun.

4. **Interpreting Graphics** Use the pie chart at right to explain why renewable resources will become more important in years to come.

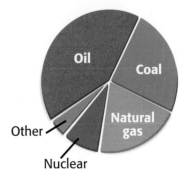

**U.S. Energy Sources**

Oil
Coal
Natural gas
Other
Nuclear

# Discovery Lab

## Finding Energy

When you coast down a big hill on a bike or skateboard, you may notice that you pick up speed. Because you are moving, you have kinetic energy—the energy of motion. Where does that energy come from? In this lab, you will find out.

MATERIALS

- 2 or 3 books
- wooden board
- masking tape
- meterstick
- metric balance
- rolling cart
- stopwatch

### Form a Hypothesis

1. Where does the kinetic energy come from when you roll down a hill? Write your hypothesis in your ScienceLog.

### Conduct an Experiment

2. Copy Table 1 into your ScienceLog or use a computer to construct a similar table.

3. Create a model of a bike on a hill. First, make a ramp with the books and board.

4. Use masking tape to make a starting line. Be sure the starting line is far enough from the top so the cart can be placed behind the line.

5. Place a strip of masking tape at the bottom of the ramp to mark the finish line.

6. Determine the height of the ramp by measuring the height of the starting line and subtracting the height of the finish line. Record the height of the ramp in meters in Table 1.

7. Measure the distance in meters between the starting line and the finish line. Record this distance as the length of the ramp in Table 1.

8. Use the metric balance to find the mass of the cart in grams. Convert this to kilograms by dividing by 1,000. Record the mass in kilograms in Table 1.

9. Multiply the mass by 10 to get the weight of the cart in newtons. Record the weight in Table 1.

| Table 1  Data Collection | | | | | | | |
|---|---|---|---|---|---|---|---|
| Height of ramp (m) | Length of ramp (m) | Mass of cart (kg) | Weight of cart (N) | Time of trial (s) | | | Average time (s) |
| | | | | 1 | 2 | 3 | |
| | | DO NOT WRITE IN BOOK | | | | | |

| Table 2  Calculations | | | |
|---|---|---|---|
| Average speed (m/s) | Final speed (m/s) | Kinetic energy at bottom (J) | Gravitational potential energy at top (J) |
| | DO NOT WRITE IN BOOK | | |

## Collect Data

**10** Set the cart behind the starting line, and release it. Use the stopwatch to time how long it takes for the cart to reach the finish line. Record the time in Table 1.

**11** Repeat step 10 twice more, and average the results. Record the average time in Table 1.

## Analyze the Results

**12** Copy Table 2 into your ScienceLog, or use a computer to construct a similar one.

**13** Using your data and the following equations, calculate and record the quantities for the cart in Table 2:

**a.** $average\ speed = \dfrac{length\ of\ ramp}{average\ time}$

**b.** $final\ speed = 2 \times average\ speed$

(This equation works because the cart accelerates smoothly from 0 m/s.)

**c.** $kinetic\ energy = \dfrac{mass \times (final\ speed)^2}{2}$

(Remember that 1 kg • $m^2/s^2$ = 1 J, the unit used to express energy.)

**d.** $gravitational\ potential\ energy = weight \times height$

(Remember that 1 N = 1 kg • $m/s^2$, so 1 N × 1 m = 1 kg • $m^2/s^2$ = 1 J.)

## Draw Conclusions

**14** How does the cart's gravitational potential energy at the top of the ramp compare with its kinetic energy at the bottom? Communicate a valid conclusion about whether or not your hypothesis was supported.

**15** You probably found that the gravitational potential energy of the cart at the top of the ramp was close but not exactly equal to the kinetic energy of the cart at the bottom. Analyze this information to construct a reasonable explanation for this finding using direct evidence.

**16** While riding your bike, you coast down both a small hill and a large hill. Compare your final speed at the bottom of the small hill with your final speed at the bottom of the large hill. Explain your answer.

# Chapter Highlights

## Vocabulary

**energy** (*p. 116*)

**kinetic energy** (*p. 117*)

**potential energy** (*p. 118*)

**mechanical energy** (*p. 119*)

## Section Notes

- Energy is the ability to do work, and work is the transfer of energy. Both energy and work are expressed in joules.

- Kinetic energy is energy of motion and depends on speed and mass.

- Potential energy is energy of position or shape. Gravitational potential energy depends on weight and height.

- Mechanical energy is the sum of kinetic energy and potential energy.

- Thermal energy, sound energy, electrical energy, and light energy can all be forms of kinetic energy.

- Chemical energy, electrical energy, sound energy, and nuclear energy can all be forms of potential energy.

## Vocabulary

**energy conversion** (*p. 124*)

## Section Notes

- An energy conversion is a change from one form of energy to another. Any form of energy can be converted into any other form of energy.

- Machines can transfer energy and convert energy into a more useful form.

- Energy conversions help to make energy useful by changing energy into the form you need.

## Labs

**Energy of a Pendulum** (*p. 198*)

# ☑ Skills Check

## Math Concepts

**GRAVITATIONAL POTENTIAL ENERGY** To calculate an object's gravitational potential energy, multiply the weight of the object by its height above the Earth's surface. For example, the gravitational potential energy (*GPE*) of a box that weighs 100 N and that is sitting in a moving truck 1.5 m above the ground is calculated as follows:

$$GPE = \text{weight} \times \text{height}$$

$$GPE = 100 \text{ N} \times 1.5 \text{ m} = 150 \text{ J}$$

## Visual Understanding

**POTENTIAL-KINETIC ENERGY CONVERSIONS** When you jump up and down on a trampoline, potential and kinetic energy are converted back and forth. Review the picture of the pendulum on page 125 for another example of potential-kinetic energy conversions.

**ENERGY RESOURCES** Look back at the diagram on page 136. Converting fossil fuels into electrical energy requires several energy conversions.

## SECTION 3

### Vocabulary

**friction** *(p. 131)*

**law of conservation of energy** *(p. 132)*

### Section Notes

- Because of friction, some energy is always converted into thermal energy during an energy conversion.

- Energy is conserved within a closed system. According to the law of conservation of energy, energy can be neither created nor destroyed.

- Perpetual motion is impossible because some of the energy put into a machine will be converted into thermal energy due to friction.

### Labs

**Eggstremely Fragile** *(p. 199)*

## SECTION 4

### Vocabulary

**energy resource** *(p. 134)*

**nonrenewable resources** *(p. 134)*

**fossil fuels** *(p. 134)*

**renewable resources** *(p. 137)*

### Section Notes

- An energy resource is a natural resource that can be converted into other forms of energy in order to do useful work.

- Nonrenewable resources cannot be replaced after they are used or can only be replaced after long periods of time. They include fossil fuels and nuclear energy.

- Fossil fuels are nonrenewable resources formed from the remains of ancient organisms. Coal, petroleum, and natural gas are fossil fuels.

- Renewable resources can be used and replaced in nature over a relatively short period of time. They include solar energy, wind energy, energy from water, geothermal energy, and biomass.

- The sun is the source of most energy on Earth.

- Depending on where you live and what you need energy for, one energy resource can be a better choice than another.

---

  **internetconnect**

**GO TO:** go.hrw.com

Visit the **HRW** Web site for a variety of learning tools related to this chapter. Just type in the keyword:

**KEYWORD:** HSTENG

**GO TO:** www.scilinks.org

Visit the **National Science Teachers Association** on-line Web site for Internet resources related to this chapter. Just type in the *sci*LINKS number for more information about the topic:

| TOPIC: | *sci*LINKS NUMBER: |
|---|---|
| What Is Energy? | HSTP205 |
| Forms of Energy | HSTP210 |
| Energy Conversions | HSTP215 |
| Law of Conservation of Energy | HSTP217 |
| Energy Resources | HSTP225 |

# Chapter Review

## USING VOCABULARY

For each pair of terms, explain the difference in their meanings.

1. potential energy/kinetic energy

2. friction/energy conversion

3. energy conversion/law of conservation of energy

4. energy resources/fossil fuels

5. renewable resources/nonrenewable resources

## UNDERSTANDING CONCEPTS

### Multiple Choice

6. Kinetic energy depends on
   a. mass and volume.
   b. speed and weight.
   c. weight and height.
   d. speed and mass.

7. Gravitational potential energy depends on
   a. mass and speed.
   b. weight and height.
   c. mass and weight.
   d. height and distance.

8. Which of the following is not a renewable resource?
   a. wind energy
   b. nuclear energy
   c. solar energy
   d. geothermal energy

9. Which of the following is a conversion from chemical energy to thermal energy?
   a. Food is digested and used to regulate body temperature.
   b. Charcoal is burned in a barbecue pit.
   c. Coal is burned to boil water.
   d. all of the above

10. Machines can
    a. increase energy.
    b. transfer energy.
    c. convert energy.
    d. Both (b) and (c)

11. In every energy conversion, some energy is always converted into
    a. kinetic energy.
    b. potential energy.
    c. thermal energy.
    d. mechanical energy.

12. An object that has kinetic energy must be
    a. at rest.
    b. lifted above the Earth's surface.
    c. in motion.
    d. None of the above

13. Which of the following is *not* a fossil fuel?
    a. gasoline          c. firewood
    b. coal              d. natural gas

### Short Answer

14. Name two forms of energy, and relate them to kinetic or potential energy.

15. Give three specific examples of energy conversions.

16. Explain how energy is conserved within a closed system.

17. How are fossil fuels formed?

## Concept Mapping

**18.** Use the following terms to create a concept map: energy, machines, energy conversions, thermal energy, friction.

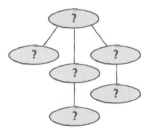

## CRITICAL THINKING AND PROBLEM SOLVING

**19.** What happens when you blow up a balloon and release it? Describe what you would see in terms of energy.

**20.** After you coast down a hill on your bike, you eventually come to a complete stop unless you keep pedaling. Relate this to the reason why perpetual motion is impossible.

**21.** Look at the photo of the pole-vaulter below. Trace the energy conversions involved in this event, beginning with the pole-vaulter's breakfast of an orange-banana smoothie.

**22.** If the sun were exhausted of its nuclear energy, what would happen to our energy resources on Earth?

**23.** A box has 400 J of gravitational potential energy.
  **a.** How much work had to be done to give the box that energy?
  **b.** If the box weighs 100 N, how far was it lifted?

**24.** Look at the illustration below, and answer the questions that follow.

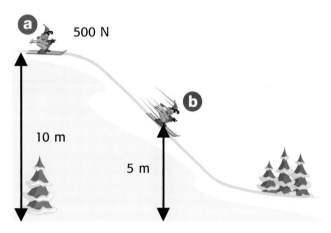

  **a.** What is the skier's gravitational potential energy at point *A*?
  **b.** What is the skier's gravitational potential energy at point *B*?
  **c.** What is the skier's kinetic energy at point *B*? (Hint: mechanical energy = potential energy + kinetic energy.)

**Reading Check-up**

Take a minute to review your answers to the Pre-Reading Questions found at the bottom of page 114. Have your answers changed? If necessary, revise your answers based on what you have learned since you began this chapter.

# Green Buildings

How do you make a building green without painting it? You make sure it does as little damage to the environment as possible. *Green,* in this case, does not refer to the color of pine trees or grass. Instead, *green* means "environmentally safe." And the "green movement" is growing quickly.

## Green Methods and Materials

One strategy that architects employ to turn a building green is to minimize its energy consumption. They also reduce water use wherever possible. One way to do this would be to create landscapes that use only native plants that require little watering. Green builders also use recycled building materials whenever possible. For example, crushed light bulbs can be recycled into floor tiles, and recycled cotton can replace fiberglass as insulation.

## Seeing Green

Although green buildings cost more than conventional buildings to construct, they save a lot of money in the long run. For example, the Audubon Building, in Manhattan, saves $100,000 in maintenance costs every year—that is $60,000 in electricity bills alone! The building uses more than 60 percent less energy and electricity than a conventional building does. Inside, the workers enjoy natural lighting, cleaner air, and an environment that is free of unnecessary chemicals.

Some designers want to create buildings that are even more environmentally friendly than the Audubon Building. Walls can be made of straw bales or packed dirt, and landscapes can be maintained with rainwater collected from rooftops. By conserving, recycling, and reducing waste, green builders are doing a great deal to help the environment.

## Design It Yourself!

▶ Design a building, a home, or even a doghouse that is made of only recycled materials. Be inventive! When you think you have the perfect design, create a scale model. Describe how your green structure saves resources.

◀ *The walls of this building are being made out of worn-out tires packed with soil. The walls will later be covered with stucco.*

# CAREERS

**POWER-PLANT MANAGER**

As a power-plant manager, **Cheryl Mele** is responsible for almost a billion watts of electric power generation at the Decker Power Plant in Austin, Texas. More than 700 MW are produced using a steam-driven turbine system with natural gas fuel and oil as a backup fuel. Another 200 MW are generated by gas turbines. The steam-driven turbine system and gas turbines together provide enough electrical energy for many homes and businesses.

**A**ccording to Cheryl Mele, her job as plant manager includes "anything that needs doing." Her training as a mechanical engineer allows her to conduct routine testing and to diagnose problems successfully. A firm believer in protecting our environment, Mele operates the plant responsibly. Mele states, "It is very important to keep the plant running properly and burning as efficiently as possible." Her previous job helping to design more-efficient gas turbines helped make her a top candidate for the job of plant manager.

## The Team Approach

Mele uses the team approach to maintain the power plant. She says, "We think better as a team. We all have areas of expertise and interest, and we maximize our effectiveness." Mele observes that working together makes everyone's job easier.

## Advice to Young People

Mele believes that mechanical engineering and managing a power plant are interesting careers because you get to work with many exciting new technologies. These professions are excellent choices for both men and women. In these careers you interact with creative people as you try to improve mechanical equipment to make it more efficient and reduce harm to the environment. Her advice for young people is to pursue what interests you. "Be sure to connect the math you learn to the science you are doing," she says. "This will help you to understand both."

## A Challenge

▶ With the help of an adult, find out how much electrical energy your home uses each month. How many homes like yours could Mele's billion-watt power plant supply energy to each month?

▶ *Cheryl Mele manages the Decker Power Plant in Austin, Texas.*

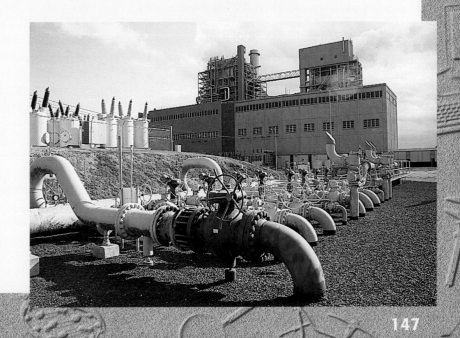

Pre-Reading
Questions

1. How do you measure how hot or cold an object is?

2. What makes an object hot or cold?

3. How can heat be used in your home?

## UP, UP, AND AWAY

A hot-air balloon race is fun to watch. The balloons start out flat, but as they fill with hot air, the balloons grow larger until they are ready to take off. Balloons don't need engines or wings. They rely on heat and thermal expansion to get them off the ground and into the sky. In this chapter, you will learn more about heat and its place in your daily life.

## SOME LIKE IT HOT

Sometimes you can tell the relative temperature of something by touching it with your hand. In this activity, you will find out how well your hand works as a thermometer!

### Procedure

1. Gather small pieces of the following materials from your teacher: **metal, wood, plastic foam, rock, plastic,** and **cardboard.**

2. Allow the materials to sit untouched on a table for several minutes.

3. Put your hands palms down on each of the various materials. Observe how warm or cool each one feels.

4. In your ScienceLog, list the materials in order from coolest to warmest.

5. Place a **thermometer strip** on the surface of each material. In your ScienceLog, record the temperature of each material.

### Analysis

6. Which material felt the warmest?

7. Which material had the highest temperature? Was it the same material as in question 6?

8. Why do you think some materials felt warmer than others?

9. Was your hand a good thermometer? Why or why not?

**Terms to Learn**

temperature
thermal expansion
absolute zero

**What You'll Do**

◆ Describe how temperature relates to kinetic energy.
◆ Give examples of thermal expansion.
◆ Compare temperatures on different temperature scales.

# Temperature

You probably put on a sweater or a jacket when it's cold outside. Likewise, you probably wear shorts in the summer when it gets hot. But how hot is hot, and how cold is cold? Think about how the knobs on a water faucet are labeled "H" for hot and "C" for cold. But does only hot water come out when the hot water knob is on? You may have noticed that when you first turn on the water, it is warm or even cool. Are you being misled by the label on the knob? The terms *hot* and *cold* are not very scientific terms. If you really want to specify how hot or cold something is, you must use temperature.

## What Is Temperature?

You probably think of temperature as a measure of how hot or cold something is. But scientifically, **temperature** is a measure of the average kinetic energy of the particles in an object. Using *temperature* instead of words like *hot* or *cold* reduces confusion. The scenario below emphasizes the importance of communicating about temperature. You can learn more about hot and cold comparisons by doing the QuickLab on the next page.

## Temperature Depends on the Kinetic Energy of Particles

All matter is made of particles—atoms or molecules—that are in constant motion. Because the particles are in motion, they have kinetic energy. The faster the particles are moving, the more kinetic energy they have. What does temperature have to do with kinetic energy? Well, as described in **Figure 1,** the more kinetic energy the particles of an object have, the higher the temperature of the object.

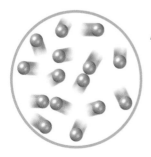

**Figure 1** *The gas particles on the right have more kinetic energy than those on the left. So, the gas on the right is at a higher temperature.*

**Temperature Is an Average Measure** Particles of matter are constantly moving, but they don't all move at the same speed and in the same direction all the time. Look back at Figure 1. As you can see, the motion of the particles is random. The particles of matter in an object move in different directions, and some particles move faster than others. As a result, some particles have more kinetic energy than others. So what determines an object's temperature? An object's temperature is the best approximation of the kinetic energy of the particles. When you measure an object's temperature, you measure the average kinetic energy of the particles in the object.

The temperature of a substance is not determined by how much of the substance you have. As shown in **Figure 2,** different amounts of the same substance can have the same temperature. However, the total kinetic energy of the particles in each amount is different. You will learn more about total kinetic energy in the next section.

**Figure 2** *Even though there is more tea in the teapot than in the mug, the temperature of the tea in the mug is the same as the temperature of the tea in the teapot.*

### Hot or Cold?

1. Put both your hands into a **bucket of warm water,** and note how it feels.

2. Now put one hand into a **bucket of cold water** and the other into a **bucket of hot water.**

3. After a minute, take your hands out of the hot and cold water and put them back in the warm water.

4. Can you rely on your hands to determine temperature? In your ScienceLog, explain your observations.

# Measuring Temperature

How would you measure the temperature of a steaming cup of hot chocolate? Would you take a sip of it or stick your finger into it? Probably not—you would use a thermometer.

**Using a Thermometer** Many thermometers are a thin glass tube filled with a liquid. Mercury and alcohol are often used in thermometers because they remain liquids over a large temperature range. Thermometers can measure temperature because of thermal expansion. **Thermal expansion** is the increase in volume of a substance due to an increase in temperature. As a substance gets hotter, its particles move faster. The particles themselves do not expand; they just spread out so that the entire substance expands. Different substances expand by different amounts for a given temperature change. When you insert a thermometer into a hot substance, the liquid inside the thermometer expands and rises. You measure the temperature of a substance by measuring the expansion of the liquid in the thermometer.

**Temperature Scales** Temperature can be expressed according to different scales. Notice how the same temperatures have different readings on the three temperature scales shown below.

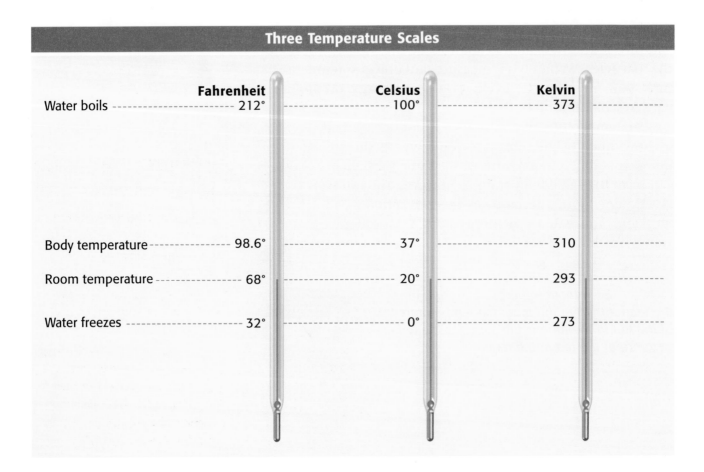

**Three Temperature Scales**

| | Fahrenheit | Celsius | Kelvin |
|---|---|---|---|
| Water boils | 212° | 100° | 373 |
| Body temperature | 98.6° | 37° | 310 |
| Room temperature | 68° | 20° | 293 |
| Water freezes | 32° | 0° | 273 |

When you hear a weather report that gives the current temperature as 65°, chances are that you are given the temperature in degrees Fahrenheit (°F). In science, the Celsius scale is used more often than the Fahrenheit scale. The Celsius scale is divided into 100 equal parts, called degrees Celsius (°C), between the freezing point and boiling point of water. A third scale, called the Kelvin (or absolute) scale, is the official SI temperature scale. The Kelvin scale is divided into units called kelvins (K)—not degrees kelvin. The lowest temperature on the Kelvin scale is 0 K, which is called **absolute zero.** It is not possible to reach a temperature lower than absolute zero. In fact, temperatures within a few billionths of a kelvin above absolute zero have been achieved in laboratories, but absolute zero itself has never been reached.

What can you do at temperatures near absolute zero? Turn to page 180 to find out!

**Temperature Conversion** As shown by the thermometers illustrated on the previous page, a given temperature is represented by different numbers on the three temperature scales. For example, the freezing point of water is 32°F, 0°C, or 273 K. As you can see, 0°C is actually a much higher temperature than 0 K, but a change of 1 K is equal to a change of one Celsius degree. In addition, 0°C is a higher temperature than 0°F, but a change of one Fahrenheit degree is *not* equal to a change of one Celsius degree. You can convert from one scale to another using the simple equations shown below. After reading the examples given, try the MathBreak on this page.

| To convert | Use this equation: | Example |
|---|---|---|
| Celsius to Fahrenheit °C ⟶ °F | $°F = \left(\frac{9}{5} \times °C\right) + 32$ | Convert 45°C to °F. $°F = \left(\frac{9}{5} \times 45°C\right) + 32 = 113°F$ |
| Fahrenheit to Celsius °F ⟶ °C | $°C = \frac{5}{9} \times (°F - 32)$ | Convert 68°F to °C. $°C = \frac{5}{9} \times (68°F - 32) = 20°C$ |
| Celsius to Kelvin °C ⟶ K | $K = °C + 273$ | Convert 45°C to K. $K = 45°C + 273 = 318$ K |
| Kelvin to Celsius K ⟶ °C | $°C = K - 273$ | Convert 32 K to °C. $°C = 32$ K $- 273 = -241°C$ |

### MATH BREAK

**Converting Temperatures**

Use the equations at left to answer the following questions:

1. What temperature on the Celsius scale is equivalent to 373 K?

2. Absolute zero is 0 K. What is the equivalent temperature on the Celsius scale? on the Fahrenheit scale?

3. Which temperature is colder, 0°F or 200 K?

**Figure 3** *The concrete segments of a bridge can expand on hot days. When the temperature drops, the segments contract.*

# More About Thermal Expansion

Have you ever gone across a highway bridge in a car? You probably heard and felt a *"thuh-thunk"* every couple of seconds as you went over the bridge. That sound occurs when the car goes over small gaps called expansion joints, shown in **Figure 3**. These joints keep the bridge from buckling as a result of thermal expansion. Recall that thermal expansion is the increase in volume of a substance due to an increase in temperature.

Thermal expansion also occurs in a thermostat, the device that controls the heater in your home. Inside a thermostat is a bimetallic strip. A *bimetallic strip* is made of two different metals stacked in a thin strip. Because different materials expand at different rates, one of the metals expands more than the other when the strip gets hot. This makes the strip coil and uncoil in response to changes in temperature. This coiling and uncoiling closes and opens an electric circuit that turns the heater on and off in your home, as shown in **Figure 4.**

**Figure 4  How a Thermostat Works**

Electrical contacts

**a** As the room temperature drops below the desired level, the bimetallic strip coils up and the glass tube tilts. A drop of mercury closes an electric circuit that turns the heater on.

**b** As the room temperature rises above the desired level, the bimetallic strip uncoils. The drop of mercury rolls back in the tube, opening the electric circuit, and the heater turns off.

## SECTION REVIEW

1. What is temperature?

2. What is the coldest temperature possible?

3. Convert 35°C to degrees Fahrenheit.

4. **Inferring Conclusions**  Why do you think heating a full pot of soup on the stove could cause the soup to overflow?

## Terms to Learn

heat                insulator
thermal energy      convection
conduction          radiation
conductor           specific heat
                    capacity

## What You'll Do

◆ Define *heat* as the transfer of energy between objects at different temperatures.

◆ Compare conduction, convection, and radiation.

◆ Use specific heat capacity to calculate heat.

◆ Explain the differences between temperature, thermal energy, and heat.

# What Is Heat?

It's time for your annual physical. The doctor comes in and begins her exam by looking down your throat using a wooden tongue depressor. Next she listens to your heart and lungs. But when she places a metal stethoscope on your back, as shown in **Figure 5,** you jump a little and say, "Whoa! That's cold!" The doctor apologizes and continues with your checkup.

Why did the metal stethoscope feel cold? After all, it was at the same temperature as the tongue depressor, which didn't make you jump. What is it about the stethoscope that made it feel cold? The answer has to do with how energy is transferred between the metal and your skin. In this section, you'll learn about this kind of energy transfer.

## Heat Is a Transfer of Energy

You might think of the word *heat* as having to do with things that feel hot. But heat also has to do with things that feel cold—like the stethoscope. In fact, heat is what causes objects to feel hot or cold or to get hot or cold under the right conditions. You probably use the word *heat* every day to mean different things. However, in this chapter, you will learn a specific meaning for it. **Heat** is the transfer of energy between objects that are at different temperatures.

Why do some things feel hot, while others feel cold? When two objects at different temperatures come in contact, energy is always transferred from the object with the higher temperature to the object with the lower temperature. When the doctor's stethoscope touches your back, energy is transferred from your back to the stethoscope because your back has a higher temperature (37°C) than the stethoscope (probably room temperature, 20°C). So to you, the stethoscope is cold, but compared to the stethoscope, you are hot! You'll learn why the tongue depressor didn't feel cold to you a little later in this section.

**Figure 5** *The reason the metal stethoscope feels cold is actually because of heat!*

**Heat and Thermal Energy** If heat is a transfer of energy, what form of energy is being transferred? The answer is thermal energy. **Thermal energy** is the total energy of the particles that make up a substance. Thermal energy, which is expressed in joules (J), depends partly on temperature. An object at a high temperature has more thermal energy than it would at a lower temperature. Thermal energy also depends on how much of a substance you have. As described in **Figure 6,** the more moving particles there are in a substance at a given temperature, the greater the thermal energy of the substance.

When you hold an ice cube, thermal energy is transferred from your hand to the ice cube. The ice cube's thermal energy increases, and it starts to melt. But your hand's thermal energy decreases. The particles in the surface of your skin move more slowly, and the surface temperature of your skin drops slightly. So your hand feels cold!

**Reaching the Same Temperature** Take a look at **Figure 7.** When objects at different temperatures come in contact, energy will always be transferred from the higher-temperature object to the lower-temperature object until both objects reach the same temperature. This point is called *thermal equilibrium* (EE kwi LIB ree uhm). When objects are at thermal equilibrium, no net change in either object's thermal energy occurs. Although one object may have more thermal energy, both objects have the same temperature.

**Figure 6** *Although both soups are at the same temperature, the soup in the pan has more thermal energy than the soup in the bowl.*

**Figure 7**
**Reaching Thermal Equilibrium**

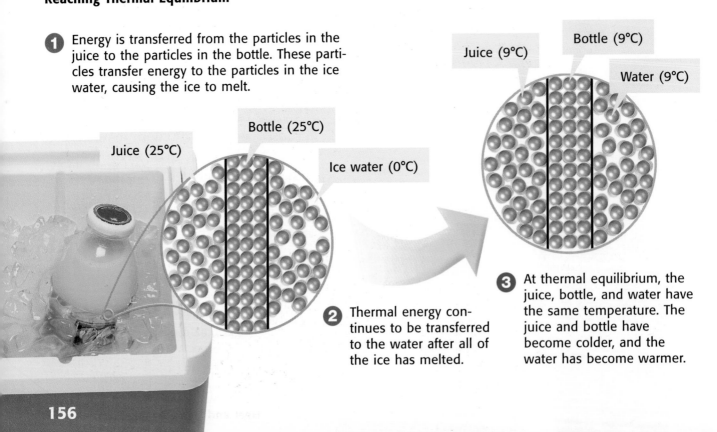

❶ Energy is transferred from the particles in the juice to the particles in the bottle. These particles transfer energy to the particles in the ice water, causing the ice to melt.

Juice (25°C)

Bottle (25°C)

Ice water (0°C)

Juice (9°C)

Bottle (9°C)

Water (9°C)

❷ Thermal energy continues to be transferred to the water after all of the ice has melted.

❸ At thermal equilibrium, the juice, bottle, and water have the same temperature. The juice and bottle have become colder, and the water has become warmer.

# Conduction, Convection, and Radiation

So far you've read about several examples of energy transfer: stoves transfer energy to substances in pots and pans; you can adjust the temperature of your bath water by adding cold or hot water to the tub; and the sun warms your skin. In the next couple of pages you'll learn about three processes involving this type of energy transfer: *conduction, convection,* and *radiation.*

**Conduction** Imagine that you put a cold metal spoon in a bowl of hot soup, as shown in **Figure 8.** Soon the handle of the spoon warms up—even though it is not in the soup! The entire spoon gets warm because of conduction. **Conduction** is the transfer of thermal energy from one substance to another through direct contact. Conduction can also occur within a substance, such as the spoon in Figure 8.

How does conduction work? As substances come in contact, particles collide and thermal energy is transferred from the higher-temperature substance to the lower-temperature substance. Remember that particles of substances at different temperatures have different average kinetic energy. So when particles collide, higher-kinetic-energy particles transfer kinetic energy to lower-kinetic-energy particles. This makes some particles slow down and other particles speed up until all particles have the same average kinetic energy. As a result, the substances have the same temperature.

## QuickLab

**Heat Exchange**

1. Fill a **film canister** with **hot water.** Insert the **thermometer apparatus** prepared by your teacher. Record the temperature.

2. Fill a **250 mL beaker** two-thirds full with **cool water.** Insert **another thermometer** in the cool water, and record its temperature.

3. Place the canister in the cool water. Record the temperature measured by each thermometer every 30 seconds.

4. When the thermometers read nearly the same temperature, stop and graph your data. Plot temperature (*y*-axis) versus time (*x*-axis).

5. In your ScienceLog, describe what happens to the rate of energy transfer as the two temperatures get closer.

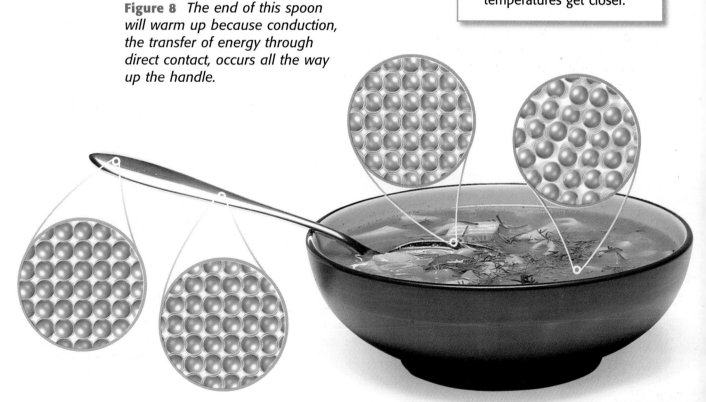

**Figure 8** *The end of this spoon will warm up because conduction, the transfer of energy through direct contact, occurs all the way up the handle.*

| Conductors | Insulators |
|---|---|
| Curling iron | Flannel shirt |
| Iron skillet | Oven mitt |
| Cookie sheet | Plastic spatula |
| Copper pipes | Fiberglass insulation |
| Stove coils | Ceramic bowl |

**Conductors and Insulators**  Substances that conduct thermal energy very well are called **conductors.** For example, the metal in a doctor's stethoscope is a conductor. Energy is transferred rapidly from your higher-temperature skin to the room-temperature stethoscope. That's why the stethoscope feels cold. Substances that do not conduct thermal energy very well are called **insulators.** For example, the doctor's wooden tongue depressor is an insulator. It has the same temperature as the stethoscope, but the tongue depressor doesn't feel cold. That's because thermal energy is transferred very slowly from your tongue to the wood. Compare some typical conductors and insulators in the chart at left.

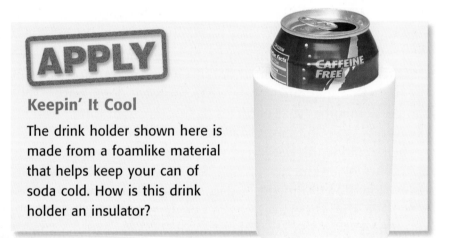

# APPLY

## Keepin' It Cool

The drink holder shown here is made from a foamlike material that helps keep your can of soda cold. How is this drink holder an insulator?

**Figure 9**  *The repeated rising and sinking of water during boiling is due to convection.*

**Convection**  When you boil a pot of water, like the one shown in **Figure 9,** the water moves in roughly circular patterns because of convection. **Convection** is the transfer of thermal energy by the movement of a liquid or a gas. The water at the bottom of a pot on a stove burner gets hot because of contact with the pot itself (conduction). As a result, the hot water becomes less dense because its higher-energy particles have spread apart. The warmer water rises through the denser, cooler water above it. At the surface, the warm water begins to cool, and the lower-energy particles move closer together, making the water denser. The denser, cooler water sinks back to the bottom, where it will be heated again. This circular motion of liquids or gases due to density differences that result from temperature differences is called a *convection current.*

**Radiation** Unlike conduction and convection, radiation can involve either an energy transfer between particles of matter or an energy transfer across empty space. **Radiation** is the transfer of energy through matter or space as electromagnetic waves, such as visible light and infrared waves.

All objects, including the heater in **Figure 10,** radiate electromagnetic waves. The sun emits mostly visible light, which you can see and your body can absorb, making you feel warmer. The Earth emits mostly infrared waves, which you cannot see but can still make you feel warmer.

**Figure 10** *The coils of this portable heater warm a room by radiating visible light and infrared waves.*

### Radiation and the Greenhouse Effect

Earth's atmosphere, like the windows of a greenhouse, allows the sun's visible light to pass through it. But like the windows of a greenhouse keep energy inside the greenhouse, the atmosphere traps some reradiated energy. This process, called the *greenhouse effect,* is illustrated in **Figure 11.** Some scientists are concerned that high levels of greenhouse gases (water vapor, carbon dioxide, and methane) in the atmosphere may trap too much energy and make Earth too warm. However, if not for the greenhouse effect, the Earth would be a cold, lifeless planet.

**Figure 11 The Greenhouse Effect**

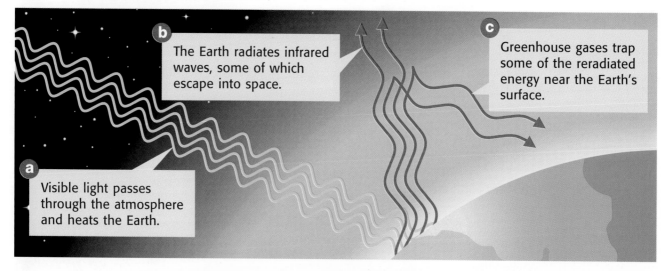

b. The Earth radiates infrared waves, some of which escape into space.

c. Greenhouse gases trap some of the reradiated energy near the Earth's surface.

a. Visible light passes through the atmosphere and heats the Earth.

## SECTION REVIEW

1. What is heat?

2. Explain how radiation is different from conduction and convection.

3. **Applying Concepts** Why do many metal cooking utensils have wooden handles?

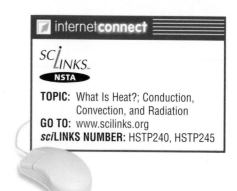

internet**connect**

SC*i*LINKS
NSTA

**TOPIC:** What Is Heat?; Conduction, Convection, and Radiation
**GO TO:** www.scilinks.org
*sci*LINKS NUMBER: HSTP240, HSTP245

Heat and Heat Technology **159**

# Heat and Temperature Change

On a hot summer day, have you ever fastened your seat belt in a car, as shown in **Figure 12**? If so, you may have noticed that the metal buckle felt hotter than the cloth belt. Why? Keep reading to learn more.

**Thermal Conductivity** Different substances have different thermal conductivities. *Thermal conductivity* is the rate at which a substance conducts thermal energy. Conductors, such as the metal buckle, have higher thermal conductivities than do insulators, such as the cloth belt. Because of the metal's higher thermal conductivity, it transfers energy more rapidly to your hand when you touch it than the cloth does. So even when the cloth and metal are the same temperature, the metal feels hotter.

**Specific Heat Capacity** Another difference between the metal and the cloth is how easily they change temperature when they absorb or lose energy. When equal amounts of energy are transferred to or from equal masses of different substances, the change in temperature for each substance will differ. **Specific heat capacity** is the amount of energy needed to change the temperature of 1 kg of a substance by 1°C.

Look at the table below. Notice that the specific heat capacity of the cloth of a seat belt is more than twice that of the metal seat belt buckle. This means that for equal masses of metal and cloth, less energy is required to change the temperature of the metal. So the metal buckle gets hot (and cools off) more quickly than an equal mass of the cloth belt.

Different substances have different specific heat capacities. Check out the specific heat capacities for various substances in the table below.

**Figure 12** *On a hot summer day, the metal part of a seat belt feels hotter than the cloth part.*

## Meteorology
### CONNECTION

Water has a higher specific heat capacity than land. This difference affects the climate of different areas on Earth. Climates in coastal areas are moderated by the ocean. Because of water's high specific heat capacity, the ocean retains a lot of thermal energy. So even in the winter, when inland temperatures drop, coastal areas stay moderately warm. Because water does not heat up as easily as land does, oceans can help to keep coastal areas cool during the summer when inland temperatures soar.

| Specific Heat Capacities of Some Common Substances | | | |
|---|---|---|---|
| Substance | Specific heat capacity (J/kg•°C) | Substance | Specific heat capacity (J/kg•°C) |
| Lead | 128 | Glass | 837 |
| Gold | 129 | Aluminum | 899 |
| Mercury | 138 | Cloth of seat belt | 1,340 |
| Silver | 234 | Wood | 1,760 |
| Copper | 387 | Steam | 2,010 |
| Iron | 448 | Ice | 2,090 |
| Metal of seat belt | 500 | Water | 4,184 |

## Heat—The Amount of Energy Transferred

Unlike temperature, energy transferred between objects cannot be measured directly—it must be calculated. When calculating energy transferred between objects, it is helpful to define *heat* as the amount of energy that is transferred between two objects that are at different temperatures. Heat can then be expressed in joules (J).

How much energy is required to heat a cup of water to make tea? To answer this question, you have to consider the water's mass, its change in temperature, and its specific heat capacity. In general, if you know an object's mass, its change in temperature, and its specific heat capacity, you can use the equation below to calculate heat (the amount of energy transferred).

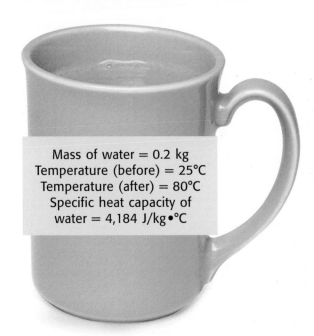

Mass of water = 0.2 kg
Temperature (before) = 25°C
Temperature (after) = 80°C
Specific heat capacity of
water = 4,184 J/kg•°C

**Figure 13** *Information used to calculate heat, the amount of energy transferred to the water, is shown above.*

Heat (J) = specific heat capacity (J/kg•°C) × mass (kg) × change in temperature (°C)

**Calculating Heat** Using the equation above and the data in **Figure 13,** you can follow the steps below to calculate the heat added to the water. Because the water's temperature increases, the value of heat is positive. You can also use this equation to calculate the heat removed from an object when it cools down. The value for heat would then be negative because the temperature decreases.

**1** **Write down what you know.**
Specific heat capacity of water = 4,184 J/kg•°C
Mass of water = 0.2 kg
Change in temperature = 80°C – 25°C = 55°C

**2** **Substitute the values into the equation.**
Heat = specific heat capacity × mass × change in temperature
= 4,184 J/kg•°C × 0.2 kg × 55°C

**3** **Solve and cancel units.**
Heat = 4,184 J/kg•°C × 0.2 kg × 55°C
= 4,184 J × 0.2 × 55
= 46,024 J

## MATH BREAK

**Calculating Energy Transfer**
Use the equation at left to solve the following problems:

1. Imagine that you heat 2 L of water to make pasta. The temperature of the water before is 40°C, and the temperature after is 100°C. What is the heat involved? (Hint: 1 L of water = 1 kg of water)

2. Suppose you put a glass filled with 180 mL of water into the refrigerator. The temperature of the water before is 25°C, and the temperature after is 10°C. How much energy was transferred away from the water as it became colder?

Build your own calorimeter! Try
the lab on page 201 of the
LabBook.

**Calorimeters** When one object transfers thermal energy to another object, the energy lost by one object is gained by the other object. This is the key to how a *calorimeter* (KAL uh RIM uh ter) works. Inside a calorimeter, shown in **Figure 14,** thermal energy is transferred from a known mass of a test substance to a known mass of another substance, usually water.

**Using a Calorimeter** If a hot test substance is placed inside the calorimeter's inner container of water, the substance transfers energy to the water until thermal equilibrium is reached. By measuring the temperature change of the water and using water's specific heat capacity, you can determine the exact amount of energy transferred by the test substance to the water. You can then use this amount of energy (heat), the change in the test substance's temperature, and the mass of the test substance to calculate that substance's specific heat capacity.

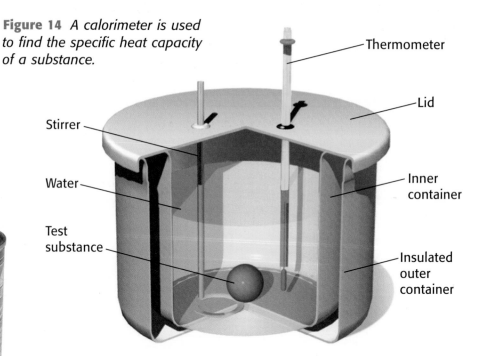

**Figure 14** *A calorimeter is used to find the specific heat capacity of a substance.*

Thermometer

Lid

Stirrer

Inner container

Water

Test substance

Insulated outer container

**Figure 15** *A serving of this fruit contains 120 Cal (502,080 J) of energy that becomes available when it is eaten and digested.*

**Calories and Kilocalories** Heat can also be expressed in units called calories. A *calorie (cal)* is the amount of energy needed to change the temperature of 0.001 kg of water by 1°C. Therefore, 1,000 calories are required to change the temperature of 1 kg of water by 1°C. One calorie is equivalent to 4.184 J. Another unit used to express heat is the *kilocalorie (kcal)*, which is equivalent to 1,000 calories. The kilocalorie is also known as a *Calorie* (with a capital *C*). These are the Calories listed on food labels, such as the label shown in **Figure 15.**

# The Differences Between Temperature, Thermal Energy, and Heat

So far in this chapter, you have been learning about some concepts that are closely related: temperature, heat, and thermal energy. But the differences between these concepts are very important.

**Temperature Versus Thermal Energy** Temperature is a measure of the average kinetic energy of an object's particles, and thermal energy is the total energy of an object's particles. While thermal energy varies with the mass of an object, temperature does not. A drop of boiling water has the same temperature as a pot of boiling water, but the pot has more thermal energy because there are more particles.

**Thermal Energy Versus Heat** Heat and thermal energy are not the same thing; heat is a transfer of thermal energy. In addition, heat can refer to the amount of energy transferred from one object to another. Objects contain thermal energy, but they do not contain heat. The table below summarizes the differences between temperature, thermal energy, and heat.

## Self-Check

How can two substances have the same temperature but different amounts of thermal energy? *(See page 232 to check your answer.)*

| Temperature | Thermal energy | Heat |
|---|---|---|
| A measure of the average kinetic energy of the particles in a substance | The total energy of the particles in a substance | The transfer of energy between objects that are at different temperatures |
| Expressed in degrees Fahrenheit, degrees Celsius, or kelvins | Expressed in joules | Amount of energy transferred expressed in joules or calories |
| Does not vary with the mass of a substance | Varies with the mass and temperature of a substance | Varies with the mass, specific heat capacity, and temperature change of a substance |

## SECTION REVIEW

1. Some objects get hot more quickly than others. Why?

2. How are temperature and heat different?

3. **Applying Concepts** Examine the photo at right. How do you think the specific heat capacities for water and air influence the temperature of a swimming pool and the area around it?

*Terms to Learn*

states of matter
change of state

*What You'll Do*

◆ Identify three states of matter.
◆ Explain how heat affects matter during a change of state.
◆ Describe how heat affects matter during a chemical change.

# Matter and Heat

Have you ever eaten a frozen juice bar outside on a hot summer day? It's pretty hard to finish the entire thing before it starts to drip and make a big mess! The juice bar melts because the sun radiates energy to the air, which transfers energy to the frozen juice bar. The energy absorbed by the juice bar increases the kinetic energy of the molecules in the juice bar, which starts to turn to a liquid. In this section, you'll learn more about how heat affects matter.

## States of Matter

The matter that makes up a frozen juice bar has the same identity whether the juice bar is frozen or has melted. The matter is just in a different form, or state. The **states of matter** are the physical forms in which a substance can exist. Recall that matter consists of particles—atoms or molecules—that can move around at different speeds. The state a substance is in depends on the speed of its particles and the attraction between them. Three familiar states of matter are solid, liquid, and gas, represented in **Figure 16.** You may recall that thermal energy is the total energy of the particles that make up a substance. Suppose you have equal masses of a substance in its three states, each at a different temperature. The substance will have the most thermal energy as a gas and the least thermal energy as a solid. That's because the particles move around fastest in a gas.

**Figure 16  Models of a Solid, a Liquid, and a Gas**

**Particles of a solid** do not move fast enough to overcome the strong attraction between them, so they are held tightly together. The particles vibrate in place.

**Particles of a liquid** move fast enough to overcome some of the attraction between them. The particles are able to slide past one another.

**Particles of a gas** move fast enough to overcome nearly all of the attraction between them. The particles move independently of one another.

## Changes of State

When you melt cheese to make a cheese dip, like that shown in **Figure 17,** the cheese changes from a solid to a thick, gooey liquid. A **change of state** is the conversion of a substance from one physical form to another. A change of state is a *physical change* that affects one or more physical properties of a substance without changing the substance's identity. Changes of state include *freezing* (liquid to solid), *melting* (solid to liquid), *boiling* (liquid to gas), and *condensing* (gas to liquid).

**Figure 17** *When you melt cheese, you change the state of the cheese but not its identity.*

**Graphing Changes of State** Suppose you put an ice cube in a pan and set the pan on a stove burner. Soon the ice will turn to water and then to steam. If you made a graph of the energy involved versus the temperature of the ice during this process, it would look something like the graph below.

As the ice is heated, its temperature increases from –25°C to 0°C. At 0°C, the ice begins to melt. Notice that the temperature of the ice remains 0°C even as more energy is added. This added energy changes the arrangement of the particles, or molecules, in the ice. The temperature of the ice remains constant until all of the ice has become liquid water. At that point, the water's temperature will start to increase from 0°C to 100°C. At 100°C, the water will begin to turn into steam. Even as more energy is added, the water's temperature stays at 100°C. The energy added at the boiling point changes the arrangement of the particles until the water has entirely changed to a gaseous state. When all of the water has become steam, the temperature again increases.

> ## ✓ Self-Check
>
> Why do you think you can get a more severe burn from steam than from boiling water? *(See page 232 to check your answer.)*

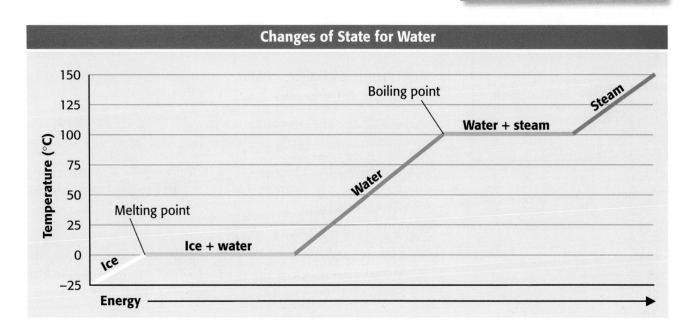

**Changes of State for Water**

# Heat and Chemical Changes

Heat is involved not only in changes of state, which are physical changes, but also in *chemical changes*—changes that occur when one or more substances are changed into entirely new substances with different properties. During a chemical change, new substances are formed. For a new substance to form, old bonds between particles must be broken and new bonds must be created. The breaking and creating of bonds between particles involves energy. Sometimes a chemical change requires that thermal energy be absorbed. For example, photosynthesis is a chemical change in which carbon dioxide and water combine to form sugar and oxygen. In order for this change to occur, energy must be absorbed. That energy is radiated by the sun. Other times, a chemical change, such as the one shown in **Figure 18,** will result in energy being released.

**Figure 18** *In a natural-gas fireplace, the methane in natural gas and the oxygen in air change into carbon dioxide and water. As a result of the change, energy is given off, making a room feel warmer.*

**internetconnect**

**SCi LINKS**
**NSTA**

**TOPIC:** Changes of State
**GO TO:** www.scilinks.org
*sci*LINKS **NUMBER:** HSTP250

## SECTION REVIEW

1. During a change of state, why doesn't the temperature of the substance change?

2. Compare the thermal energy of 10 g of ice with the thermal energy of the same amount of water.

3. When water evaporates (changes from a liquid to a gas), the air near the water's surface becomes cooler. Explain why.

4. **Applying Concepts** Many cold packs used for sports injuries are activated by bending the package, causing the substances inside to interact. How is heat involved in this process?

## Terms to Learn

insulation
heat engine
thermal pollution

## What You'll Do

◆ Analyze several kinds of heating systems.
◆ Describe how a heat engine works.
◆ Explain how a refrigerator keeps food cold.
◆ Give examples of some effects of heat technology on the environment.

# Heat Technology

You probably wouldn't be surprised to learn that the heater in your home is an example of heat technology. But did you know that automobiles, refrigerators, and air conditioners are also examples of heat technology? It's true! You can travel long distances, you can keep your food cold, and you can feel comfortable indoors during the summer—all because of heat technology.

## Heating Systems

Many homes and buildings have a central heating system that controls the temperature in every room. On the next few pages, you will see some different central heating systems.

**Hot-Water Heating** The high specific heat capacity of water makes it useful for heating systems. In a hot-water heating system, shown in **Figure 19,** water is heated by burning fuel (usually natural gas or fuel oil) in a hot-water heater. The hot water is pumped through pipes that lead to radiators in each room. The hot water heats the radiators, and the radiators then heat the colder air surrounding them. The water returns to the hot-water heater to be heated again. A *steam-heating system* is similar, except that steam is used in place of water.

**Figure 19**
**A Hot-Water Heating System**

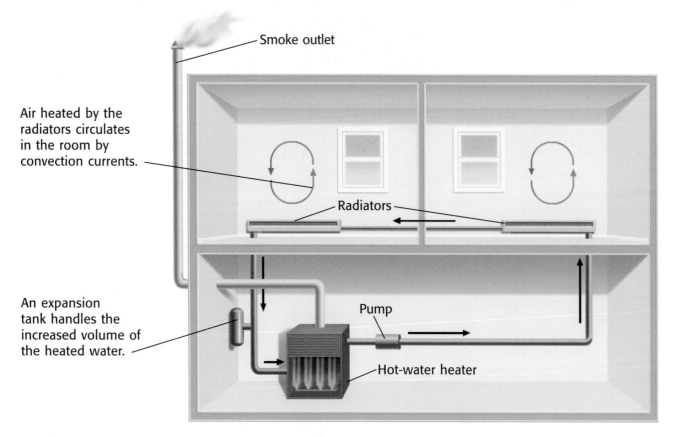

Smoke outlet

Air heated by the radiators circulates in the room by convection currents.

Radiators

An expansion tank handles the increased volume of the heated water.

Pump

Hot-water heater

**Warm-Air Heating** Although air has a lower specific heat capacity than water, warm-air heating systems are used in many homes and offices in the United States. In a warm-air heating system, shown in **Figure 20,** air is heated in a separate chamber by burning fuel (usually natural gas) in a furnace. The warm air travels through ducts to different rooms, which it enters through vents. The warm air heats air in the rooms. Cooler air sinks below the warm air and enters a vent near the floor. Then a fan forces the cooler air into the furnace, where the air will be heated and returned to the ducts. An air filter cleans the air as it circulates through the system.

**Figure 20**
**A Warm-Air Heating System**

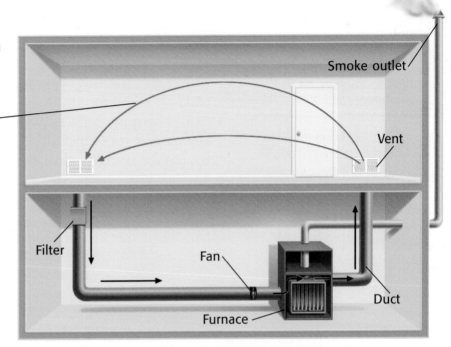

Warm air is circulated in the rooms by convection currents.

Smoke outlet

Vent

Filter

Fan

Duct

Furnace

**Heating and Insulation** Thermal energy may be transferred out of a house during cold weather and into a house during hot weather. To keep the house comfortable, a heating system must run almost continuously during the winter, and air conditioners often do the same during the summer. This can be wasteful. That's where insulation comes in. **Insulation** is a substance that reduces the transfer of thermal energy. Insulation, such as the fiberglass insulation shown in **Figure 21,** is made of insulators—materials that do not conduct thermal energy very well. Insulation that is used in walls, ceilings, and floors helps a house stay warm in the winter and cool in the summer.

Insulation is made of a variety of materials. The effectiveness of an insulating material is its R-value. The higher the R-value, the greater the insulating effectiveness. The R-value of a material depends on the type of material, its thickness, and its density.

**Figure 21** *Millions of tiny air pockets in this insulation help prevent thermal energy from flowing into or out of a building.*

**Solar Heating** The sun radiates an enormous amount of energy. Solar heating systems use this energy to heat houses and buildings. *Passive solar heating* systems do not have moving parts. They rely on a building's structural design and materials to use energy from the sun as a means of heating. *Active solar heating* systems do have moving parts. They use pumps and fans to distribute the sun's energy throughout a building.

Look at the house in **Figure 22.** The large windows on the south side of the house are part of the passive solar heating system. These windows receive maximum sunlight, and energy is radiated through the windows into the rooms. Thick, well-insulated concrete walls absorb energy and heat the house at night or when it is cloudy. In the active solar heating system, water is pumped to the solar collector, where it is heated. The hot water is pumped through pipes and transfers its energy to them. A fan blowing over the pipes helps the pipes transfer their thermal energy to the air. Warm air is then sent into rooms through vents. Cooler water returns to the water storage tank to be pumped back through the solar collector.

**Figure 22** *Passive and active solar heating systems work together to use the sun's energy to heat an entire house.*

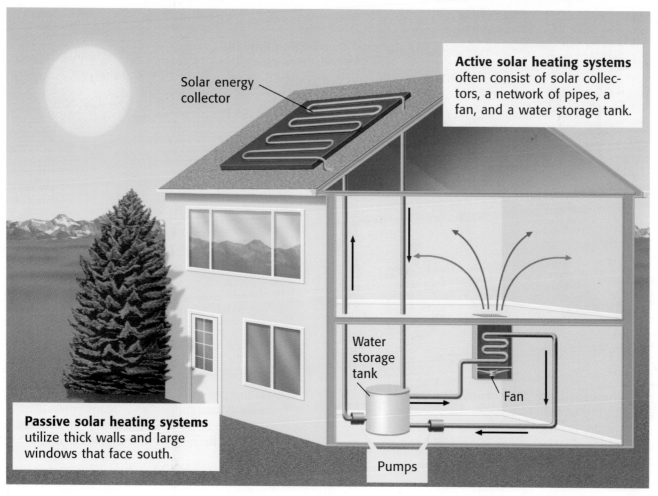

Solar energy collector

**Active solar heating systems** often consist of solar collectors, a network of pipes, a fan, and a water storage tank.

Water storage tank

Fan

**Passive solar heating systems** utilize thick walls and large windows that face south.

Pumps

## Oceanography

# CONNECTION

Ocean engineers are developing a new technology known as Ocean Thermal Energy Conversion, or OTEC. OTEC uses temperature differences between surface water and deep water in the ocean to do work like a heat engine does. Warm surface water vaporizes a fluid, such as ammonia, causing it to expand. Then cool water from ocean depths causes the fluid to condense and contract. The continuous cycle of vaporizing and condensing converts thermal energy into kinetic energy that can be used to generate electrical energy.

# Heat Engines

Did you know that automobiles work because of heat? A car has a **heat engine,** a machine that uses heat to do work. In a heat engine, fuel combines with oxygen in a chemical change that produces thermal energy. This process, called *combustion,* is how engines burn fuel. Heat engines that burn fuel outside the engine are called *external combustion engines*. Heat engines that burn fuel inside the engine are called *internal combustion engines*. In both types of engines, fuel is burned to produce thermal energy that can be used to do work.

**External Combustion Engine** A simple steam engine, shown in **Figure 23,** is an example of an external combustion engine. Coal is burned to heat water in a boiler and change the water to steam. When water changes to steam, it expands. The expanding steam is used to drive a piston, which can be attached to other mechanisms that do work, such as a flywheel. Modern steam engines, such as those used to generate electrical energy at a power plant, drive turbines instead of pistons.

**Figure 23 An External Combustion Engine**

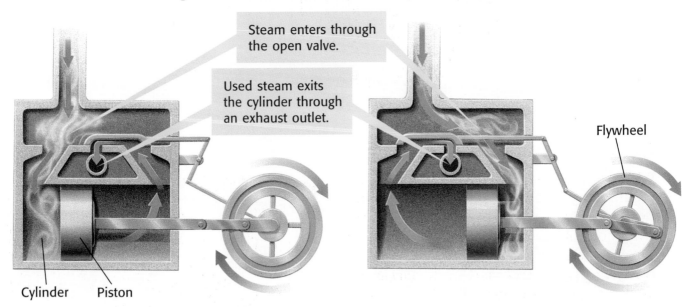

Steam enters through the open valve.

Used steam exits the cylinder through an exhaust outlet.

Flywheel

Cylinder     Piston

**a** The expanding steam enters the cylinder from one side. The steam does work on the piston, forcing the piston to move.

**b** As the piston moves to the other side, a second valve opens and steam enters. The steam does work on the piston and moves it back. The motion of the piston turns a flywheel.

**Internal Combustion Engine** In the six-cylinder car engine shown in **Figure 24,** fuel is burned inside the engine. During the intake stroke, a mixture of gasoline and air enters each cylinder as the piston moves down. Next the crankshaft turns and pushes the piston up, compressing the fuel mixture. This is called the compression stroke. Next comes the power stroke, in which the spark plug uses electrical energy to ignite the compressed fuel mixture, causing the mixture to expand and force the piston down. Finally, during the exhaust stroke, the crankshaft turns and the piston is forced back up, pushing exhaust gases out of the cylinder.

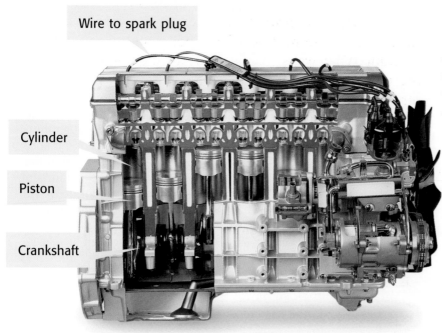

Wire to spark plug

Cylinder

Piston

Crankshaft

**Figure 24** *The continuous cycling of the four strokes in the cylinders converts thermal energy into the kinetic energy required to make a car move.*

## Cooling Systems

When it gets hot in the summer, an air-conditioned room can feel very refreshing. Cooling systems are used to transfer thermal energy out of a particular area so that it feels cooler. An air conditioner, shown in **Figure 25,** is a cooling system that transfers thermal energy from a warm area inside a building or car to an area outside, where it is often even warmer. But wait a minute—doesn't that go against the natural direction of heat—from higher temperatures to lower temperatures? Well, yes. A cooling system moves thermal energy from cooler temperatures to warmer temperatures. But in order to do that, the cooling system must do work.

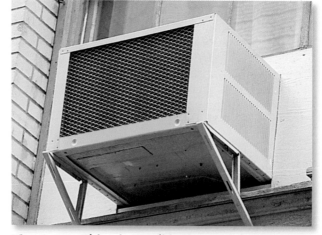

**Figure 25** *This air conditioning unit keeps a building cool by moving thermal energy from inside the building to the outside.*

**Cooling Takes Energy** Most cooling systems require electrical energy to do the work of cooling. The electrical energy is used by a device called a compressor. The compressor does the work of compressing the refrigerant, a gas that has a boiling point below room temperature. This property of the refrigerant allows it to condense easily.

To keep many foods fresh, you store them in a refrigerator. A refrigerator is another example of a cooling system. **Figure 26** shows how a refrigerator continuously transfers thermal energy from inside the refrigerator to the condenser coils on the outside of the refrigerator. That's why the area near the back of a refrigerator feels warm.

**Figure 26  How a Refrigerator Works**

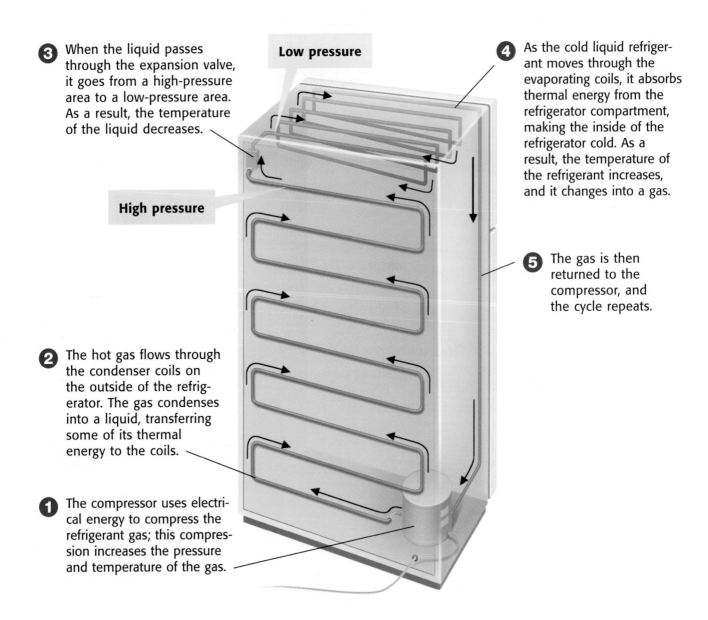

**3** When the liquid passes through the expansion valve, it goes from a high-pressure area to a low-pressure area. As a result, the temperature of the liquid decreases.

**Low pressure**

**High pressure**

**4** As the cold liquid refrigerant moves through the evaporating coils, it absorbs thermal energy from the refrigerator compartment, making the inside of the refrigerator cold. As a result, the temperature of the refrigerant increases, and it changes into a gas.

**5** The gas is then returned to the compressor, and the cycle repeats.

**2** The hot gas flows through the condenser coils on the outside of the refrigerator. The gas condenses into a liquid, transferring some of its thermal energy to the coils.

**1** The compressor uses electrical energy to compress the refrigerant gas; this compression increases the pressure and temperature of the gas.

## Heat Technology and Thermal Pollution

Heating systems, car engines, and cooling systems all transfer thermal energy to the environment. Unfortunately, too much thermal energy can have a negative effect on the environment.

One of the negative effects of excess thermal energy is **thermal pollution,** the excessive heating of a body of water. Thermal pollution can occur near large power plants, which are often located near a body of water. Electric power plants burn fuel to produce thermal energy that is used to generate electrical energy. Unfortunately, it is not possible for all of that thermal energy to do work, so some waste thermal energy results. **Figure 27** shows how a cooling tower helps remove this waste thermal energy in order to keep the power plants operating smoothly. In extreme cases, the increase in temperature downstream from a power plant can adversely affect the ecosystem of the river or lake. Some power plants reduce thermal pollution by reducing the temperature of the water before it is returned to the river.

## Environment
### CONNECTION

Large cities can exhibit something called a heat island effect when excessive amounts of waste thermal energy are added to the urban environment. This thermal energy comes from automobiles, factories, home heating and cooling, lighting, and even just the number of people living in a relatively small area. The heat island effect can make the temperature of the air in a city higher than that of the air in the surrounding countryside.

**Figure 27** *Cool water is circulated through a power plant to absorb waste thermal energy.*

Cool water

Warm water

## SECTION REVIEW

1. Compare a hot-water heating system with a warm-air heating system.

2. What is the difference between an external combustion engine and an internal combustion engine?

3. **Analyzing Relationships** How are changes of state an important part of the way a refrigerator works?

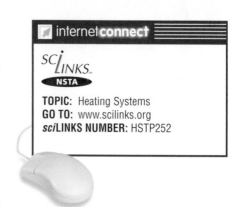

**internetconnect**

*sci*LINKS
NSTA

TOPIC: Heating Systems
GO TO: www.scilinks.org
*sci*LINKS NUMBER: HSTP252

# Discovery Lab

## Feel the Heat

Heat is the transfer of energy between objects at different temperatures. Energy moves from objects at higher temperatures to objects at lower temperatures. If two objects are left in contact for a while, the warmer object will cool down and the cooler object will warm up until they eventually reach the same temperature. In this activity, you will combine equal masses of water and iron nails at different temperatures to determine which has a greater effect on the final temperature.

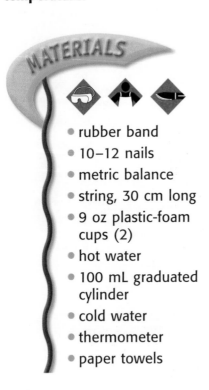

**MATERIALS**

- rubber band
- 10–12 nails
- metric balance
- string, 30 cm long
- 9 oz plastic-foam cups (2)
- hot water
- 100 mL graduated cylinder
- cold water
- thermometer
- paper towels

## Make a Prediction

**1** When you combine substances at different temperatures, will the final temperature be closer to the initial temperature of the warmer substance or the colder substance, or halfway in between? Write your prediction in your ScienceLog.

## Conduct an Experiment/Collect Data

**2** Copy the table on the next page into your ScienceLog.

**3** Use the rubber band to bundle the nails together. Find and record the mass of the bundle. Tie a length of string around the bundle, leaving one end of the string 15 cm long.

**4** Put the bundle of nails into one of the cups. Hang the string outside the cup. Fill the cup with enough hot water to cover the nails, and set it aside for at least 5 minutes.

**5** In the graduated cylinder, measure cold water exactly equal to the mass of the nails (1 mL of water = 1 g). Record this volume in the table.

**6** Measure and record the temperature of the hot water with the nails, and the temperature of the cold water.

**7** Use the string to move the bundle of nails to the cup of cold water. Use the thermometer to monitor the temperature of this water-nail mixture. When the temperature stops changing, record this final temperature in the table.

**8** Empty the cups, and dry the nails.

## Data Collection Table

| Trial | Mass of nails (g) | Volume of water that equals mass of nails (mL) | Initial temp. of water and nails (°C) | Initial temp. of water to which nails will be transferred (°C) | Final temp. of water and nails combined (°C) |
|-------|-------------------|------------------------------------------------|---------------------------------------|---------------------------------------------------------------|----------------------------------------------|
| 1 | | | | | |
| 2 | | | | | |

DO NOT WRITE IN BOOK

9 For Trial 2, repeat steps 3 through 8, but switch the order of the hot and cold water. Record all of your measurements.

## Analyze the Results

10 In Trial 1, you used equal masses of cold water and nails. Did the final temperature support your initial prediction? Explain.

11 In Trial 2, you used equal masses of hot water and nails. Did the final temperature support your initial prediction? Explain.

12 In Trial 1, which substance—the water or the nails—changed temperature the most after you transferred the nails? What about in Trial 2? Explain your answers.

## Draw Conclusions

13 The cold water in Trial 1 gained energy. Infer where the energy came from.

14 Evaluate how the energy gained by the nails in Trial 2 compares with the energy lost by the hot water in Trial 2. Explain.

15 Which material seems to be able to hold energy better? Explain your answer.

16 Specific heat capacity is a property of matter that indicates how much energy is required to change the temperature of 1 kg of a material by 1°C. Which material in this activity has a higher specific heat capacity (changes temperature less for the same amount of energy)—the nails or the water?

17 Would it be better to have pots and pans made from a material with a high specific heat capacity or a low specific heat capacity? Explain your answer.

## Communicate Results

18 Discuss with classmates how you would change your initial prediction to include specific heat capacity.

# Chapter Highlights

## SECTION 1

### Vocabulary

**temperature** *(p. 150)*
**thermal expansion** *(p. 152)*
**absolute zero** *(p. 153)*

### Section Notes

• Temperature is a measure of the average kinetic energy of the particles of a substance. It is a specific measurement of how hot or cold a substance is.

• Thermal expansion is the increase in volume of a substance due to an increase in temperature. Temperature is measured according to the expansion of the liquid in a thermometer.

• Fahrenheit, Celsius, and Kelvin are three temperature scales.

• Absolute zero—0 K, or –273°C— is the lowest possible temperature.

• A thermostat works according to the thermal expansion of a bimetallic strip.

## SECTION 2

### Vocabulary

**heat** *(p. 155)*
**thermal energy** *(p. 156)*
**conduction** *(p. 157)*
**conductor** *(p. 158)*
**insulator** *(p. 158)*
**convection** *(p. 158)*
**radiation** *(p. 159)*
**specific heat capacity** *(p. 160)*

### Section Notes

• Heat is the transfer of energy between objects that are at different temperatures.

• Thermal energy is the total energy of the particles that make up a substance.

• Energy transfer will always occur from higher temperatures to lower temperatures until thermal equilibrium is reached.

# ☑ Skills Check

## Math Concepts

**TEMPERATURE CONVERSION** To convert between different temperature scales, you can use the equations found on page 153. The example below shows you how to convert a Fahrenheit temperature to a Celsius temperature.

Convert 41°F to °C.

$$°C = \frac{5}{9} \times (°F - 32)$$

$$°C = \frac{5}{9} \times (41°F - 32)$$

$$°C = \frac{5}{9} \times 9 = 5°C$$

## Visual Understanding

**HEAT—A TRANSFER OF ENERGY**
Remember that thermal energy is transferred between objects at different temperatures until both objects reach the same temperature. Look back at Figure 7, on page 156, to review what you've learned about heat.

## SECTION 2

- Conduction, convection, and radiation are three methods of energy transfer.

- Specific heat capacity is the amount of energy needed to change the temperature of 1 kg of a substance by 1°C. Different substances have different specific heat capacities.

- Energy transferred by heat cannot be measured directly. It must be calculated using specific heat capacity, mass, and change in temperature.

- A calorimeter is used to determine the specific heat capacity of a substance.

**Labs**

**Save the Cube!** (*p. 200*)
**Counting Calories** (*p. 201*)

## SECTION 3

**Vocabulary**

**states of matter** (*p. 164*)
**change of state** (*p. 165*)

**Section Notes**

- A substance's state is determined by the speed of its particles and the attraction between them.

- Thermal energy transferred during a change of state does not change a substance's temperature. Rather, it causes a substance's particles to be rearranged.

- Chemical changes can cause thermal energy to be absorbed or released.

## SECTION 4

**Vocabulary**

**insulation** (*p. 168*)
**heat engine** (*p. 170*)
**thermal pollution** (*p. 173*)

**Section Notes**

- Central heating systems include hot-water heating systems and warm-air heating systems.

- Solar heating systems can be passive or active.

- Heat engines use heat to do work. External combustion engines burn fuel outside the engine. Internal combustion engines burn fuel inside the engine.

- A cooling system transfers thermal energy from cooler temperatures to warmer temperatures by doing work.

- Transferring excess thermal energy to lakes and rivers can result in thermal pollution.

---

**internet connect**

**GO TO:** go.hrw.com

Visit the **HRW** Web site for a variety of learning tools related to this chapter. Just type in the keyword:

**KEYWORD:** HSTHOT

**GO TO:** www.scilinks.org

Visit the **National Science Teachers Association** on-line Web site for Internet resources related to this chapter. Just type in the *sci*LINKS number for more information about the topic:

**TOPIC:** What Is Temperature?    ***sci*LINKS NUMBER:** HSTP230
**TOPIC:** What Is Heat?    ***sci*LINKS NUMBER:** HSTP240
**TOPIC:** Conduction, Convection, and Radiation    ***sci*LINKS NUMBER:** HSTP245
**TOPIC:** Changes of State    ***sci*LINKS NUMBER:** HSTP250
**TOPIC:** Heating Systems    ***sci*LINKS NUMBER:** HSTP252

# Chapter Review

## USING VOCABULARY

For each pair of terms, explain the difference in their meanings.

1. temperature/thermal energy

2. heat/thermal energy

3. conductor/insulator

4. conduction/convection

5. states of matter/change of state

## UNDERSTANDING CONCEPTS

### Multiple Choice

6. Which of the following temperatures is the lowest?
   - **a.** 100°C
   - **b.** 100°F
   - **c.** 100 K
   - **d.** They are the same.

7. Compared with the Pacific Ocean, a cup of hot chocolate has
   - **a.** more thermal energy and a higher temperature.
   - **b.** less thermal energy and a higher temperature.
   - **c.** more thermal energy and a lower temperature.
   - **d.** less thermal energy and a lower temperature.

8. The energy units on a food label are
   - **a.** degrees.
   - **b.** Calories.
   - **c.** calories.
   - **d.** joules.

9. Which of the following materials would not be a good insulator?
   - **a.** wood
   - **b.** cloth
   - **c.** metal
   - **d.** rubber

10. The engine in a car is a(n)
    - **a.** heat engine.
    - **b.** external combustion engine.
    - **c.** internal combustion engine.
    - **d.** Both (a) and (c)

11. Materials that warm up or cool down very quickly have a
    - **a.** low specific heat capacity.
    - **b.** high specific heat capacity.
    - **c.** low temperature.
    - **d.** high temperature.

12. In an air conditioner, thermal energy is
    - **a.** transferred from higher to lower temperatures.
    - **b.** transferred from lower to higher temperatures.
    - **c.** used to do work.
    - **d.** taken from air outside a building and transferred to air inside the building.

### Short Answer

13. How does temperature relate to kinetic energy?

14. What is specific heat capacity?

15. Explain how heat affects matter during a change of state.

16. Describe how a bimetallic strip works in a thermostat.

## Concept Mapping

**17.** Use the following terms to create a concept map: thermal energy, temperature, radiation, heat, conduction, convection.

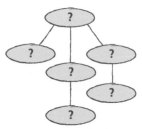

## CRITICAL THINKING AND PROBLEM SOLVING

**18.** Why does placing a jar under warm running water help loosen the lid on the jar?

**19.** Why do you think a down-filled jacket keeps you so warm? (Hint: Think about what insulation does.)

**20.** Would opening the refrigerator cool a room in a house? Why or why not?

**21.** In a hot-air balloon, air is heated by a flame. Explain how this enables the balloon to float in the air.

## MATH IN SCIENCE

**22.** The weather forecast calls for a temperature of 86°F. What is the corresponding temperature in degrees Celsius? in kelvins?

**23.** Suppose 1,300 mL of water are heated from 20°C to 100°C. How much energy was transferred to the water? (Hint: Water's specific heat capacity is 4,184 J/kg•°C.)

## INTERPRETING GRAPHICS

Examine the graph below, and then answer the questions that follow.

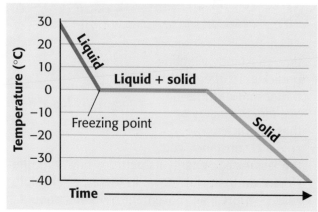

**24.** What physical change does this graph illustrate?

**25.** What is the freezing point of this liquid?

**26.** What is happening at the point where the line is horizontal?

Reading Check-up

Take a minute to review your answers to the Pre-Reading Questions found at the bottom of page 148. Have your answers changed? If necessary, revise your answers based on what you have learned since you began this chapter.

# Science, Technology, and Society

## The Deep Freeze

In the dark reaches of outer space, temperatures can drop below −270°C. Perhaps the only place colder is a laboratory here on Earth!

### The Quest for Zero

All matter is made up of tiny, constantly vibrating particles. Temperature is a measure of the average kinetic energy of these particles. The colder a substance gets, the less kinetic energy its particles have and the slower the particles move. In theory, at absolute zero (−273°C), all movement of matter should stop. Scientists are working in laboratories to slow down matter so much that the temperature approaches absolute zero.

### How Low Can They Go?

Using lasers, along with magnets, mirrors, and supercold chemicals, scientists have cooled matter to within a few billionths of a degree of absolute zero. In one method, scientists aim lasers at tiny gas particles inside a special chamber. The lasers hold the particles so still that their temperature approaches −272.999998°C.

To get an idea of what takes place, imagine turning on several garden hoses as high as they can go. Then direct the streams of water at a soccer ball so that each stream pushes the ball from a different angle. If the hoses are aimed properly, the ball won't roll in any direction. That's similar to what happens to the particles in the scientists' experiment.

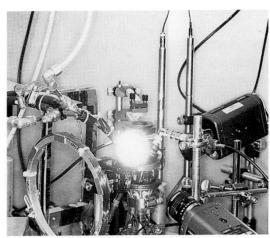

▲ *This laser device is used to cool matter to nearly absolute zero.*

### Cryogenics–Cold Temperature Technology

Supercold temperatures have led to some super-cool technology. Cryosurgery, which is surgery that uses extremely low temperatures, allows doctors to seal off tiny blood vessels during an operation or to freeze diseased cells and destroy them.

Cooling materials to near absolute zero has also led to the discovery of superconductors. Superconductors are materials that lose all of their electrical resistance when they are cooled to a low enough temperature. Imagine the possibilities for materials that could conduct electricity indefinitely without any energy loss. Unfortunately, it takes a great deal of energy to cool such materials. Right now, applications for superconductors are still just the stuff of dreams.

### Freezing Fun on Your Own

▶ You can try your hand at cryoinvestigation. Place 50 mL of tap water, 50 mL of salt water (50 mL of water plus 15 g of salt), and 50 mL of rubbing alcohol (isopropanol) in three separate plastic containers. Then put all three containers in your freezer at the same time. Check the containers every 5 minutes for 40 minutes. Which liquid freezes first? How can you explain any differences?

# DiAPLEX®: The Intelligent Fabric

Wouldn't it be great if you had a winter coat that could automatically adjust to keep you cozy regardless of the outside temperature? Well, scientists have developed a new fabric, called DiAPLEX, that can be used to make such a coat!

## With Pores or Without?

Winter adventurers usually wear nylon fabrics to keep warm. These nylon fabrics are laminated with a thin coating that contains thousands of tiny pores, or openings. The pores allow moisture, such as sweat from your body, and excess thermal energy to escape. You might think the pores would let moisture and cold air into the fabric, but that's not the case. Because the pores are so small, the nylon fabric is windproof and waterproof.

DiAPLEX is also made from laminated nylon, but the coating is different. DiAPLEX doesn't have pores; it is a solid film. This film makes DiAPLEX even more waterproof and breathable than other laminated nylon fabrics. So how does it work?

## Moving Particles

DiAPLEX keeps you warm by taking advantage of how particles move. When the air outside is cold, the particles of DiAPLEX arrange themselves into a solid sheet, forming an insulator and preventing the transfer of thermal energy from your body to colder surroundings. As your body gets warm, such as after exercising, the fabric's particles respond to your body's increased thermal energy. Their kinetic energy increases, and they rearrange to create millions of tiny openings that allow excess thermal energy and moisture to escape.

## Donning DiAPLEX

DiAPLEX has a number of important advantages over traditional nylon fabrics. Salts in perspiration and ice can clog the pores of traditional nylon fabrics, decreasing their ability to keep you warm and dry. But DiAPLEX does not have this problem because it contains no pores. Because DiAPLEX is unaffected by UV light and is machine washable, it is also a durable fabric that is easy to care for.

## Anatomy Connection

▶ Do some research to find out how your skin lets thermal energy and moisture escape.

▶ *When your body is cold, the DiAPLEX garment adjusts to prevent the transfer of thermal energy from your body to its surroundings, and you feel warmer.*

▶ *When your body gets too warm, the DiAPLEX garment adjusts to allow your body to transfer excess thermal energy and moisture to your surroundings, and you feel cooler.*

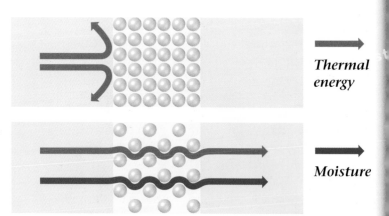

*Thermal energy*

*Moisture*

# SAFETY FIRST!

Exploring, inventing, and investigating are essential to the study of science. However, these activities can also be dangerous. To make sure that your experiments and explorations are safe, you must be aware of a variety of safety guidelines.

You have probably heard of the saying, "It is better to be safe than sorry." This is particularly true in a science classroom where experiments and explorations are being performed. Being uninformed and careless can result in serious injuries. Don't take chances with your own safety or with anyone else's.

Following are important guidelines for staying safe in the science classroom. Your teacher may also have safety guidelines and tips that are specific to your classroom and laboratory. Take the time to be safe.

## Safety Rules!

### Start Out Right

Always get your teacher's permission before attempting any laboratory exploration. Read the procedures carefully, and pay particular attention to safety information and caution statements. If you are unsure about what a safety symbol means, look it up or ask your teacher. You cannot be too careful when it comes to safety. If an accident does occur, inform your teacher immediately, regardless of how minor you think the accident is.

### Safety Symbols

All of the experiments and investigations in this book and their related worksheets include important safety symbols to alert you to particular safety concerns. Become familiar with these symbols so that when you see them, you will know what they mean and what to do. It is important that you read this entire safety section to learn about specific dangers in the laboratory.

If you are instructed to note the odor of a substance, wave the fumes toward your nose with your hand. Never put your nose close to the source.

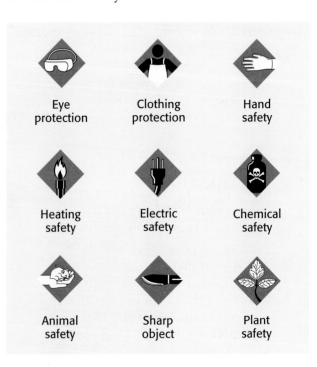

Eye protection

Clothing protection

Hand safety

Heating safety

Electric safety

Chemical safety

Animal safety

Sharp object

Plant safety

## Eye Safety

Wear safety goggles when working around chemicals, acids, bases, or any type of flame or heating device. Wear safety goggles any time there is even the slightest chance that harm could come to your eyes. If any substance gets into your eyes, notify your teacher immediately, and flush your eyes with running water for at least 15 minutes. Treat any unknown chemical as if it were a dangerous chemical. Never look directly into the sun. Doing so could cause permanent blindness.

Avoid wearing contact lenses in a laboratory situation. Even if you are wearing safety goggles, chemicals can get between the contact lenses and your eyes. If your doctor requires that you wear contact lenses instead of glasses, wear eye-cup safety goggles in the lab.

## Safety Equipment

Know the locations of the nearest fire alarms and any other safety equipment, such as fire blankets and eyewash fountains, as identified by your teacher, and know the procedures for using them.

Be extra careful when using any glassware. When adding a heavy object to a graduated cylinder, tilt the cylinder so the object slides slowly to the bottom.

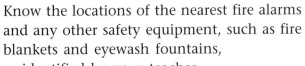

## Neatness

Keep your work area free of all unnecessary books and papers. Tie back long hair, and secure loose sleeves or other loose articles of clothing, such as ties and bows. Remove dangling jewelry. Don't wear open-toed shoes or sandals in the laboratory. Never eat, drink, or apply cosmetics in a laboratory setting. Food, drink, and cosmetics can easily become contaminated with dangerous materials.

Certain hair products (such as aerosol hair spray) are flammable and should not be worn while working near an open flame. Avoid wearing hair spray or hair gel on lab days.

## Sharp/Pointed Objects

Use knives and other sharp instruments with extreme care. Never cut objects while holding them in your hands. Place objects on a suitable work surface for cutting.

## Heat

Wear safety goggles when using a heating device or a flame. Whenever possible, use an electric hot plate as a heat source instead of an open flame. When heating materials in a test tube, always angle the test tube away from yourself and others. In order to avoid burns, wear heat-resistant gloves whenever instructed to do so.

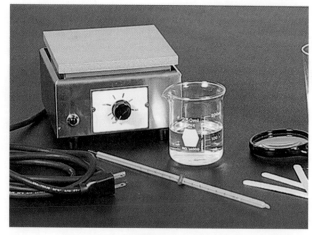

## Chemicals

Wear safety goggles when handling any potentially dangerous chemicals, acids, or bases. If a chemical is unknown, handle it as you would a dangerous chemical. Wear an apron and safety gloves when working with acids or bases or whenever you are told to do so. If a spill gets on your skin or clothing, rinse it off immediately with water for at least 5 minutes while calling to your teacher.

Never mix chemicals unless your teacher tells you to do so. Never taste, touch, or smell chemicals unless you are specifically directed to do so. Before working with a flammable liquid or gas, check for the presence of any source of flame, spark, or heat.

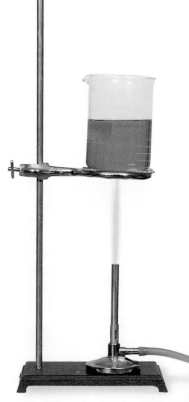

## Electricity

Be careful with electrical cords. When using a microscope with a lamp, do not place the cord where it could trip someone. Do not let cords hang over a table edge in a way that could cause equipment to fall if the cord is accidentally pulled. Do not use equipment with damaged cords. Be sure your hands are dry and that the electrical equipment is in the "off" position before plugging it in. Turn off and unplug electrical equipment when you are finished.

## Animal Safety

Always obtain your teacher's permission before bringing any animal into the school building. Handle animals only as your teacher directs. Always treat animals carefully and with respect. Wash your hands thoroughly after handling any animal.

## Plant Safety

Do not eat any part of a plant or plant seed used in the laboratory. Wash hands thoroughly after handling any part of a plant. When in nature, do not pick any wild plants unless your teacher instructs you to do so.

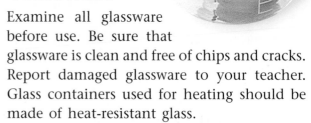

## Glassware

Examine all glassware before use. Be sure that glassware is clean and free of chips and cracks. Report damaged glassware to your teacher. Glass containers used for heating should be made of heat-resistant glass.

# Built for Speed

Imagine that you are an engineer at GoCarCo, a toy-vehicle company. GoCarCo is trying to beat the competition by building a new toy vehicle. Several new designs are being tested. Your boss has given you one of the new toy vehicles and instructed you to measure its speed as accurately as possible with the tools you have. Other engineers (your classmates) are testing the other designs. Your results could decide the fate of the company!

## Materials

- toy vehicle
- meterstick
- masking tape
- stopwatch

## Procedure

1. How will you accomplish your goal? Write a paragraph in your ScienceLog to describe your goal and your procedure for this experiment. Be sure that your procedure includes several trials.

2. Show your plan to your boss (teacher). Get his or her approval to carry out your procedure.

3. Perform your stated procedure. Record all data in your ScienceLog. Be sure to express all data in the correct units.

## Analysis

4. What was the average speed of your vehicle? How does your result compare with the results of the other engineers?

5. Compare your technique for determining the speed of your vehicle with the techniques of the other engineers. Which technique do you think is the most effective?

6. Was your toy vehicle the fastest? Explain why or why not.

### Going Further

Think of several conditions that could affect your vehicle's speed. Design an experiment to test your vehicle under one of those conditions. Write a paragraph in your ScienceLog to explain your procedure. Be sure to include an explanation of how that condition changes your vehicle's speed.

# Relating Mass and Weight

Why do objects with more mass weigh more than objects with less mass? All objects have weight on Earth because their mass is affected by Earth's gravitational force. Because the mass of an object on Earth is constant, the relationship between the mass of an object and its weight is also constant. You will measure the mass and weight of several objects to verify the relationship between mass and weight on the surface of Earth.

## Materials

- metric balance
- small classroom objects
- spring scale (force meter)
- string
- scissors
- graph paper

## Collect Data

1. Copy the table below into your ScienceLog.

| Mass and Weight Measurements | | |
|---|---|---|
| **Object** | **Mass (g)** | **Weight (N)** |
| | | |
| | | |
| | | |
| | | |
| | | |
| | | |

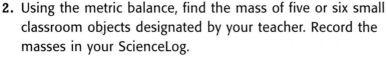

2. Using the metric balance, find the mass of five or six small classroom objects designated by your teacher. Record the masses in your ScienceLog.

3. Using the spring scale, find the weight of each object. Record the weights in your ScienceLog. (You may need to use the string to create a hook with which to hang some objects from the spring scale, as shown at right.)

## Analyze the Results

4. Using your data, construct a graph of weight (*y*-axis) versus mass (*x*-axis). Draw a line that best fits all your data points.

5. Does the graph confirm the relationship between mass and weight on Earth? Explain your answer.

# A Marshmallow Catapult

Catapults use projectile motion to launch objects across distances. A variety of factors can affect the distance an object can be launched, such as the weight of the object, how far the catapult is pulled back, and the catapult's strength. In this lab, you will build a simple catapult and determine the angle at which the catapult will launch an object the farthest.

## Materials

- plastic spoon
- block of wood, 3.5 cm × 3.5 cm × 1 cm
- duct tape
- miniature marshmallows
- protractor
- meterstick

## Form a Hypothesis

1. At what angle, from 10° to 90°, will a catapult launch a marshmallow the farthest?

## Test the Hypothesis

2. Copy the table below into your ScienceLog. In your table, add one row each for 20°, 30°, 40°, 50°, 60°, 70°, 80°, and 90° angles.

| Angle | Distance 1 (cm) | Distance 2 (cm) | Average distance (cm) |
|-------|-----------------|-----------------|-----------------------|
| 10° | DO NOT WRITE IN BOOK | | |

3. Attach the plastic spoon to the 1 cm side of the block with duct tape. Use enough tape so that the spoon is attached securely.

4. Place one marshmallow in the center of the spoon, and tape it to the spoon. This serves as a ledge to hold the marshmallow that will be launched.

5. Line up the bottom corner of the block with the bottom center of the protractor, as shown in the photograph. Start with the block at 10°.

6. Place a marshmallow in the spoon, on top of the taped marshmallow. Pull back lightly, and let go. Measure and record the distance from the catapult that the marshmallow lands. Repeat the measurement, and calculate an average.

7. Repeat step 6 for each angle up to 90°.

## Analyze the Results

8. At what angle did the catapult launch the marshmallow the farthest? Compare this with your hypothesis. Explain any differences.

## Draw Conclusions

9. Does the path of an object's projectile motion depend on the catapult's angle? Support your answer with your data.

10. At what angle should you throw a ball or shoot an arrow so that it will fly the farthest? Why? Support your answer with your data.

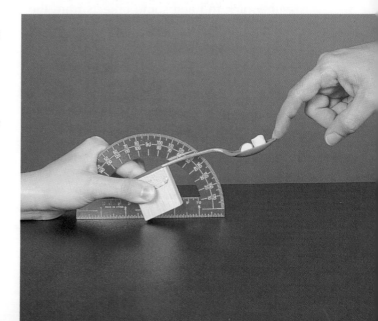

# Blast Off!

You have been hired as a rocket scientist for NASA. Your job is to design a rocket that will have a controlled flight while carrying a payload. Keep in mind that Newton's laws will have a powerful influence on your rocket.

## Materials

- tape
- 3 m fishing line
- pencil
- small paper cup
- 15 cm pieces of string (2)
- long, thin balloon
- twist tie
- drinking straw
- meterstick
- pennies

## Procedure

1. When you begin your experiment, your teacher will tape one end of the fishing line to the ceiling.

2. Use a pencil to poke a small hole in each side of the cup near the top. Place a 15 cm piece of string through each hole, and tape down the ends inside.

3. Inflate the balloon, and use the twist tie to hold it closed.

4. Tape the free ends of the strings to the sides of the balloon near the bottom. The cup should hang below the balloon. Your model rocket should look like a hot-air balloon.

5. Thread the fishing line that is hanging from the ceiling through the straw. Tape the balloon securely to the straw.

6. Tape the loose end of the fishing line to the floor.

## Collect Data

7. Untie the twist tie while holding the end of the balloon closed. When you are ready, release the end of the balloon. Mark and record the maximum height of the rocket.

8. Repeat the procedure, adding a penny to the cup each time until your rocket cannot lift any more pennies.

## Analysis

9. In a paragraph, describe how all three of Newton's laws influenced the flight of your rocket.

10. Draw a diagram of your rocket. Label the action and reaction forces.

### Going Further

Brainstorm ways to modify your rocket so that it will carry the most pennies to the maximum height. Select the best design. When your teacher has approved all the designs, each team will build and launch their rocket. Which variable did you modify? How did this variable affect your rocket's flight?

# Quite a Reaction

Catapults have been used for centuries to throw objects great distances. You may already be familiar with catapults after doing the marshmallow catapult lab. According to Newton's third law of motion (whenever one object exerts a force on a second object, the second object exerts an equal and opposite force on the first), when an object is launched, something must also happen to the catapult. In this activity, you will build a kind of catapult that will allow you to observe the effects of Newton's third law of motion and the law of conservation of momentum.

## Materials

- glue
- 10 cm × 15 cm rectangles of cardboard (3)
- 3 pushpins
- string
- rubber band
- 6 plastic straws
- marble
- scissors
- meterstick

## Conduct an Experiment

1. Glue the cardboard rectangles together to make a stack of three.

2. Push two of the pushpins into the cardboard stack near the corners at one end, as shown below. These will be the anchors for the rubber band.

3. Make a small loop of string.

4. Put the rubber band through the loop of string, and then place the rubber band over the two pushpin anchors. The rubber band should be stretched between the two anchors with the string loop in the middle.

5. Pull the string loop toward the end of the cardboard stack opposite the end with the anchors, and fasten the loop in place with the third pushpin.

6. Place the six straws about 1 cm apart on a tabletop or on the floor. Then carefully center the catapult on top of the straws.

7. Put the marble in the closed end of the V formed by the rubber band.

8. Use scissors to cut the string holding the rubber band, and observe what happens. (Be careful not to let the scissors touch the cardboard catapult when you cut the string.)

9. Reset the catapult with a new piece of string. Try launching the marble several times to be sure that you have observed everything that happens during a launch. Record all your observations in your ScienceLog.

## Analyze the Results

10. Which has more mass, the marble or the catapult?

11. What happened to the catapult when the marble was launched?

12. How far did the marble fly before it landed?

13. Did the catapult move as far as the marble did?

## Draw Conclusions

14. Explain why the catapult moved backward.

15. If the forces that made the marble and the catapult move apart are equal, why didn't the marble and the catapult move apart the same distance? (Hint: The fact that the marble can roll after it lands is not the answer.)

16. The momentum of an object depends on the mass and velocity of the object. What is the momentum of the marble before it is launched? What is the momentum of the catapult? Explain your answers.

17. Using the law of conservation of momentum, explain why the marble and the catapult move in opposite directions after the launch.

### Going Further

How would you modify the catapult if you wanted to keep it from moving backward as far as it did? (It still has to rest on the straws.) Using items that you can find in the classroom, design a catapult that will move backward less than the original design.

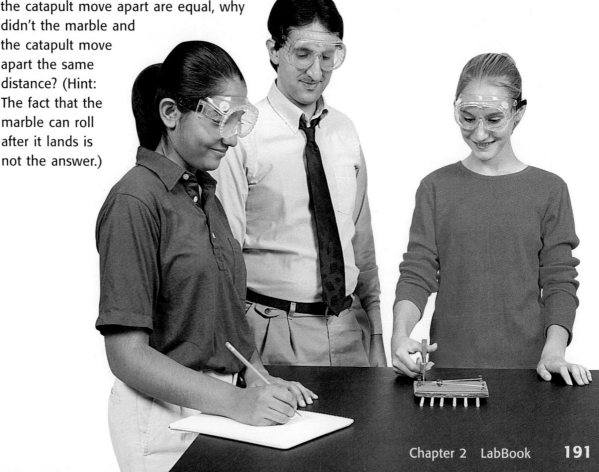

# Using Scientific Methods

## Density Diver

Crew members of a submarine can control the submarine's density underwater by allowing water to flow into and out of special tanks. These changes in density affect the submarine's position in the water. In this lab, you'll control a "density diver" to learn for yourself how the density of an object affects its position in a fluid.

### Materials

- 2 L plastic bottle with screw-on cap
- water
- medicine dropper

### Form a Hypothesis

1. How does the density of an object determine whether the object floats, sinks, or maintains its position in a fluid? Write your hypothesis in your ScienceLog.

### Test the Hypothesis

2. Completely fill the 2 L plastic bottle with water.

3. Fill the diver (medicine dropper) approximately halfway with water, and place it in the bottle. The diver should float with only part of the rubber bulb above the surface of the water. If the diver floats too high, carefully remove it from the bottle and add a small amount of water to the diver. Place the diver back in the bottle. If you add too much water and the diver sinks, empty out the bottle and diver and go back to step 2.

4. Put the cap on the bottle tightly so that no water leaks out.

5. Apply various pressures to the bottle. Carefully watch the water level inside the diver as you squeeze and release the bottle. Record what happens in your ScienceLog.

6. Try to make the diver rise, sink, or stop at any level. Record your technique and your results.

### Analyze the Results

7. How do the changes inside the diver affect its position in the surrounding fluid?

8. What is the relationship between the water level inside the diver and the diver's density? Explain.

### Draw Conclusions

9. What relationship did you observe between the diver's density and the diver's position in the fluid?

10. Explain how your density diver is like a submarine.

11. Explain how pressure on the bottle is related to the diver's density. Be sure to include Pascal's principle in your explanation.

12. What was the variable in this experiment? What factors were controlled?

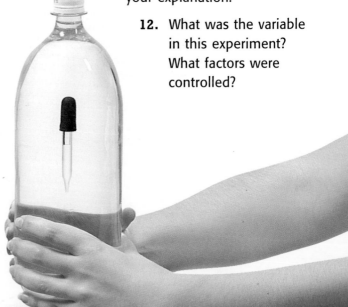

# Out the Spouts

Although many undersea vessels explore the ocean depths, few are able to descend to the deepest parts of the ocean. The reason? Water exerts tremendous pressure at these depths. In this lab you'll witness one of the effects of this pressure firsthand.

## Materials

- pencil
- cardboard milk container
- masking tape
- water
- large plastic tray or sink

## Procedure

1. With a sharp pencil, punch a small hole in the center of one side of an empty cardboard milk container.

2. Make another hole 4 cm above the center hole. Then make another hole 8 cm above the center hole.

3. With a single piece of masking tape, carefully cover the holes. Leave a little tape free at the bottom for easy removal.

4. Fill the container with water, and place it in a large plastic tray or sink.

5. Quickly pull the tape off the container.

6. Record your observations in your ScienceLog.

## Analysis

7. Did the same thing happen at each hole after you removed the tape? If not, what do you think caused the different results? Record your answers in your ScienceLog.

# Inclined to Move

In this lab, you will examine a simple machine—an inclined plane. Your task is to compare the work done with and without the inclined plane and to analyze the effects of friction.

## Collect Data

1. Copy the table below into your ScienceLog.

2. Tie a piece of string around a book. Attach the spring scale to the string. Use the spring scale to slowly lift the book to a height of 50 cm. Record the output force (the force needed to lift the book). The output force is constant throughout the lab.

3. Use the board and blocks to make a ramp 10 cm high at the highest point. Measure and record the ramp length.

4. Keeping the spring scale parallel to the ramp, as shown below, slowly raise the book. Record the input force (the force needed to pull the book up the ramp).

5. Increase the height of the ramp by 10 cm. Repeat step 4. Repeat this step for each ramp height up to 50 cm.

## Analyze the Results

6. The *real* work done includes the work done to overcome friction. Calculate the real work at each height by multiplying the ramp length (converted to meters) by the input force. Graph your results, plotting work (*y*-axis) versus height (*x*-axis).

7. The *ideal* work is the work you would do if there were no friction. Calculate the ideal work at each height by multiplying the ramp height (m) by the output force. Plot the data on your graph.

## Materials

- string
- small book
- spring scale
- meterstick
- wooden board
- blocks
- graph paper

| Force vs. Height | | | |
|---|---|---|---|
| Ramp height (cm) | Output force (N) | Ramp length (cm) | Input force (N) |
| 10 | | | |
| 20 | | | |
| 30 | | | |
| 40 | | | |
| 50 | | | |

DO NOT WRITE IN BOOK

## Draw Conclusions

8. Does it require more or less force and work to raise the book using the ramp? Explain, using your calculations and graphs.

9. What is the relationship between the height of the inclined plane and the input force?

10. Write a statement that summarizes why the slopes of the two graphs are different.

# Building Machines

You are surrounded by machines. Some are simple machines, such as ramps for wheelchair access to a building. Others are compound machines, like elevators and escalators, that are made of two or more simple machines. In this lab, you will design and build several simple machines and a compound machine.

## Procedure

1. Use the listed materials to build a model of each simple machine: inclined plane, lever, wheel and axle, pulley, screw, and wedge. Describe and draw each model in your ScienceLog.

2. In your ScienceLog, design a compound machine using the materials listed. You may design a machine that already exists, or you may invent your own machine—be creative!

3. After your teacher approves your design, build your compound machine.

## Analysis

4. List a possible use for each of your simple machines.

5. Compare your simple machines with those created by your classmates.

6. How many simple machines are in your compound machine? List them.

7. Compare your compound machine with those created by your classmates.

8. What is a possible use for your compound machine? Why did you design it as you did?

9. A compound machine is listed in the Materials list. What is it?

## Materials

- bottle caps
- cardboard
- craft sticks
- empty thread spools
- glue
- modeling clay
- paper
- pencils
- rubber bands
- scissors
- shoe boxes
- stones
- straws
- string
- tape
- other materials available in your classroom that are approved by your teacher

## Going Further

Design a compound machine that has all the simple machines in it. Explain what the machine will do and how it will make work easier. With your teacher's approval, build your machine.

# Wheeling and Dealing

A wheel and axle is one type of simple machine. A crank handle, such as that used in pencil sharpeners, ice-cream makers, and water wells is one kind of wheel and axle. In this lab, you will use a crank handle to find out how a wheel and axle helps you do work. You will also determine what effect the length of the handle has on the operation of the machine.

## Materials

- wheel and axle assembly
- meterstick
- large mass
- spring scale
- handles
- 0.5 m string
- 2 C-clamps

## Procedure

1. Copy Table 1 into your ScienceLog.

2. Measure the radius (in meters) of the large dowel in the wheel and axle assembly. Record this in Table 1 as the axle radius, which remains constant throughout the lab. (Hint: Measure the diameter and divide by two.)

3. Using the spring scale, measure the weight of the large mass. Record this in Table 1 as the output force, which remains constant throughout the lab.

4. Use two C-clamps to secure the wheel and axle assembly to the table, as shown at right.

## Collect Data

5. Measure the length (in meters) of handle 1. Record this as a wheel radius in Table 1.

6. Insert the handle into the hole in the axle. Attach one end of the string to the large mass and the other end to the screw in the axle. The mass should hang down and the handle should turn freely.

7. Turn the handle to lift the mass off the floor. Hold the spring scale upside down, and attach it to the end of the handle. Measure the force (in newtons) as the handle pulls up on the spring scale. Record this as the input force.

| Table 1 Data Collection | | | | |
|---|---|---|---|---|
| Handle | Axle radius (m) | Output force (N) | Wheel radius (m) | Input force (N) |
| 1 | | | | |
| 2 | | | | |
| 3 | | DO NOT WRITE IN BOOK | | |
| 4 | | | | |

8. Remove the spring scale, and lower the mass to the floor. Remove the handle.

9. Repeat steps 5 through 8 with the other three handles. Record all data in Table 1.

## Analyze the Results

10. Copy Table 2 into your ScienceLog.

| Table 2 Calculations | | | | | | |
|---|---|---|---|---|---|---|
| Handle | Axle distance (m) | Wheel distance (m) | Work input (J) | Work output (J) | Mechanical efficiency (%) | Mechanical advantage |
| 1 | | | | | | |
| 2 | | | | | | |
| 3 | | | | | | |
| 4 | | | | | | |

DO NOT WRITE IN BOOK

11. Calculate the following for each handle using the equations given. Record your answers in Table 2.

   a. Distance axle rotates =
      $2 \times \pi \times$ axle radius

      Distance wheel rotates =
      $2 \times \pi \times$ wheel radius

      (Use 3.14 for the value of $\pi$.)

   b. Work input =
      input force $\times$ wheel distance

      Work output =
      output force $\times$ axle distance

   c. Mechanical efficiency =
      $\dfrac{\text{work output}}{\text{work input}} \times 100$

   d. Mechanical advantage =
      $\dfrac{\text{wheel radius}}{\text{axle radius}}$

## Draw Conclusions

12. What happens to work output and work input as the handle length increases? Why?

13. What happens to mechanical efficiency as the handle length increases? Why?

14. What happens to mechanical advantage as the handle length increases? Why?

15. What will happen to mechanical advantage if the handle length is kept constant and the axle radius gets larger?

16. What factors were controlled in this experiment? What was the variable?

# Energy of a Pendulum

A pendulum clock is a compound machine that uses stored energy to do work. A spring stores energy, and with each swing of the pendulum, some of that stored energy is used to move the hands of the clock. In this lab you will take a close look at the energy conversions that occur as a pendulum swings.

## Materials

- 1 m of string
- 100 g hooked mass
- marker
- meterstick

## Collect Data

1. Make a pendulum by tying the string around the hook of the mass. Use the marker and the meterstick to mark points on the string that are 50 cm, 70 cm, and 90 cm away from the mass.

2. Hold the string at the 50 cm mark. Gently pull the mass to the side, and release it without pushing it. Observe at least 10 swings of the pendulum.

3. In your ScienceLog, record your observations. Be sure to note how fast and how high the pendulum swings.

4. Repeat steps 2 and 3 while holding the string at the 70 cm mark and again while holding the string at the 90 cm mark.

## Analyze the Results

5. In your ScienceLog, list similarities and differences in the motion of the pendulum during all three trials.

6. At which point (or points) of the swing was the pendulum moving the slowest? the fastest?

## Draw Conclusions

7. In each trial, at which point (or points) of the swing did the pendulum have the greatest potential energy? the smallest potential energy? (Hint: Think about your answers to question 6.)

8. At which point (or points) of the swing did the pendulum have the greatest kinetic energy? the smallest kinetic energy? Explain your answers.

9. Describe the relationship between the pendulum's potential energy and its kinetic energy on its way down. Explain.

10. What improvements might reduce the amount of energy used to overcome friction so that the pendulum would swing for a longer period of time?

# Eggstremely Fragile

All moving objects have kinetic energy. The faster an object is moving, the more kinetic energy it has. When a falling object hits the floor, the law of conservation of energy requires that the energy be transferred to another object or changed into another form of energy.

When an unprotected egg hits the ground from a height of 1 m, most of the kinetic energy of the falling egg is transferred to the pieces of the shell—with messy results. In this lab you will design a protection system for an egg.

## Materials

- raw egg
- empty half-pint milk carton
- assorted materials provided by your teacher

## Conduct an Experiment

1. Using the materials provided by your teacher, design a protection system that will prevent the egg from breaking when it is dropped from heights of 1, 2, and 3 m. Keep the following points in mind while developing your egg-protection system:

   a. The egg and its protection system must fit inside the closed milk carton. (Note: The milk carton will not be dropped with the egg.)

   b. The protective materials don't have to be soft.

   c. The protective materials can surround the egg or can be attached to the egg at various points.

2. In your ScienceLog, explain why you chose your materials.

3. You will perform the three trials at a time and location specified by your teacher. Record your results for each trial in your ScienceLog.

## Analyze the Results

4. Did your egg survive all three trials? If it did not, why did your egg-protection system fail? If your egg did survive, what features of your egg-protecting system transferred or absorbed the energy?

## Draw Conclusions

5. How do egg cartons like those you find in a grocery store protect eggs from mishandling?

# Save the Cube!

The biggest enemy of an ice cube is the transfer of thermal energy—heat. Energy can be transferred to an ice cube in three ways: conduction (the transfer of energy through direct contact), convection (the transfer of energy by the movement of a liquid or gas), and radiation (the transfer of energy through matter or space). Your challenge in this activity is to design a way to protect an ice cube as much as possible from all three types of energy transfer.

## Materials

- small plastic bag
- ice cube
- assorted materials provided by your teacher
- empty half-pint milk carton
- metric balance
- small plastic or paper cup

## Procedure

1. Follow these guidelines: Use a plastic bag to hold the ice cube and any water from its melting. You may use any of the materials to protect the ice cube. The ice cube, bag, and protection must all fit inside the milk carton.

2. Describe your proposed design in your ScienceLog. Explain how your design protects against each type of energy transfer.

3. Find the mass of the empty cup, and record it in your ScienceLog. Then find and record the mass of an empty plastic bag.

4. Place an ice cube in the bag. Quickly find and record their mass together.

5. Quickly wrap the bag (and the ice cube inside) in its protection. Remember that the package must fit in the milk carton.

6. Place your protected ice cube in the "thermal zone" set up by your teacher. After 10 minutes, remove the package from the zone and remove the protective material from the plastic bag and ice cube.

7. Open the bag. Pour any water into the cup. Find and record the mass of the cup and water together.

8. Find and record the mass of the water by subtracting the mass of the empty cup from the mass of the cup and water.

9. Use the same method to find and record the mass of the ice cube.

10. Find the percentage of the ice cube that melted using the following equation:

$$\% \text{ melted} = \frac{\text{mass of water}}{\text{mass of ice cube}} \times 100$$

11. Record this percentage in your ScienceLog and on the board.

## Analysis

12. Compared with other designs in your class, how well did your design protect against each type of energy transfer? How could you improve your design?

13. Why is a white plastic-foam cooler so useful for keeping ice frozen?

# Counting Calories

Energy transferred by heat is often expressed in units called calories. In this lab, you will build a model of a device called a calorimeter. Scientists often use calorimeters to measure the amount of energy that can be transferred by a substance. In this experiment, you will construct your own calorimeter and test it by measuring the energy released by a hot penny.

## Materials

- small plastic-foam cup with lid
- thermometer
- large plastic-foam cup
- water
- 100 mL graduated cylinder
- tongs
- heat source
- penny
- stopwatch

## Procedure

1. Copy the table below into your ScienceLog.

| Data Collection Table | | | | | | | | | |
|---|---|---|---|---|---|---|---|---|---|
| **Seconds** | 0 | 15 | 30 | 45 | 60 | 75 | 90 | 105 | 120 |
| **Water temp. (°C)** | | | | | | | | | |

DO NOT WRITE IN BOOK

2. Place the lid on the small plastic-foam cup, and insert a thermometer through the hole in the top of the lid. (The thermometer should not touch the bottom of the cup.) Place the small cup inside the large cup to complete the calorimeter.

3. Remove the lid from the small cup, and add 50 mL of room-temperature water to the cup. Measure the water's temperature, and record the value in the first column (0 seconds) of the table.

4. Using tongs, heat the penny carefully. Add the penny to the water in the small cup, and replace the lid. Start your stopwatch.

5. Every 15 seconds, measure and record the temperature. Gently swirl the large cup to stir the water, and continue recording temperatures for 2 minutes (120 seconds).

## Analysis

6. What was the total temperature change of the water after 2 minutes?

7. The number of calories absorbed by the water is the mass of the water (in grams) multiplied by the temperature change (in °C) of the water. How many calories were absorbed by the water? (Hint: 1 mL of water = 1 g of water)

8. In terms of heat, explain where the calories to change the water temperature came from.

# Concept Mapping: A Way to Bring Ideas Together

## What Is a Concept Map?

Have you ever tried to tell someone about a book or a chapter you've just read and found that you can remember only a few isolated words and ideas? Or maybe you've memorized facts for a test and then weeks later discovered you're not even sure what topics those facts covered.

In both cases, you may have understood the ideas or concepts by themselves but not in relation to one another. If you could somehow link the ideas together, you would probably understand them better and remember them longer. This is something a concept map can help you do. A concept map is a way to see how ideas or concepts fit together. It can help you see the "big picture."

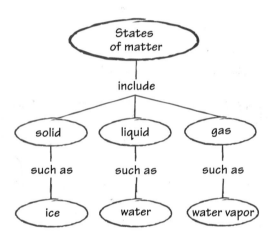

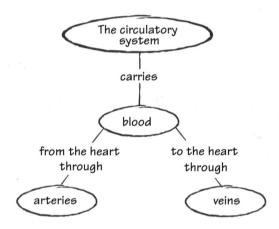

## How to Make a Concept Map

❶ **Make a list of the main ideas or concepts.**

It might help to write each concept on its own slip of paper. This will make it easier to rearrange the concepts as many times as necessary to make sense of how the concepts are connected. After you've made a few concept maps this way, you can go directly from writing your list to actually making the map.

❷ **Arrange the concepts in order from the most general to the most specific.**

Put the most general concept at the top and circle it. Ask yourself, "How does this concept relate to the remaining concepts?" As you see the relationships, arrange the concepts in order from general to specific.

❸ **Connect the related concepts with lines.**

❹ **On each line, write an action word or short phrase that shows how the concepts are related.**

Look at the concept maps on this page, and then see if you can make one for the following terms:

**plants, water, photosynthesis, carbon dioxide, sun's energy**

One possible answer is provided at right, but don't look at it until you try the concept map yourself.

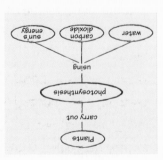

# SI Measurement

The International System of Units, or SI, is the standard system of measurement used by many scientists. Using the same standards of measurement makes it easier for scientists to communicate with one another.

SI works by combining prefixes and base units. Each base unit can be used with different prefixes to define smaller and larger quantities. The table below lists common SI prefixes.

| SI Prefixes | | | |
|---|---|---|---|
| Prefix | Abbreviation | Factor | Example |
| kilo- | k | 1,000 | kilogram, 1 kg = 1,000 g |
| hecto- | h | 100 | hectoliter, 1 hL = 100 L |
| deka- | da | 10 | dekameter, 1 dam = 10 m |
| | | 1 | meter, liter |
| deci- | d | 0.1 | decigram, 1 dg = 0.1 g |
| centi- | c | 0.01 | centimeter, 1 cm = 0.01 m |
| milli- | m | 0.001 | milliliter, 1 mL = 0.001 L |
| micro- | µ | 0.000 001 | micrometer, 1 µm = 0.000 001 m |

| SI Conversion Table | | |
|---|---|---|
| SI units | From SI to English | From English to SI |
| **Length** | | |
| kilometer (km) = 1,000 m | 1 km = 0.621 mi | 1 mi = 1.609 km |
| meter (m) = 100 cm | 1 m = 3.281 ft | 1 ft = 0.305 m |
| centimeter (cm) = 0.01 m | 1 cm = 0.394 in. | 1 in. = 2.540 cm |
| millimeter (mm) = 0.001 m | 1 mm = 0.039 in. | |
| micrometer (µm) = 0.000 001 m | | |
| nanometer (nm) = 0.000 000 001 m | | |
| **Area** | | |
| square kilometer ($km^2$) = 100 hectares | 1 $km^2$ = 0.386 $mi^2$ | 1 $mi^2$ = 2.590 $km^2$ |
| hectare (ha) = 10,000 $m^2$ | 1 ha = 2.471 acres | 1 acre = 0.405 ha |
| square meter ($m^2$) = 10,000 $cm^2$ | 1 $m^2$ = 10.765 $ft^2$ | 1 $ft^2$ = 0.093 $m^2$ |
| square centimeter ($cm^2$) = 100 $mm^2$ | 1 $cm^2$ = 0.155 $in.^2$ | 1 $in.^2$ = 6.452 $cm^2$ |
| **Volume** | | |
| liter (L) = 1,000 mL = 1 $dm^3$ | 1 L = 1.057 fl qt | 1 fl qt = 0.946 L |
| milliliter (mL) = 0.001 L = 1 $cm^3$ | 1 mL = 0.034 fl oz | 1 fl oz = 29.575 mL |
| microliter (µL) = 0.000 001 L | | |
| **Mass** | | |
| kilogram (kg) = 1,000 g | 1 kg = 2.205 lb | 1 lb = 0.454 kg |
| gram (g) = 1,000 mg | 1 g = 0.035 oz | 1 oz = 28.349 g |
| milligram (mg) = 0.001 g | | |
| microgram (µg) = 0.000 001 g | | |

# Temperature Scales

Temperature can be expressed using three different scales: Fahrenheit, Celsius, and Kelvin. The SI unit for temperature is the kelvin (K).

Although 0 K is much colder than 0°C, a change of 1 K is equal to a change of 1°C.

## Three Temperature Scales

| | Fahrenheit | Celsius | Kelvin |
|---|---|---|---|
| Water boils | 212° | 100° | 373 |
| Body temperature | 98.6° | 37° | 310 |
| Room temperature | 68° | 20° | 293 |
| Water freezes | 32° | 0° | 273 |

## Temperature Conversions Table

| To convert | Use this equation: | Example |
|---|---|---|
| Celsius to Fahrenheit °C ⟶ °F | $°F = \left(\dfrac{9}{5} \times °C\right) + 32$ | Convert 45°C to °F. $°F = \left(\dfrac{9}{5} \times 45°C\right) + 32 = 113°F$ |
| Fahrenheit to Celsius °F ⟶ °C | $°C = \dfrac{5}{9} \times (°F - 32)$ | Convert 68°F to °C. $°C = \dfrac{5}{9} \times (68°F - 32) = 20°C$ |
| Celsius to Kelvin °C ⟶ K | $K = °C + 273$ | Convert 45°C to K. $K = 45°C + 273 = 318\ K$ |
| Kelvin to Celsius K ⟶ °C | $°C = K - 273$ | Convert 32 K to °C. $°C = 32\ K - 273 = -241°C$ |

# Measuring Skills

## Using a Graduated Cylinder

When using a graduated cylinder to measure volume, keep the following procedures in mind:

**1** Make sure the cylinder is on a flat, level surface.

**2** Move your head so that your eye is level with the surface of the liquid.

**3** Read the mark closest to the liquid level. On glass graduated cylinders, read the mark closest to the center of the curve in the liquid's surface.

## Using a Meterstick or Metric Ruler

When using a meterstick or metric ruler to measure length, keep the following procedures in mind:

**1** Place the ruler firmly against the object you are measuring.

**2** Align one edge of the object exactly with the zero end of the ruler.

**3** Look at the other edge of the object to see which of the marks on the ruler is closest to that edge. **Note:** Each small slash between the centimeters represents a millimeter, which is one-tenth of a centimeter.

## Using a Triple-Beam Balance

When using a triple-beam balance to measure mass, keep the following procedures in mind:

**1** Make sure the balance is on a level surface.

**2** Place all of the countermasses at zero. Adjust the balancing knob until the pointer rests at zero.

**3** Place the object you wish to measure on the pan. **Caution:** Do not place hot objects or chemicals directly on the balance pan.

**4** Move the largest countermass along the beam to the right until it is at the last notch that does not tip the balance. Follow the same procedure with the next-largest countermass. Then move the smallest countermass until the pointer rests at zero.

**5** Add the readings from the three beams together to determine the mass of the object.

**6** When determining the mass of crystals or powders, use a piece of filter paper. First find the mass of the paper. Then add the crystals or powder to the paper and re-measure. The actual mass of the crystals or powder is the total mass minus the mass of the paper. When finding the mass of liquids, first find the mass of the empty container. Then find the mass of the liquid and container together. The mass of the liquid is the total mass minus the mass of the container.

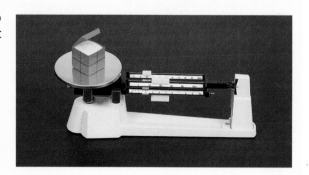

# Scientific Method

The series of steps that scientists use to answer questions and solve problems is often called the **scientific method.** The scientific method is not a rigid procedure. Scientists may use all of the steps or just some of the steps of the scientific method. They may even repeat some of the steps. The goal of the scientific method is to come up with reliable answers and solutions.

## Six Steps of the Scientific Method

**1** **Ask a Question** Good questions come from careful **observations.** You make observations by using your senses to gather information. Sometimes you may use instruments, such as microscopes and telescopes, to extend the range of your senses. As you observe the natural world, you will discover that you have many more questions than answers. These questions drive the scientific method.

Questions beginning with *what, why, how,* and *when* are very important in focusing an investigation, and they often lead to a hypothesis. (You will learn what a hypothesis is in the next step.) Here is an example of a question that could lead to further investigation.

**Question:** How does acid rain affect plant growth?

**2** **Form a Hypothesis** After you come up with a question, you need to turn the question into a **hypothesis.** A hypothesis is a clear statement of what you expect the answer to your question to be. Your hypothesis will represent your best "educated guess" based on your observations and what you already know. A good hypothesis is testable. If observations and information cannot be gathered or if an experiment cannot be designed to test your hypothesis, it is untestable, and the investigation can go no further.

Here is a hypothesis that could be formed from the question, "How does acid rain affect plant growth?"

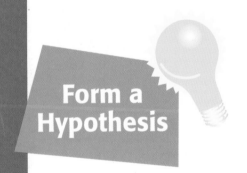

**Hypothesis:** Acid rain causes plants to grow more slowly.

Notice that the hypothesis provides some specifics that lead to methods of testing. The hypothesis can also lead to predictions. A **prediction** is what you think will be the outcome of your experiment or data collection. Predictions are usually stated in an "if . . . then" format. For example, **if** meat is kept at room temperature, **then** it will spoil faster than meat kept in the refrigerator. More than one prediction can be made for a single hypothesis. Here is a sample prediction for the hypothesis that acid rain causes plants to grow more slowly.

**Prediction:** If a plant is watered with only acid rain (which has a pH of 4), then the plant will grow at half its normal rate.

**3** **Test the Hypothesis** After you have formed a hypothesis and made a prediction, you should test your hypothesis. There are different ways to do this. Perhaps the most familiar way is to conduct a **controlled experiment.** A controlled experiment tests only one factor at a time. A controlled experiment has a **control group** and one or more **experimental groups.** All the factors for the control and experimental groups are the same except for one factor, which is called the **variable.** By changing only one factor, you can see the results of just that one change.

Sometimes, the nature of an investigation makes a controlled experiment impossible. For example, dinosaurs have been extinct for millions of years, and the Earth's core is surrounded by thousands of meters of rock. It would be difficult, if not impossible, to conduct controlled experiments on such things. Under such circumstances, a hypothesis may be tested by making detailed observations. Taking measurements is one way of making observations.

**Test the Hypothesis**

**4** **Analyze the Results** After you have completed your experiments, made your observations, and collected your data, you must analyze all the information you have gathered. Tables and graphs are often used in this step to organize the data.

**Analyze the Results**

**5** **Draw Conclusions** Based on the analysis of your data, you should conclude whether or not your results support your hypothesis. If your hypothesis is supported, you (or others) might want to repeat the observations or experiments to verify your results. If your hypothesis is not supported by the data, you may have to check your procedure for errors. You may even have to reject your hypothesis and make a new one. If you cannot draw a conclusion from your results, you may have to try the investigation again or carry out further observations or experiments.

**Draw Conclusions**

**Do they support your hypothesis?**

**No**

**Yes**

**6** **Communicate Results** After any scientific investigation, you should report your results. By doing a written or oral report, you let others know what you have learned. They may want to repeat your investigation to see if they get the same results. Your report may even lead to another question, which in turn may lead to another investigation.

**Communicate Results**

## Scientific Method in Action

The scientific method is not a "straight line" of steps. It contains loops in which several steps may be repeated over and over again, while others may not be necessary. For example, sometimes scientists will find that testing one hypothesis raises new questions and new hypotheses to be tested. And sometimes, testing the hypothesis leads directly to a conclusion. Furthermore, the steps in the scientific method are not always used in the same order. Follow the steps in the diagram below, and see how many different directions the scientific method can take you.

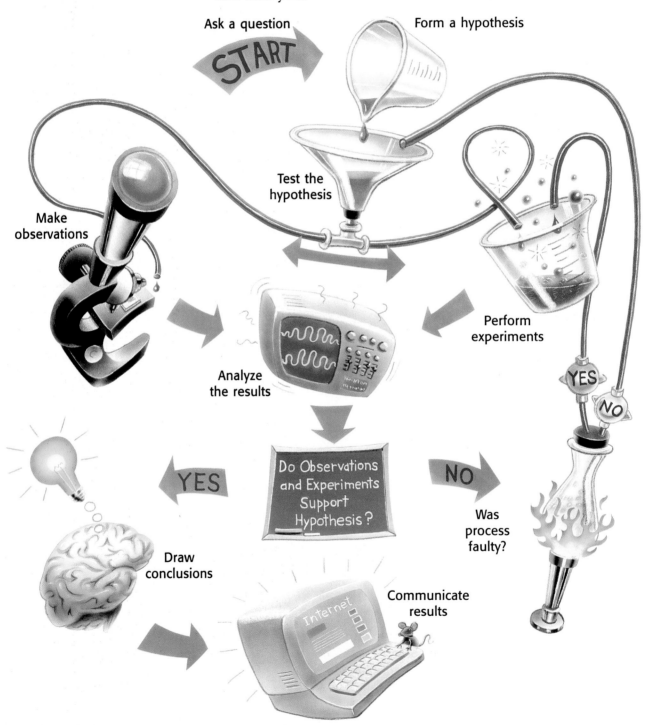

Ask a question

START

Form a hypothesis

Test the hypothesis

Make observations

Perform experiments

Analyze the results

YES

NO

YES

Do Observations and Experiments Support Hypothesis?

NO

Draw conclusions

Was process faulty?

Communicate results

Internet

# Making Charts and Graphs

## Circle Graphs

A circle graph, or pie chart, shows how each group of data relates to all of the data. Each part of the circle represents a category of the data. The entire circle represents all of the data. For example, a biologist studying a hardwood forest in Wisconsin found that there were five different types of trees. The data table at right summarizes the biologist's findings.

| Wisconsin Hardwood Trees | |
|---|---|
| **Type of tree** | **Number found** |
| Oak | 600 |
| Maple | 750 |
| Beech | 300 |
| Birch | 1,200 |
| Hickory | 150 |
| Total | 3,000 |

## How to Make a Circle Graph

**1** In order to make a circle graph of this data, first find the percentage of each type of tree. To do this, divide the number of individual trees by the total number of trees and multiply by 100.

$$\frac{600 \text{ oak}}{3,000 \text{ trees}} \times 100 = 20\%$$

$$\frac{750 \text{ maple}}{3,000 \text{ trees}} \times 100 = 25\%$$

$$\frac{300 \text{ beech}}{3,000 \text{ trees}} \times 100 = 10\%$$

$$\frac{1,200 \text{ birch}}{3,000 \text{ trees}} \times 100 = 40\%$$

$$\frac{150 \text{ hickory}}{3,000 \text{ trees}} \times 100 = 5\%$$

**2** Now determine the size of the pie shapes that make up the chart. Do this by multiplying each percentage by 360°. Remember that a circle contains 360°.

$20\% \times 360° = 72°$    $25\% \times 360° = 90°$
$10\% \times 360° = 36°$    $40\% \times 360° = 144°$
$5\% \times 360° = 18°$

**3** Then check that the sum of the percentages is 100 and the sum of the degrees is 360.

$20\% + 25\% + 10\% + 40\% + 5\% = 100\%$
$72° + 90° + 36° + 144° + 18° = 360°$

**4** Use a compass to draw a circle and mark its center.

**5** Then use a protractor to draw angles of 72°, 90°, 36°, 144°, and 18° in the circle.

**6** Finally, label each part of the graph, and choose an appropriate title.

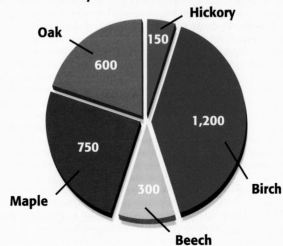

**A Community of Wisconsin Hardwood Trees**

| Population of Appleton, 1900–2000 | |
|---|---|
| Year | Population |
| 1900 | 1,800 |
| 1920 | 2,500 |
| 1940 | 3,200 |
| 1960 | 3,900 |
| 1980 | 4,600 |
| 2000 | 5,300 |

## Line Graphs

Line graphs are most often used to demonstrate continuous change. For example, Mr. Smith's science class analyzed the population records for their hometown, Appleton, between 1900 and 2000. Examine the data at left.

Because the year and the population change, they are the *variables*. The population is determined by, or dependent on, the year. Therefore, the population is called the **dependent variable**, and the year is called the **independent variable**. Each set of data is called a **data pair**. To prepare a line graph, data pairs must first be organized in a table like the one at left.

## How to Make a Line Graph

❶ Place the independent variable along the horizontal (*x*) axis. Place the dependent variable along the vertical (*y*) axis.

❷ Label the *x*-axis "Year" and the *y*-axis "Population." Look at your largest and smallest values for the population. Determine a scale for the *y*-axis that will provide enough space to show these values. You must use the same scale for the entire length of the axis. Find an appropriate scale for the *x*-axis too.

❸ Choose reasonable starting points for each axis.

❹ Plot the data pairs as accurately as possible.

❺ Choose a title that accurately represents the data.

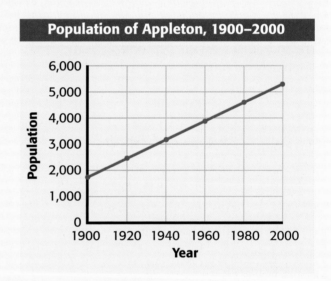

Population of Appleton, 1900–2000

## How to Determine Slope

Slope is the ratio of the change in the *y*-axis to the change in the *x*-axis, or "rise over run."

❶ Choose two points on the line graph. For example, the population of Appleton in 2000 was 5,300 people. Therefore, you can define point *a* as (2000, 5,300). In 1900, the population was 1,800 people. Define point *b* as (1900, 1,800).

❷ Find the change in the *y*-axis.
(*y* at point *a*) − (*y* at point *b*)
5,300 people − 1,800 people = 3,500 people

❸ Find the change in the *x*-axis.
(*x* at point *a*) − (*x* at point *b*)
2000 − 1900 = 100 years

❹ Calculate the slope of the graph by dividing the change in *y* by the change in *x*.

$$\text{slope} = \frac{\text{change in } y}{\text{change in } x}$$

$$\text{slope} = \frac{3{,}500 \text{ people}}{100 \text{ years}}$$

$$\text{slope} = 35 \text{ people per year}$$

In this example, the population in Appleton increased by a fixed amount each year. The graph of this data is a straight line. Therefore, the relationship is **linear.** When the graph of a set of data is not a straight line, the relationship is **nonlinear.**

## Using Algebra to Determine Slope

The equation in step 4 may also be arranged to be:

$$y = kx$$

where $y$ represents the change in the $y$-axis, $k$ represents the slope, and $x$ represents the change in the $x$-axis.

$$\text{slope} = \frac{\text{change in } y}{\text{change in } x}$$

$$k = \frac{y}{x}$$

$$k \times x = \frac{y \times x}{x}$$

$$kx = y$$

## Bar Graphs

Bar graphs are used to demonstrate change that is not continuous. These graphs can be used to indicate trends when the data are taken over a long period of time. A meteorologist gathered the precipitation records at right for Hartford, Connecticut, for April 1–15, 1996, and used a bar graph to represent the data.

### Precipitation in Hartford, Connecticut April 1–15, 1996

| Date | Precipitation (cm) | Date | Precipitation (cm) |
|------|--------------------|------|--------------------|
| April 1 | 0.5 | April 9 | 0.25 |
| April 2 | 1.25 | April 10 | 0.0 |
| April 3 | 0.0 | April 11 | 1.0 |
| April 4 | 0.0 | April 12 | 0.0 |
| April 5 | 0.0 | April 13 | 0.25 |
| April 6 | 0.0 | April 14 | 0.0 |
| April 7 | 0.0 | April 15 | 6.50 |
| April 8 | 1.75 | | |

## How to Make a Bar Graph

**1** Use an appropriate scale and a reasonable starting point for each axis.

**2** Label the axes, and plot the data.

**3** Choose a title that accurately represents the data.

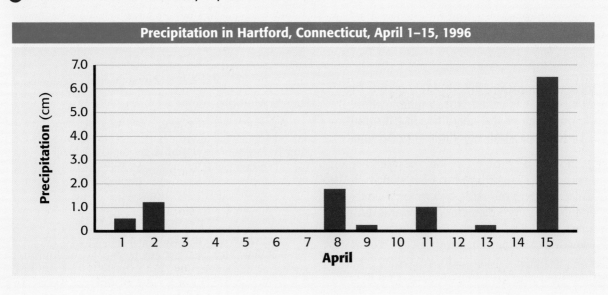

Precipitation in Hartford, Connecticut, April 1–15, 1996

# Math Refresher

Science requires an understanding of many math concepts. The following pages will help you review some important math skills.

## Averages

An **average**, or **mean**, simplifies a list of numbers into a single number that *approximates* their value.

> **Example:** Find the average of the following set of numbers: 5, 4, 7, and 8.

**Step 1:** Find the sum.

$$5 + 4 + 7 + 8 = 24$$

**Step 2:** Divide the sum by the amount of numbers in your set. Because there are four numbers in this example, divide the sum by 4.

$$\frac{24}{4} = 6$$

The average, or mean, is **6.**

## Ratios

A **ratio** is a comparison between numbers, and it is usually written as a fraction.

> **Example:** Find the ratio of thermometers to students if you have 36 thermometers and 48 students in your class.

**Step 1:** Make the ratio.

$$\frac{36 \text{ thermometers}}{48 \text{ students}}$$

**Step 2:** Reduce the fraction to its simplest form.

$$\frac{36}{48} = \frac{36 \div 12}{48 \div 12} = \frac{3}{4}$$

The ratio of thermometers to students is **3 to 4,** or $\frac{3}{4}$. The ratio may also be written in the form 3:4.

## Proportions

A **proportion** is an equation that states that two ratios are equal.

$$\frac{3}{1} = \frac{12}{4}$$

To solve a proportion, first multiply across the equal sign. This is called cross-multiplication. If you know three of the quantities in a proportion, you can use cross-multiplication to find the fourth.

> **Example:** Imagine that you are making a scale model of the solar system for your science project. The diameter of Jupiter is 11.2 times the diameter of the Earth. If you are using a plastic-foam ball with a diameter of 2 cm to represent the Earth, what diameter does the ball representing Jupiter need to be?
>
> $$\frac{11.2}{1} = \frac{x}{2 \text{ cm}}$$

**Step 1:** Cross-multiply.

$$\frac{11.2}{1} \diagdown\!\!\!\!\diagup \frac{x}{2}$$

$$11.2 \times 2 = x \times 1$$

**Step 2:** Multiply.

$$22.4 = x \times 1$$

**Step 3:** Isolate the variable by dividing both sides by 1.

$$x = \frac{22.4}{1}$$
$$x = 22.4 \text{ cm}$$

You will need to use a ball with a diameter of **22.4 cm** to represent Jupiter.

## Percentages

A **percentage** is a ratio of a given number to 100.

> **Example:** What is 85 percent of 40?

**Step 1:** Rewrite the percentage by moving the decimal point two places to the left.

$$.85$$

**Step 2:** Multiply the decimal by the number you are calculating the percentage of.

$$0.85 \times 40 = 34$$

85 percent of 40 is **34.**

## Decimals

To **add** or **subtract decimals,** line up the digits vertically so that the decimal points line up. Then add or subtract the columns from right to left, carrying or borrowing numbers as necessary.

> **Example:** Add the following numbers: 3.1415 and 2.96.

**Step 1:** Line up the digits vertically so that the decimal points line up.

$$\begin{array}{r} 3.1415 \\ + \ 2.96 \\ \hline \end{array}$$

**Step 2:** Add the columns from right to left, carrying when necessary.

$$\begin{array}{r} {}^{1\ 1}\phantom{00} \\ 3.1415 \\ + \ 2.96 \\ \hline 6.1015 \end{array}$$

The sum is **6.1015.**

## Fractions

Numbers tell you how many; **fractions** tell you *how much of a whole.*

> **Example:** Your class has 24 plants. Your teacher instructs you to put 5 in a shady spot. What fraction does this represent?

**Step 1:** Write a fraction with the total number of parts in the whole as the denominator.

$$\frac{?}{24}$$

**Step 2:** Write the number of parts of the whole being represented as the numerator.

$$\frac{5}{24}$$

$\frac{5}{24}$ of the plants will be in the shade.

## Reducing Fractions

It is usually best to express a fraction in simplest form. This is called *reducing* a fraction.

> **Example:** Reduce the fraction $\frac{30}{45}$ to its simplest form.

**Step 1:** Find the largest whole number that will divide evenly into both the numerator and denominator. This number is called the greatest common factor (GCF).

*factors of the numerator* 30: 1, 2, 3, 5, 6, 10, **15,** 30

*factors of the denominator* 45: 1, 3, 5, 9, **15,** 45

**Step 2:** Divide both the numerator and the denominator by the GCF, which in this case is 15.

$$\frac{30}{45} = \frac{30 \div 15}{45 \div 15} = \frac{2}{3}$$

$\frac{30}{45}$ reduced to its simplest form is $\frac{2}{3}$.

# Adding and Subtracting Fractions

To **add** or **subtract fractions** that have the **same denominator,** simply add or subtract the numerators.

> **Examples:**
> $$\frac{3}{5} + \frac{1}{5} = ? \quad \text{and} \quad \frac{3}{4} - \frac{1}{4} = ?$$

**Step 1:** Add or subtract the numerators.

$$\frac{3}{5} + \frac{1}{5} = \frac{4}{} \quad \text{and} \quad \frac{3}{4} - \frac{1}{4} = \frac{2}{}$$

**Step 2:** Write the sum or difference over the denominator.

$$\frac{3}{5} + \frac{1}{5} = \frac{4}{5} \quad \text{and} \quad \frac{3}{4} - \frac{1}{4} = \frac{2}{4}$$

**Step 3:** If necessary, reduce the fraction to its simplest form.

$$\frac{4}{5} \text{ cannot be reduced, and } \frac{2}{4} = \frac{1}{2}.$$

To **add** or **subtract fractions** that have **different denominators,** first find the least common denominator (LCD).

> **Examples:**
> $$\frac{1}{2} + \frac{1}{6} = ? \quad \text{and} \quad \frac{3}{4} - \frac{2}{3} = ?$$

**Step 1:** Write the equivalent fractions with a common denominator.

$$\frac{3}{6} + \frac{1}{6} = ? \quad \text{and} \quad \frac{9}{12} - \frac{8}{12} = ?$$

**Step 2:** Add or subtract.

$$\frac{3}{6} + \frac{1}{6} = \frac{4}{6} \quad \text{and} \quad \frac{9}{12} - \frac{8}{12} = \frac{1}{12}$$

**Step 3:** If necessary, reduce the fraction to its simplest form.

$$\frac{4}{6} = \frac{2}{3}, \text{ and } \frac{1}{12} \text{ cannot be reduced.}$$

# Multiplying Fractions

To **multiply fractions,** multiply the numerators and the denominators together, and then reduce the fraction to its simplest form.

> **Example:**
> $$\frac{5}{9} \times \frac{7}{10} = ?$$

**Step 1:** Multiply the numerators and denominators.

$$\frac{5}{9} \times \frac{7}{10} = \frac{5 \times 7}{9 \times 10} = \frac{35}{90}$$

**Step 2:** Reduce.

$$\frac{35}{90} = \frac{35 \div 5}{90 \div 5} = \frac{7}{18}$$

# Dividing Fractions

To **divide fractions,** first rewrite the divisor (the number you divide *by*) upside down. This is called the reciprocal of the divisor. Then you can multiply and reduce if necessary.

> **Example:**
> $$\frac{5}{8} \div \frac{3}{2} = ?$$

**Step 1:** Rewrite the divisor as its reciprocal.

$$\frac{3}{2} \rightarrow \frac{2}{3}$$

**Step 2:** Multiply.

$$\frac{5}{8} \times \frac{2}{3} = \frac{5 \times 2}{8 \times 3} = \frac{10}{24}$$

**Step 3:** Reduce.

$$\frac{10}{24} = \frac{10 \div 2}{24 \div 2} = \frac{5}{12}$$

## Scientific Notation

**Scientific notation** is a short way of representing very large and very small numbers without writing all of the place-holding zeros.

> **Example:** Write 653,000,000 in scientific notation.

**Step 1:** Write the number without the place-holding zeros.

653

**Step 2:** Place the decimal point after the first digit.

6.53

**Step 3:** Find the exponent by counting the number of places that you moved the decimal point.

6̰.53000000

The decimal point was moved eight places to the left. Therefore, the exponent of 10 is positive 8. Remember, if the decimal point had moved to the right, the exponent would be negative.

**Step 4:** Write the number in scientific notation.

$$\textbf{6.53} \times \textbf{10}^{\textbf{8}}$$

## Area

**Area** is the number of square units needed to cover the surface of an object.

> **Formulas:**
> Area of a square = side × side
> Area of a rectangle = length × width
> Area of a triangle = $\frac{1}{2}$ × base × height
>
> **Examples:** Find the areas.

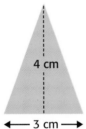

**Triangle**
Area = $\frac{1}{2}$ × base × height
Area = $\frac{1}{2}$ × 3 cm × 4 cm
Area = **6 cm²**

4 cm
3 cm

**Rectangle**
Area = length × width
Area = 6 cm × 3 cm
Area = **18 cm²**

3 cm
6 cm

**Square**
Area = side × side
Area = 3 cm × 3 cm
Area = **9 cm²**

3 cm
3 cm

## Volume

**Volume** is the amount of space something occupies.

> **Formulas:**
> Volume of a cube =
> side × side × side
>
> Volume of a prism =
> area of base × height
>
> **Examples:**
> Find the volume
> of the solids.

**Cube**
Volume = side × side × side
Volume = 4 cm × 4 cm × 4 cm
Volume = **64 cm³**

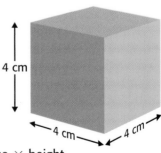

4 cm
4 cm
4 cm

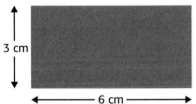

4 cm
3 cm
5 cm

**Prism**
Volume = area of base × height
Volume = (area of triangle) × height
Volume = $\left( \frac{1}{2} \times 3 \text{ cm} \times 4 \text{ cm} \right) \times 5 \text{ cm}$
Volume = 6 cm² × 5 cm
Volume = **30 cm³**

# Periodic Table of the Elements

Each square on the table includes an element's name, chemical symbol, atomic number, and atomic mass.

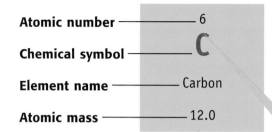

Atomic number —— 6

Chemical symbol —— C

Element name —— Carbon

Atomic mass —— 12.0

The background color indicates the type of element. Carbon is a nonmetal.

The color of the chemical symbol indicates the physical state at room temperature. Carbon is a solid.

**Background**
Metals
Metalloids
Nonmetals

**Chemical Symbol**
Solid
Liquid
Gas

**Period 1**

| 1 |
|---|
| **H** |
| Hydrogen |
| 1.0 |

| | Group 1 | Group 2 |
|---|---|---|
| **Period 2** | 3 **Li** Lithium 6.9 | 4 **Be** Beryllium 9.0 |
| **Period 3** | 11 **Na** Sodium 23.0 | 12 **Mg** Magnesium 24.3 |

| | Group 3 | Group 4 | Group 5 | Group 6 | Group 7 | Group 8 | Group 9 |
|---|---|---|---|---|---|---|---|
| **Period 4** | 21 **Sc** Scandium 45.0 | 22 **Ti** Titanium 47.9 | 23 **V** Vanadium 50.9 | 24 **Cr** Chromium 52.0 | 25 **Mn** Manganese 54.9 | 26 **Fe** Iron 55.8 | 27 **Co** Cobalt 58.9 |
| **Period 5** | 39 **Y** Yttrium 88.9 | 40 **Zr** Zirconium 91.2 | 41 **Nb** Niobium 92.9 | 42 **Mo** Molybdenum 95.9 | 43 **Tc** Technetium (97.9) | 44 **Ru** Ruthenium 101.1 | 45 **Rh** Rhodium 102.9 |
| **Period 6** | 57 **La** Lanthanum 138.9 | 72 **Hf** Hafnium 178.5 | 73 **Ta** Tantalum 180.9 | 74 **W** Tungsten 183.8 | 75 **Re** Rhenium 186.2 | 76 **Os** Osmium 190.2 | 77 **Ir** Iridium 192.2 |
| **Period 7** | 89 **Ac** Actinium (227.0) | 104 **Rf** Rutherfordium (261.1) | 105 **Db** Dubnium (262.1) | 106 **Sg** Seaborgium (263.1) | 107 **Bh** Bohrium (262.1) | 108 **Hs** Hassium (265) | 109 **Mt** Meitnerium (266) |

(Period 4, Groups 1–2: 19 **K** Potassium 39.1, 20 **Ca** Calcium 40.1)
(Period 5, Groups 1–2: 37 **Rb** Rubidium 85.5, 38 **Sr** Strontium 87.6)
(Period 6, Groups 1–2: 55 **Cs** Cesium 132.9, 56 **Ba** Barium 137.3)
(Period 7, Groups 1–2: 87 **Fr** Francium (223.0), 88 **Ra** Radium (226.0))

A row of elements is called a period.

A column of elements is called a group or family.

| **Lanthanides** | 58 **Ce** Cerium 140.1 | 59 **Pr** Praseodymium 140.9 | 60 **Nd** Neodymium 144.2 | 61 **Pm** Promethium (144.9) | 62 **Sm** Samarium 150.4 |
|---|---|---|---|---|---|
| **Actinides** | 90 **Th** Thorium 232.0 | 91 **Pa** Protactinium 231.0 | 92 **U** Uranium 238.0 | 93 **Np** Neptunium (237.0) | 94 **Pu** Plutonium 244.1 |

These elements are placed below the table to allow the table to be narrower.

**Group 18**

| 2 | | | | | |
|---|---|---|---|---|---|
| **He** | | | | | |
| Helium | | | | | |
| 4.0 | | | | | |

This zigzag line reminds you where the metals, nonmetals, and metalloids are.

| **Group 13** | **Group 14** | **Group 15** | **Group 16** | **Group 17** |
|---|---|---|---|---|
| 5 | 6 | 7 | 8 | 9 | 10 |

| 5 **B** Boron 10.8 | 6 **C** Carbon 12.0 | 7 **N** Nitrogen 14.0 | 8 **O** Oxygen 16.0 | 9 **F** Fluorine 19.0 | 10 **Ne** Neon 20.2 |
|---|---|---|---|---|---|
| 13 **Al** Aluminum 27.0 | 14 **Si** Silicon 28.1 | 15 **P** Phosphorus 31.0 | 16 **S** Sulfur 32.1 | 17 **Cl** Chlorine 35.5 | 18 **Ar** Argon 39.9 |

| **Group 10** | **Group 11** | **Group 12** | | | | | |
|---|---|---|---|---|---|---|---|
| 28 **Ni** Nickel 58.7 | 29 **Cu** Copper 63.5 | 30 **Zn** Zinc 65.4 | 31 **Ga** Gallium 69.7 | 32 **Ge** Germanium 72.6 | 33 **As** Arsenic 74.9 | 34 **Se** Selenium 79.0 | 35 **Br** Bromine 79.9 | 36 **Kr** Krypton 83.8 |
| 46 **Pd** Palladium 106.4 | 47 **Ag** Silver 107.9 | 48 **Cd** Cadmium 112.4 | 49 **In** Indium 114.8 | 50 **Sn** Tin 118.7 | 51 **Sb** Antimony 121.8 | 52 **Te** Tellurium 127.6 | 53 **I** Iodine 126.9 | 54 **Xe** Xenon 131.3 |
| 78 **Pt** Platinum 195.1 | 79 **Au** Gold 197.0 | 80 **Hg** Mercury 200.6 | 81 **Tl** Thallium 204.4 | 82 **Pb** Lead 207.2 | 83 **Bi** Bismuth 209.0 | 84 **Po** Polonium (209.0) | 85 **At** Astatine (210.0) | 86 **Rn** Radon (222.0) |
| 110 **Uun\*** Ununnilium (271) | 111 **Uuu\*** Unununium (272) | 112 **Uub\*** Ununbium (277) | | 114 **Uuq\*** Ununquadium (285) | | 116 **Uuh\*** Ununhexium (289) | | 118 **Uuo\*** Ununoctium (293) |

A number in parenthesis is the mass number of the most stable form of that element.

| 63 **Eu** Europium 152.0 | 64 **Gd** Gadolinium 157.3 | 65 **Tb** Terbium 158.9 | 66 **Dy** Dysprosium 162.5 | 67 **Ho** Holmium 164.9 | 68 **Er** Erbium 167.3 | 69 **Tm** Thulium 168.9 | 70 **Yb** Ytterbium 173.0 | 71 **Lu** Lutetium 175.0 |
|---|---|---|---|---|---|---|---|---|
| 95 **Am** Americium (243.1) | 96 **Cm** Curium (247.1) | 97 **Bk** Berkelium (247.1) | 98 **Cf** Californium (251.1) | 99 **Es** Einsteinium (252.1) | 100 **Fm** Fermium (257.1) | 101 **Md** Mendelevium (258.1) | 102 **No** Nobelium (259.1) | 103 **Lr** Lawrencium (262.1) |

*The official names and symbols for the elements greater than 109 will eventually be approved by a committee of scientists.*

# Physical Science Laws and Principles

## Law of Conservation of Energy

**The law of conservation of energy states that energy can be neither created nor destroyed.**

The total amount of energy in a closed system is always the same. Energy can be changed from one form to another, but all the different forms of energy in a system always add up to the same total amount of energy, no matter how many energy conversions occur.

## Law of Universal Gravitation

**The law of universal gravitation states that all objects in the universe attract each other by a force called gravity. The size of the force depends on the masses of the objects and the distance between them.**

The first part of the law explains why a bowling ball is much harder to lift than a table-tennis ball. Because the bowling ball has a much larger mass than the table-tennis ball, the amount of gravity between the Earth and the bowling ball is greater than the amount of gravity between the Earth and the table-tennis ball.

The second part of the law explains why a satellite can remain in orbit around the Earth. The satellite is carefully placed at a distance great enough to prevent the Earth's gravity from immediately pulling it down but small enough to prevent it from completely escaping the Earth's gravity and wandering off into space.

## Newton's Laws of Motion

**Newton's first law of motion states that an object at rest remains at rest and an object in motion remains in motion at constant speed and in a straight line unless acted on by an unbalanced force.**

The first part of the law explains why a football will remain on a tee until it is kicked off or until a gust of wind blows it off.

The second part of the law explains why a bike's rider will continue moving forward after the bike tire runs into a crack in the sidewalk and the bike comes to an abrupt stop until gravity and the sidewalk stop the rider.

**Newton's second law of motion states that the acceleration of an object depends on the mass of the object and the amount of force applied.**

The first part of the law explains why the acceleration of a 4 kg bowling ball will be greater than the acceleration of a 6 kg bowling ball if the same force is applied to both.

The second part of the law explains why the acceleration of a bowling ball will be larger if a larger force is applied to it.

The relationship of acceleration ($a$) to mass ($m$) and force ($F$) can be expressed mathematically by the following equation:

$$\text{acceleration} = \frac{\text{force}}{\text{mass}}, \text{ or } a = \frac{F}{m}$$

This equation is often rearranged to the form:

$$\text{force} = \text{mass} \times \text{acceleration},$$
$$\text{or}$$
$$F = m \times a$$

**Newton's third law of motion states that whenever one object exerts a force on a second object, the second object exerts an equal and opposite force on the first.**

This law explains that a runner is able to move forward because of the equal and opposite force the ground exerts on the runner's foot after each step.

# Law of Reflection

**The law of reflection** states that the angle of incidence is equal to the angle of reflection. This law explains why light reflects off of a surface at the same angle it strikes the surface.

A line perpendicular to the mirror's surface is called the *normal*.

The beam of light reflected off the mirror is called the *reflected beam*.

The beam of light traveling toward the mirror is called the *incident beam*.

The angle between the incident beam and the normal is called the *angle of incidence*.

The angle between the reflected beam and the normal is called the *angle of reflection*.

## Charles's Law

**Charles's law** states that for a fixed amount of gas at a constant pressure, the volume of the gas increases as its temperature increases. Likewise, the volume of the gas decreases as its temperature decreases.

If a basketball that was inflated indoors is left outside on a cold winter day, the air particles inside of the ball will move more slowly. They will hit the sides of the basketball less often and with less force. The ball will get smaller as the volume of the air decreases. If a basketball that was inflated outdoors on a cold winter day is brought indoors, the air particles inside of the ball will move more rapidly. They will hit the sides of the basketball more often and with more force. The ball will get larger as the volume of the air increases.

## Boyle's Law

**Boyle's law** states that for a fixed amount of gas at a constant temperature, the volume of a gas increases as its pressure decreases. Likewise, the volume of a gas decreases as its pressure increases.

This law explains why the pressure of the gas in a helium balloon decreases as the balloon rises from the Earth's surface.

## Pascal's Principle

**Pascal's principle** states that a change in pressure at any point in an enclosed fluid will be transmitted equally to all parts of that fluid.

When a mechanic uses a hydraulic jack to raise an automobile off the ground, he or she increases the pressure on the fluid in the jack by pushing on the jack handle. The pressure is transmitted equally to all parts of the fluid-filled jacking system. The fluid presses the jack plate against the frame of the car, lifting the car off the ground.

## Archimedes' Principle

**Archimedes' principle** states that the buoyant force on an object in a fluid is equal to the weight of the volume of fluid that the object displaces.

A person floating in a swimming pool displaces 20 L of water. The weight of that volume of water is about 200 N. Therefore, the buoyant force on the person is 200 N.

# Bernoulli's Principle

**Bernoulli's principle states that as the speed of a moving fluid increases, its pressure decreases.**

Bernoulli's principle helps to explain how a wing gives lift to an airplane or even how a Frisbee® can fly through the air. Because of the shape of the Frisbee, the air moving over the top of the Frisbee travels faster than the air below the Frisbee. This faster-moving air above the Frisbee exerts less pressure than the slower-moving air below it. The resulting increased pressure below exerts an upward force, pushing the Frisbee up.

# Useful Equations

## Average speed

$$\text{Average speed} = \frac{\text{total distance}}{\text{total time}}$$

**Example:** A bicycle messenger traveled a distance of 136 km in 8 hours. What was the messenger's average speed?

$$\frac{136 \text{ km}}{8 \text{ h}} = 17 \text{ km/h}$$

The messenger's average speed was **17 km/h.**

## Average acceleration

$$\frac{\text{Average}}{\text{acceleration}} = \frac{\text{final velocity} - \text{starting velocity}}{\text{time it takes to change velocity}}$$

**Example:** Calculate the average acceleration of an Olympic 100 m dash sprinter who reaches a velocity of 20 m/s south at the finish line. The race was in a straight line and lasted 10 s.

$$\frac{20 \text{ m/s} - 0 \text{ m/s}}{10 \text{ s}} = 2 \text{ m/s/s}$$

The sprinter's average acceleration is **2 m/s/s south.**

## Net force

### Forces in the Same Direction

When forces are in the same direction, add the forces together to determine the net force.

**Example:** Calculate the net force on a stalled car that is being pushed by two people. One person is pushing with a force of 13 N northwest and the other person is pushing with a force of 8 N in the same direction.

$$13 \text{ N} + 8 \text{ N} = 21 \text{ N}$$

The net force is **21 N northwest.**

### Forces in Opposite Directions

When forces are in opposite directions, subtract the smaller force from the larger force to determine the net force.

**Example:** Calculate the net force on a rope that is being pulled on each end. One person is pulling on one end of the rope with a force of 12 N south. Another person is pulling on the opposite end of the rope with a force of 7 N north.

$$12 \text{ N} - 7 \text{ N} = 5 \text{ N}$$

The net force is **5 N south.**

## Work

**Work** is done by exerting a force through a distance. Work has units of joules (J), which are equivalent to Newton-meters.

$$W = F \times d$$

**Example:** Calculate the amount of work done by a man who lifts a 100 N toddler 1.5 m off the floor.

$$W = 100 \text{ N} \times 1.5 \text{ m} = 150 \text{ N} \bullet \text{m} = 150 \text{ J}$$

The man did **150 J** of work.

## Power

**Power** is the rate at which work is done. Power is measured in watts (W), which are equivalent to joules per second.

$$P = \frac{W}{t}$$

**Example:** Calculate the power of a weightlifter who raises a 300 N barbell 2.1 m off the floor in 1.25 s.

$$W = 300 \text{ N} \times 2.1 \text{ m} = 630 \text{ N} \bullet \text{m} = 630 \text{ J}$$
$$P = \frac{630 \text{ J}}{1.25 \text{ s}} = 504 \text{ J/s} = 504 \text{ W}$$

The weightlifter has **504 W** of power.

## Pressure

**Pressure** is the force exerted over a given area. The SI unit for pressure is the pascal, which is abbreviated Pa.

$$\text{Pressure} = \frac{\text{force}}{\text{area}}$$

**Example:** Calculate the pressure of the air in a soccer ball if the air exerts a force of 10 N over an area of 0.5 m².

$$\text{Pressure} = \frac{10 \text{ N}}{0.5 \text{ m}^2} = 20 \text{ N/m}^2 = 20 \text{ Pa}$$

The pressure of the air inside of the soccer ball is **20 Pa.**

## Density

$$\text{Density} = \frac{\text{mass}}{\text{volume}}$$

**Example:** Calculate the density of a sponge with a mass of 10 g and a volume of 40 mL.

$$\frac{10 \text{ g}}{40 \text{ mL}} = 0.25 \text{ g/mL}$$

The density of the sponge is **0.25 g/mL.**

## Concentration

$$\text{Concentration} = \frac{\text{mass of solute}}{\text{volume of solvent}}$$

**Example:** Calculate the concentration of a solution in which 10 g of sugar is dissolved in 125 mL of water.

$$\frac{10 \text{ g of sugar}}{125 \text{ mL of water}} = 0.08 \text{ g/mL}$$

The concentration of this solution is **0.08 g/mL.**

# Glossary

## A

**absolute zero** the lowest possible temperature (0 K, −273°C) (153)

**acceleration** (ak SEL uhr AY shuhn) the rate at which velocity changes; an object accelerates if its speed changes, if its direction changes, or if both its speed and its direction change (8)

**active solar heating** a solar-heating system consisting of solar collectors and a network of pipes that distributes energy from the sun throughout a building (169)

**Archimedes'** (ahr kuh MEE deez) **principle** the principle that states that the buoyant force on an object in a fluid is an upward force equal to the weight of the volume of fluid that the object displaces (68)

**atmospheric pressure** the pressure caused by the weight of the atmosphere (63)

**average speed** the overall rate at which an object moves; average speed can be calculated by dividing total distance by total time (5)

## B

**balanced forces** forces on an object that cause the net force to be zero; balanced forces do not cause a change in motion or acceleration (14)

**Bernoulli's** (buhr NOO leez) **principle** the principle that states that as the speed of a moving fluid increases, its pressure decreases (73)

**bimetallic** (BIE muh TAL ik) **strip** a strip made by stacking two different metals in a long thin strip; because the different metals expand at different rates, a bimetallic strip can coil and uncoil with changes in temperature; bimetallic strips are used in devices such as thermostats (154)

**biomass** organic matter, such as plants, wood, and waste, that contains stored energy (138)

**block and tackle** a fixed pulley and a movable pulley used together; it can have a large mechanical advantage if several pulleys are used (104)

**Boyle's law** the law that states that for a fixed amount of gas at a constant temperature, the volume of a gas increases as its pressure decreases (219)

**buoyant force** the upward force that fluids exert on all matter; buoyant force opposes gravitational force (68)

## C

**calorie** the amount of energy needed to change the temperature of 0.001 kg of water by 1°C; 1 calorie is equivalent to 4.184 J (162)

**calorimeter** (KAL uh RIM uht uhr) a device used to determine the specific heat capacity of a substance (162)

**centripetal** (sen TRIP uht uhl) **acceleration** the acceleration that occurs in circular motion; an object traveling in a circle is constantly changing directions, so acceleration occurs continuously (10)

**change of state** the conversion of a substance from one physical form to another (165)

**Charles's law** the law that states that for a fixed amount of gas at a constant pressure, the volume of a gas increases as its temperature increases (219)

**chemical change** a change that occurs when one or more substances are changed into entirely new substances with different properties; cannot be reversed using physical means (166)

**chemical energy** the energy of a compound that changes as its atoms are rearranged to form a new compound; chemical energy is a form of potential energy (120)

**combustion** the burning of fuel; specifically, the process in which fuel combines with oxygen in a chemical change that produces thermal energy (170)

**compound machine** a machine that is made of two or more simple machines (104)

**conduction (thermal)** the transfer of thermal energy from one substance to another through direct contact; conduction can also occur within a substance (157)

**conductor (thermal)** a substance that conducts thermal energy well (158)

**convection** the transfer of thermal energy by the movement of a liquid or a gas (158)

**convection current** the circular motion of liquids or gases due to density differences that result from temperature differences (158)

## D

**density** the amount of matter in a given space; mass per unit volume (65)

**drag** the force that opposes or restricts motion in a fluid; drag opposes thrust (76)

## E

**energy** the ability to do work (116)

**energy conversion** a change from one form of energy into another (124)

**energy efficiency** (e FISH uhn see) a comparison of the amount of energy before a conversion and the amount of useful energy after a conversion (130)

**energy resource** a natural resource that can be converted by humans into other forms of energy in order to do useful work (134)

**external combustion engine** a heat engine that burns fuel outside the engine, such as a steam engine (170)

## F

**fixed pulley** a pulley that is attached to something that does not move; fixed pulleys change the direction of a force but do not increase the force (103)

**fluid** any material that can flow and that takes the shape of its container (62)

**force** a push or a pull; all forces have both size and direction (11)

**fossil fuels** nonrenewable energy resources that form in the Earth's crust over millions of years from the buried remains of once-living organisms (134)

**free fall** the condition an object is in when gravity is the only force acting on it (39)

**friction** a force that opposes motion between two surfaces that are touching (15, 131)

**fulcrum** the fixed point about which a lever pivots (98)

## G

**geothermal energy** energy resulting from the heating of the Earth's crust (138)

**gravitational potential energy** energy due to an object's position above the Earth's surface (118)

**gravity** a force of attraction between objects that is due to their masses (21)

**greenhouse effect** the natural heating process of a planet, such as the Earth, by which gases in the atmosphere trap thermal energy (159)

## H

**heat** the transfer of energy between objects that are at different temperatures; energy is always transferred from higher-temperature objects to lower-temperature objects until thermal equilibrium is reached (155); *also* the amount of energy that is transferred between objects that are at different temperatures (161)

**heat engine** a machine that uses heat to do work (170)

**hydraulic** (hie DRAW lik) **device** a device that uses liquids to transmit pressure from one point to another (67)

## I

**ideal machine** a machine that has 100 percent mechanical efficiency (97)

**inertia** the tendency of all objects to resist any change in motion (45)

**input force** the force applied to a machine (93)

**insulation** a substance that reduces the transfer of thermal energy (168)

**insulator (thermal)** a substance that does not conduct thermal energy well (158)

**internal combustion engine** a heat engine that burns fuel inside the engine; for example, an automobile engine (171)

## J

**joule** (J) the unit used to express work and energy; equivalent to the newton-meter (N•m) (90)

## K

**kilocalorie** the unit of energy equal to 1,000 calories; the kilocalorie can also be referred to as the Calorie, which is the unit of energy listed on food labels (162)

**kinetic** (ki NET ik) **energy** the energy of motion; kinetic energy depends on speed and mass (117)

## L

**law of conservation of energy** the law that states that energy is neither created nor destroyed (132)

**law of universal gravitation** the law that states that all objects in the universe attract each other through gravitational force; the size of the force depends on the masses of the objects and the distance between them (22)

**lever** a simple machine consisting of a bar that pivots at a fixed point, called a fulcrum; there are three classes of levers, based on where the input force, output force, and fulcrum are placed in relation to the load: first class levers, second class levers, and third class levers (98)

**lift** an upward force on an object (such as a wing) that opposes the downward pull of gravity; differences in pressure above and below the object contribute to lift (74)

**light energy** the energy produced by the vibrations of electrically charged particles (122)

**lubricant** (LOO bri kuhnt) a substance applied to surfaces to reduce the friction between them (19)

## M

**machine** a device that helps make work easier by changing the size or direction (or both) of a force (92)

**mass** the amount of matter that something is made of (25)

**mechanical advantage** a number that tells how many times a machine multiplies force; can be calculated by dividing the output force by the input force (96)

**mechanical efficiency** (e FISH uhn see) a comparison—expressed as a percentage—of a machine's work output with the work input; can be calculated by dividing work output by work input and then multiplying by 100 (97)

**mechanical energy** the total energy of motion and position of an object (119)

**momentum** a property of a moving object that depends on the object's mass and velocity (50)

**motion** an object's change in position over time when compared with a reference point (4)

**movable pulley** a pulley attached to the object being moved; movable pulleys increase force (103)

## N

**negative acceleration** acceleration in which velocity decreases; also called deceleration (9)

**net force** the force that results from combining all the forces exerted on an object (12)

**newton** (N) the SI unit of force (11)

**nonrenewable resource** a natural resource that cannot be replaced or that can be replaced only over thousands or millions of years (134)

**nuclear energy** the form of energy associated with changes in the nucleus of an atom (123)

**nuclear fission** the process in which a large nucleus splits into two smaller nuclei (137)

**nuclear fusion** the process in which two or more nuclei with small masses join together, or fuse, to form a larger, more massive nucleus (123)

## O

**output force** the force applied by a machine (93)

## P

**pascal** (Pa) the SI unit of pressure; equal to the force of 1 N exerted over an area of one square meter (62)

**Pascal's principle** the principle that states that a change in pressure at any point in an enclosed fluid is transmitted equally to all parts of that fluid (67)

**passive solar heating** a solar-heating system that relies on thick walls and large windows to use energy from the sun as a means of heating (169)

**perpetual** (puhr PECH oo uhl) **motion machine** a machine that runs forever without any additional energy input; perpetual motion machines are impossible to create (133)

**physical change** a change that affects one or more physical properties of a substance; many physical changes are easy to undo (165)

**positive acceleration** acceleration in which velocity increases (9)

**potential energy** the energy of position or shape (118)

**power** the rate at which work is done (91)

**pressure** the amount of force exerted on a given area; expressed in pascals (Pa) (62)

**projectile** (proh JEK tuhl) **motion** the curved path an object follows when thrown or propelled near the surface of the Earth (41)

**pulley** a simple machine consisting of a grooved wheel that holds a rope or a cable (103)

## R

**radiation** the transfer of energy through matter or space as electromagnetic waves, such as visible light and infrared waves (159)

**reference point** an object that appears to stay in place in relation to an object being observed for motion (4)

**renewable resource** a natural resource that can be used and replaced over a relatively short time (137)

**resultant velocity** the combination of two or more velocities (7)

## S

**screw** a simple machine that is an inclined plane wrapped in a spiral (101)

**simple machines** the six machines from which all other machines are constructed: a lever, an inclined plane, a wedge, a screw, a wheel and axle, and a pulley (98)

**sound energy** the energy caused by an object's vibrations (122)

**specific heat capacity** the amount of energy needed to change the temperature of 1 kg of a substance by 1°C (160)

**speed** the rate at which an object moves; speed depends on the distance traveled and the time taken to travel that distance (5)

**states of matter** the physical forms in which a substance can exist; states include solid, liquid, gas, and plasma (164)

## T

**temperature** a measure of how hot (or cold) something is; specifically, a measure of the average kinetic energy of the particles in an object (150)

**terminal velocity** the constant velocity of a falling object when the size of the upward force of air resistance matches the size of the downward force of gravity (38)

**thermal energy** the total energy of the particles that make up an object (120, 156)

**thermal equilibrium** the point at which two objects reach the same temperature (156)

**thermal expansion** the increase in volume of a substance due to an increase in temperature (152)

**thermal pollution** the excessive heating of a body of water (173)

**thrust** the forward force produced by an airplane's engines; thrust opposes drag (75)

**turbulence** an irregular or unpredictable flow of fluids that can cause drag; lift is often reduced by turbulence (76)

## U

**unbalanced forces** forces on an object that cause the net force to be other than zero; unbalanced forces produce a change in motion or acceleration (13)

## V

**velocity** (vuh LAHS uh tee) the speed of an object in a particular direction (6)

## W

**watt** (W) the unit used to express power; equivalent to joules per second (J/s) (91)

**wedge** a simple machine that is a double inclined plane that moves; a wedge is often used for cutting (101)

**weight** a measure of the gravitational force exerted on an object, usually by the Earth (24)

**wheel and axle** a simple machine consisting of two circular objects of different sizes; the wheel is the larger of the two circular objects (102)

**work** the action that results when a force causes an object to move in the direction of the force (88)

**work input** the work done on a machine; the product of the input force and the distance through which it is exerted (93)

**work output** the work done by a machine; the product of the output force and the distance through which it is exerted (93)

# Index

# Credits

**Abbreviations used:** (t) top, (c) center, (b) bottom, (l) left, (r) right, (bkgd) background

## ILLUSTRATIONS

All illustrations, unless noted below, by Holt, Rinehart and Winston.

**Chapter One** Page 5, Preface, Inc.; 7, Marty Roper/Planet Rep; 8, Gary Locke/Suzanne Craig; 9(t), Mike Carroll/Steve Edsey & Sons; 10(cr), Preface, Inc.; 15(t), Blake Thornton/Rita Marie; 15(b), 16, 17, Gary Ferster; 22, Doug Henry/American Artists; 23, Stephen Durke/Washington Artists; 24, Craig Attebery/Frank & Jeff Lavaty; 25, Terry Guyer; 28(br), Stephen Durke/Washington Artists; 29, Terry Guyer; 31(r), Preface, Inc.

**Chapter Two** Page 37, 38, Gary Ferster; 40, Craig Attebery/Frank & Jeff Lavaty; 42(tl), Mike Carroll/Steve Edsey & Sons; 44, Marty Roper/Planet Rep; 46, Charles Thomas; 49(tr), Gary Ferster; 54(br), Craig Attebery/Frank & Jeff Lavaty; 55, Marty Roper/Planet Rep; 58, James Pfeffer.

**Chapter Three** Page 62, 63, Stephen Durke/ Washington Artists; 64, 65, Rainey Kirk/The Neis Group; 66, Christy Krames; 67, Mark Heine; 68, Preface, Inc.; 69, Will Nelson/Sweet Reps; 71, Preface, Inc.; 72, Sam Collins/Art & Science, Inc.; 74, Craig Attebery/Jeff Lavaty Artist Agent; 76(l), Marty Roper/Planet Rep; 77, Terry Guyer; 80, Craig Attebery/Frank & Jeff Lavaty; 83(tr), Jared Schneidman/ Wilkinson Studios; 83(bl), Keith Locke/Suzanne Craig.

**Chapter Four** Page 89(tr), Blake Thornton/Rita Marie; 90, John White/The Neis Group; 95(l), Annie Bissett; 95(r), John White/The Neis Group; 96, Keith Locke/Suzanne Craig; 98(l), 99(tl, bl), Annie Bissett; 101(cl), Preface, Inc.; 103(t), Gary Ferster; 103(c,b), 104, John White/The Neis Group; 108, Blake Thornton/Rita Marie.

**Chapter Five** Page 117(b), Dave Joly; 118, John White/The Neis Group; 120, Stephen Durke/Washington Artists; 121(t), Dave Joly; 121(b), Stephen Durke/Washington Artists; 122(t), Gary Ferster; 126, Will Nelson/Sweet Reps; 127, Dan Stuckenschneider/Uhl Studios Inc.; 128(t), Blake Thornton/Rita Marie; 129, Dan Stuckenschneider/Uhl Studios Inc.; 131, Dan McGeehan/Koralik Associates; 132(t), Marty Roper/Planet Rep; 132(b), 134(b), Dan Stuckenschneider/Uhl Studios Inc.; 135(r), Preface, Inc.; 136, Patrick Gnan/Deborah Wolfe; 137(br), Michael Moore; 138(cr), Dan Stuckenschneider/Uhl Studios Inc.; 139(b), Preface, Inc.; 145(r), Dave Joly.

**Chapter Six** Page 150, Blake Thornton/Rita Marie; 151, Stephen Durke/Washington Artists; 152, Terry Guyer; 153(tr), Dave Joly; 154, Dan Stuckenschneider/Uhl Studios Inc.; 156, 157, Stephen Durke/Washington Artists; 158(bl), Mark Heine; 159, Jared Schneidman/Wilkinson Studios; 162, 164, Stephen Durke/Washington Artists; 165, Preface, Inc.; 167, 168, 169, 170, 172, 173, Dan Stuckenschneider/Uhl Studios Inc.; 176(c), Dave Joly; 178(br), Dan Stuckenschneider/Uhl Studios Inc.; 179(cr), Preface, Inc.; 181, Stephen Durke/Washington Artists.

**Lab** Page 195, John White/The Weis Group; 199, Marty Roper; 200, Dave Joly; 204, Terry Guyer; 208, Mark Mille/Sharon Langley; 209, 210, 211, Preface; 216, 217, Kristy Sprott.

**Appendix** Page 204(t), Terry Guyer; 208(b), Mark Mille/Sharon Langley Artist Rep.; 209, 210, 211, Preface, Inc.; 216, 217, Kristy Sprott; 219(t), Dan Stuckenschneider/Uhl Studios Inc.

## PHOTOGRAPHY

**Cover and Tile page** Jose Fuste Raga/The Stock Market

**Table of Contents** Page iv(t), Gene Peach/The Picture Cube; iv(c), SuperStock; iv(b), Michelle Bridwell/HRW Photo; v(t), Scott Van Osdol/HRW; v(c), Richard Nowitz/Phototake; v(b), Victoria Smith/HRW Photo; vi(t), T. Mein/N & M Mishler/ Stone; vi(c), Al Bello/Allsport; vi(b), Michelle Bridwell/HRW Photo; vii(t), Robert Wolf; vii(b), John Langford/HRW Photo.

**Feature Borders** Unless otherwise noted below, all images ©2001 PhotoDisc/ HRW; "Across the Sciences" Pages 33, 146, 181, all images by HRW; "Careers" 59, 147, sand bkgd and saturn, Corbis Images, DNA, Morgan Cain & Associates, scuba gear, ©1997 Radlund & Associates for Artville; "Eureka" 58, 84, 113, ©2001 PhotoDisc/HRW; "Science Fiction" 85, saucers, Ian Christopher/Greg Geisler, book, HRW, bkgd, Stock Illustration Source; "Science, Technology, and Society" 32, 112, 180, robot, Greg Geisler.

**Chapter One** Page 4(all), SuperStock; 6(t), Tom Tietz/Stone; 6(b), Robert Ginn/PhotoEdit; 9, Sergio Putrell/Foca; 10(t), Gene Peach/The Picture Cube; 11, 12(b), Michelle Bridwell/HRW Photos; 13, Daniel Schaefer/HRW Photo; 14(t), David Young-Wolff/PhotoEdit; 14(b), Arthur C. Smith/Grant Heilman Photography; 17(all), Michelle Bridwell/HRW Photos; 17(insets), Stephanie Morris/HRW Photos; 18, Tony Freedman/PhotoEdit; 20(cl), Michelle Bridwell/HRW Photo; 21, NASA; 24, Image ©2001 PhotoDisc; 28(c), Superstock; 31, Mavournea Hay/HRW Photo; 32, Hunter Hoffman; 33, Bruce Hands/Stone.

**Chapter Two** Page 36, Richard Megna/Fundamental Photographs; 37, Doug Armand/Stone; 38, Robert Daemmrich/Stone; 39(t), James Sugar/Black Star; 39(b), NASA; 41(l), Michelle Bridwell/Frontera Fotos; 41(r), Image ©2001 PhotoDisc, Inc.; 41(b), James Balog/Stone; 42(t), Richard Megna/Fundamental Photographs; 44, Marc Asnin/SABA Press Photos, Inc.; 45(l), Mavournea Hay/HRW Photo; 45(r), Michelle Bridwell/Frontera Fotos; 47(all), Image ©2001 PhotoDisc, Inc.; 48, David Madison; 49(tl), Gerard Lacz/Animals Animals/Earth Sciences; 49(tc), Coronado Rodney Jones/HRW Photo; 49(tr), Image ©2001 PhotoDisc, Inc.; 49(bl), NASA; 49(br), Lance Schriner/HRW Photo; 50(all), Michelle Bridwell/HRW Photo; 51(t), Zigy Kaluzny/Stone; 51(b), Michelle Bridwell/HRW Photo; 54, Robert Daemmrich/Stone; 56(t), James Balog/Stone; 56(b), David Madison/Stone; 57(l), NASA; 58(t), Courtesy of Steve Okamoto; 58(b), Lee Schwabe; 59, R.N. Metheny/The Christian Science Monitor.

**Chapter Three** Page 59(t), Courtesy of Steve Okamoto; 59(b), Lee Schwabe; 64(t), I. M. House/Stone; 64(tc), David R. Frazier Photolibrary, Inc.; 64(c), Deiter and Mary Plage/Bruce Coleman; 64(bc), Wolfgang Kaeler/Corbis; 64(b), Martin Barraud/Stone; 65(t), SuperStock; 65(tc), Daniel A. Nord; 65(r), Ken Marschall/Madison Press Books; 65(bc), Bassot/Photo Researchers Inc.; 65(b), Bettmann Archive; 68, Michelle Bridwell/HRW Photo; 70, Bruno P. Zehnder/Peter Arnold, Inc.; 73, Richard Megna/Fundamental Photographs; 75(tr), Larry L. Miller/Photo Researchers, Inc.; 75(t), Larry L. Miller/Photo Researchers, Inc.; 75(c), Richard Neville/Check Six; 75(bl), T. Mein/N&M Mishler/Stone; 76 (t), Ron Kimball/Ron Kimball Photography, Inc.; 76(b), Michelle Bridwell/HRW Photo; 77(b), George Hall/Check Six; 81(t), Ron Kimball/Ron Kimball Photography, Inc.; 84 (t), Victor Malafronte.

**Chapter Four** Page 92(cl,cr,bc,br,t) Robert Wolf; 92(bl), Image © 2001 PhotoDisc, Inc.; 97, 98(l,r), 99 (c), Robert Wolf; 100, Lisa Davis; 101(b,c), 102(t,b), Robert Wolf; 104, Russell Dian/HRW Photo; 104(b), Robert Wolf; 105(tl), Image © 1998 PhotoDisc, Inc.; 105(tc), 110(t), Robert Wolf; 111(l), Helmut Gritscher/Peter Arnold, Inc.; 111(b), Stephanie Morris/HRW Photo; 112, Courtesy of IBM Corp., Research Division, Almaden Research; 113, A.W. Stegmeyer/Upstream.

**Chapter Five** Page 116, Al Bello/Allsport; 118, Earl Kowall/Corbis; 120(c), Paul A. Souders/Corbis; 120(r), Tony Freeman/Photo Edit; 123(t), NASA; 123(b), Mark C. Burnett/Photo Researchers, Inc.; 124(l,cl,cr,r), Peter Van Steen/HRW Photo; 130, Morton Beebe/Corbis; 133, Victoria Smith/HRW Photo; 134, Ted Clutter/Photo Researchers, Inc.; 135(t), Tom Carroll/ Phototake; 135(cl), Mark E. Gibson; 135(br), John Kaprielian/Photo Researchers, Inc.; 136(t), Robert Wolf; 137(t), D.O.E./Science Source/Photo Researchers, Inc.; 137(cl), H.P. Merton/The Stock Market; 137(bl), Tom Carroll/Phototake; 138(tl), Bob Gomel/The Stock Market; 138(tr), Ed Young/Corbis; 138(c), Richard Nowitz/ Phototake; 138(bl), Coronado Rodney Jones/HRW Photo; 138 (br), Kevin R. Morris/Corbis; 143, Ed Young/Corbis; 144(b), Ted Clutter/Photo Researchers, Inc.; 145(bl), Mike Powell/Allsport; 146, Solar Survival Architecture; 147(t,b), Robert Wolf.

**Chapter Six** Page 154, Mark Burnett/Photo Researchers, Inc.; 163, L.D. Gordon/The Image Bank; 166, Peter Van Steen/HRW Photo; 171(t), Dorling Kindersley LTD; 171(b), Peter Arnold Inc., NY; 178, Dorling Kindersley LTD; 179, Kees van den Berg/Photo Researchers, Inc.; 180, Dan Winters/ Discover Magazine.

**LabBook** "LabBook Header": "L," Corbis Images, "a," Letraset Phototone, "b" and "B," HRW, "o" and "k," Images ©2001 PhotoDisc/HRW; 183(c), Michelle Bridwell/HRW Photo; 183(b), Image © 2001 PhotoDisc, Inc.; 184(cl), Victoria Smith/HRW Photo; 184(bl), Stephanie Morris/HRW Photo; 185(tr), Jana Birchum/HRW Photo; 185(b), Peter Van Steen/HRW Photo; 189, NASA; 195(l,r), Robert Wolf; 198, Victoria Smith/HRW Photo.

**Appendix** Page 205(b), Sam Dudgeon/HRW Photo; 205(t), Peter Van Steen/HRW Photo; 220, Sam Dudgeon/HRW Photo.

**Sam Dudgeon/HRW Photo** Page viii-1, 8(b); 10(b); 12(t); 14(c); 19; 20(bl); 30; 57(r); 77(t); 82; 84(b); 95(c); 98, 99(bl); 117; 119; 122; 142; 144(t); 155; 160; 182; 183(b); 184(br,t); 185(tl); 188; 191; 193; 194; 201; 205; 220.

**John Langford/HRW Photo** Page 43; 88-89; 91; 93; 95(t); 99(t); 101(t); 105(tr); 108; 109; 110(b); 111(tr); 120(l); 121; 122(b); 125; 126; 128; 135(cl,r,bl); 137(cr); 151; 156-159; 161; 162; 164-165; 168; 176; 183(t); 195(b); 196.

**Scott Van Osdol/HRW Photo** Page 63; 66; 75(br); 94; 96; 99(br).

# Self-Check Answers

## Chapter 1—Matter in Motion

**Page 6:** Numbers 1 and 3 are examples of velocity.

**Page 13:** 2 N north

**Page 18:** sliding friction

**Page 22:** Gravity is a force of attraction between objects that is due to the masses of the objects.

## Chapter 2—Forces in Motion

**Page 38:** A leaf is more affected by air resistance.

**Page 45:** This can be answered in terms of either Newton's first law or inertia.

Newton's first law: When the bus is still, both you and the bus are at rest. The bus started moving, but no unbalanced force acted on your body, so your body stayed at rest.

Inertia: You have inertia, and that makes you difficult to move. As a result, when the bus started to move, you didn't move with it.

## Chapter 3—Forces in Fluids

**Page 75:** Air travels faster over the top of a wing.

## Chapter 4—Work and Machines

**Page 89:** Pulling a wheeled suitcase is doing work because the force applied and the motion of the suitcase are in the same direction.

## Chapter 5—Energy and Energy Resources

**Page 125:** A roller coaster has the greatest potential energy at the top of the highest hill (usually the first hill) and the greatest kinetic energy at the bottom of the highest hill.

## Chapter 6—Heat and Heat Technology

**Page 163:** Two substances can have the same temperature but different amounts of thermal energy because temperature, unlike thermal energy, does not depend on mass. A small amount of a substance at a particular temperature will have less thermal energy than a large amount of the substance at the same temperature.

**Page 165:** Steam can cause a more severe burn than boiling water because steam contains more energy per unit mass than does boiling water.